THE PHILOSOPHY

OF

WILLIAM JAMES

THE PHILOSOPHY
OF
WILLIAM JAMES

Selected from His Chief Works

WITH AN INTRODUCTION BY

HORACE M. KALLEN

OF THE NEW SCHOOL
FOR SOCIAL RESEARCH

THE MODERN LIBRARY · NEW YORK

Random House IS THE PUBLISHER OF

THE MODERN LIBRARY

BENNETT A. CERF · DONALD S. KLOPFER · ROBERT K. HAAS

Manufactured in the United States of America

By H. Wolff

PREFACE

WHAT William James thinks about man, and the world, and man's place in it, he has said in many books and many scattered papers. These do not present a complete system of philosophy, but rather special and intensive studies of problems Mr. James felt to be momentous and living at the time. The systematic statement of his position which he aimed at in "Some Problems of Philosophy" was denied him; he died before the book was half done. The completed sections, published in 1911, serve only to carry farther and to restate the results of his earlier studies in the nature of the One and the Many, Freedom, Novelty, Causation.

His teachings on manifold other matters of high import exist scattered through his various volumes. Particularly, there are subjects which occupy the foreground of contemporary thought, themes like the relations between individuals taken distributively and taken collectively which are nowadays lumped as social psychology; themes like the American temper and the American scene, the labor question, war and peace and nationalism, education and democracy, on which James has expressed reasoned opinions. These expressions often occur incidentally, in the course of a discussion of other topics at the time more interesting, in letters, in occasional addresses. In so far as they are complete in themselves they have been assembled together in separate chapters under appropriate headings.

They, and the other selections which make up this book have been chosen with the view of presenting the philosophy of William James systematically in his own words and in convenient compass, with some approximation to that rounded wholeness he himself would have given it had he lived to complete his work.

In this presentation regard has been had rather for the continuity and recurrence of a metaphysical or social view than for its place in the historical order of Mr. James's writings. This has been the guiding principle most especially in the selections from his letters. For letters are responses to immediate and passing occasions; they are specific responses to specific persons, under particular circumstances, voices of moods, situations, conditions, never to recur as easily as lasting attitudes. And William James wrote thousands of letters. Those printed are a selection in which the temper and propensity of the selector must needs automatically enter into the picture they make up. How much more care then, is required, if a selection from a selection is to be typical and adequately representative!

Readers of William James will observe that in the selections from his printed books, footnotes have usually been omitted. Occasionally they have been retained, abbreviated, and less frequently, they have been kept as the author set them down. Of the text proper, passages have now and then been slightly condensed, while at other times, when the differences in context seemed to require it, repetitions have been allowed to stand.

Acknowledgments are due to the publishers of the works of William James for permission to reprint the selections in this volume. It could not have been put together without the generous interest and coöperation of his son, Mr. Henry James, to whose advice and suggestions the book owes much.

H. M. KALLEN.

CONTENTS

CONTENTS

INTRODUCTION

THE MEANING OF WILLIAM JAMES FOR "US MODERNS"

I

To none of the great endeavors of the mind does the spirit of irony so attach itself as to that which in the high tradition of our many cultures goes by the name of philosophy. In America or in China art, religion, science, war, government and industry are each sufficiently penetrated by the joke which actual capacity makes of pretense; actual purpose, of declared intention; real workings, of claims of every sort. These institutions of our daily life have, however, their moments of genuine efficacy amid the secular stretch of their fatuous attainments; they forcibly alter the world from within and add a veritable new dimension to the stuffs of which it is made up. Not so philosophy. With claims of the greatest, its achievements are of the slightest. Offering its views as insight and grasp upon the immutable and eternal, they are outmoded in a generation; they die like ephemeridæ overnight. Where, outside of the mausoleums we call colleges, are the philosophers of yesteryear? The life of a philosophy is so brief, its claim to hold the deathless and the everlasting is so assured, how can the pity and laughter whose compenetration is irony not attach to the philosopher's story, not find meat and drink in the philosopher's themes! Fortunate he whose thought reaches the heart of his own generation! If, outside the schools, the generation that follows also heeds him, he has won what immortality his craft attains to.

For the enterprise which the philosopher is engaged upon is at once the most heroic and the most illusory the spirit undertakes. It is to find reasons in a world which does not care any more than a dead donkey whether we live or die, are happy or unhappy or bond or free, for believing that we are assured eternal life in happiness and freedom. It is to reconcile the world we live in with the heart's desire, so that, soon or late nothing we aspire to shall be unattained, nothing we reject shall be undestroyed. Ah, the unending procession of convinced enlightened ones, announcing their discoveries of this reconciliation! Ah, the long, long line of systems of philosophy, each a reasoned justification of the never-to-be-doubted attainment of the heart's desire, each an exposure of the failure of those that have gone before, and each convicted of failure in its own turn! The history of philosophy is a Saragosso sea; it simply counts the tale of this wreckage of magnificent argosies of thought by the winds and waves of the real; the tale of the foredoomed failure to reconcile the old original irreconcilables, ever renewing their form and their strength with the blood of the new experience and the new knowledge gathered by the new generation whom each new philosophy signalizes. The problems of philosophy have been persistent problems ever with us; the solutions of philosophy have passed in the night. The solutions are what each age and generation makes for itself; many individuals contribute to them, deriving their especial stuffs and spirit from the common intellectual treasure-house of the time. Every age has to build its philosophy anew. Each finds itself anew required to establish the One, the Eternal, the Free, the Happy, the Immortal—any or all of them; and to sustain and to vindicate these desirables against all-consuming time, against all-disillusioning experience.

William James, more than any other the philosophic spokesman for the whole age that passed with the Great War and, there is good reason to believe, for the generation yet to come, has, as any true philosopher must, made his own unique endeavor at reconciling the heart of the world and the heart of man. In so far forth he has simply carried a stage farther the ancient torch passed him by the thinkers who have run their course before. But the manner in which he has done this, the materials he has used, the methods he has applied, set him apart from the tradition. It is another road he travels. Not alone are the solutions he has offered new; his treatment has mollified the asperities of the problems; it has imparted to them a viability and transitiveness they used not to have; it has assimilated them to the problems of science; it has given them a greater kinship with the solutions that used never to resolve them. It has rendered them amenable as they are, in their own natures. And this, in philosophy, is revolution. Because of William James, the philosophic endeavor receives a new significance and a new status; it becomes the peer of the arts and the sciences, and while it may, and no doubt will, continue to share their secular fatuity, it will now also have its own moments of genuine efficacy and transforming power upon the stuffs and dimensions of the world.

Paradoxically, this enhancement of the power of philosophy arises directly out of a recognition of its limitations: the limitations of its wishful originative and driving energies, the limitations of its materials, the limitations of its instruments. By recognizing that philosophers had been endeavoring to make their art execute more than it was able to, James enabled it to perform more than it was accustomed to. He thus liberated the powers of philosophy and validated its task. He vindicated the values of humanity without denying the dynamics of nature; he acknowledged the realities that arise in experience, as they arise, without reducing the heart to resignation or despair. The systems of the tradition—the idealisms, the materialisms, the theodicies and naturalisms of such thinkers as Plato or Diderot or Epicurus or Bergson or Haeckel or Hegel or Nietzsche or Kant, have been perforce compelled to do one thing or the other: to belie reality or to deny the heart. James is as deeply preoccupied with the aspirations of the heart as any; in fact, the entire development of his philosophy often seems an unrelaxing endeavor to install them victorious in this world that was not made for them; but an obstinate conviction of the unharmonizable variety that composes this same world saves him from denaturing it. He refuses to rationalize its brute contingencies into an agreeable order; he rejects the pretense of a transformation of evil into good, and of conflict and aliency into inwardness and harmony, by means of dialectic. It is for this reason useless to seek a system in James's writings in the customary meaning of the word "system." His works are as unarchitectural as the realities they point to and light up. The changing life of the latter flows also in the former, and such direction and climax as they, the former, have, is a continuation of the same qualities of the felt stream of existence itself.

Consequently, James's philosophy has a living immediacy of appeal which those in the classic tradition of this art lack. It talks straight to your good sense; you do not need to be persuaded of it by an elaborate logic, a complicated technique of inference and illation. Only late does it come to you that you are assenting to discrete observations which keep doing violence to your feeling of syllogism and sense of ratiocination: Bertrand Russell once said that reading "Pragmatism" was like taking a bath in water which heated up so imperceptibly that you didn't know when to scream. Such is the natural outcome when you give up the endeavor by means of dialectic to reweave the world into a pattern whose motives are drawn from your needs and not from its nature. Then reality is no longer replaced by rationalization; events and desires can be harmonized according to their natures, without being "sublated" or otherwise metaphysically metamorphosed by the magic wand of Logic or Reason written with capital letters. Then, indeed, Reason becomes recognized for the rationality that it in fact is, a human sentiment, not a cosmic law or a metaphysical power, a sentiment with ambiguous data and variable applications. You see then that the very nature of rationality keeps you from looking for literal agreement among mankind as to *what* is rational. Anything may be. For you recognize that the utmost of rationality, says James, is the "feeling of sufficiency of the present moment," the simple, flat acquiescence in the moment that might be brought about merely by the custom of the country or personal habituation or just the absence of competitors to challenge and displace.

The philosophies of the tradition cannot in the nature of things be insights into reality and accurate perceptions of the going continuance of events. They are projections of the heart's desire and works of the imagination that survive or perish by the same standards as other forms of fiction. What with their insistence on the world's being through and through One (whether one Spirit or one Matter is immaterial); what with the necessity which followed from this insistence to explain away change and chance and freedom and novelty and individuality and evil, to explain away the

whole procession of pathos and laughter whose alternations make up the poignant drama of even the dullest
and most routine daily life—these traditional philosophies, James saw, are ever under the challenge of precisely those things they explain away. A richer and
deeper rationality comes to be when those things are
acknowledged and taken account of as they step out
and present themselves, with all their imperfections—
their opacity, their arbitrariness and unaccountability—
on their heads. You do not need, says James, an Unseen to account for what you see, or a One beyond
experience to give birth to the Many of experience and
hold them together. The visible multitudes of our
action and passion exist in their own right and hold
together in their own ways and of their own power; and
the ways and the power are as visible as the multitudes
themselves. Acquiesce in them, and they are rational
as anything can be rational; set up some particular
interest or ideal for special regard among them and they
become rational or irrational by their congruity with
that. But it is your need, not theirs, which requires
them thus congruous; your need either to exist yourself
or to establish a rationality for them. Rationality is a
term of appreciation, not of description; it does not
analyze; it judges.

These ideas give the framework within which the
philosophy of William James is developed. Broadly
speaking, it has two branches.

One is the polemic he conducts, from the very beginning, against the classic tradition of philosophy—the monism, the eternalism, the intellectualism, the necessitarianism and metaphysical optimism or pessimism of the historical idealists and materialists.

The other is the development of his own positive doctrine. The points of this doctrine, when separated from the polemic which their exposition was involved in, are in fact very uncomplex. They are the summary simply of that which we observe and rely on when we take experience at its face value as it comes, radically, in its living fullness.

1. Our experience, taken thus simply, is of multitudes of separate and distinct individuals, persons, qualities, matters, immaterialities, and of the relations between them, each confluently existent and real in its own way and on its own account. The objects of religious experience and relations of value are among them. And the relations are as fully there as the individuals they relate, and the individuals as the relations.

2. The spontaneities, the chance comings and goings, the freedoms and unpredictabilities that we feel in our experience are as real as we feel them. We make mistakes in placing them, not in recognizing what they are and that they happen.

3. The same thing holds for causality, for creative energy and for novelties. Our inveterate belief that they are what we think they are is no error; we make

mistakes about *where,* not *what,* they are; about their locations, not their natures.

4. Truth and error are relations between things or events or ideas used as signs, symbols, or meanings, and other things and events and ideas that they symbolize. Their nature is to be instruments in our struggle to live; their function is to lead from the symbol or idea to its object. Successful leading is truth; unsuccessful, error. Consequences are the essential content of truth, error, or meaning.

These points, taken together, make up all that William James includes in the philosophy that he calls Radical Empiricism and Pragmatism. It is a philosophy that does justice at once to the hunger of the heart within us, and to our sense of the ineluctable world around us, its continuities and breaks, its coercions and spontaneities, its responsiveness and impenetrability; a philosophy that recognizes the tasks such a world imposes on the spirit of man, the call it makes upon courage, upon effort, upon a readiness to adventure on hazard—hazard of belief and hazard of enterprise—if life is to be lived not only, but won to excellency.

This is why, among the philosophers of America, William James has no peer in the eyes of the world. Whether it be in China or Great Britain, in Italy or Russia, or all the nations of the earth between, men celebrate him not merely as the greatest American philosopher, but as the great philosopher of America.

And this, in its turn, is a paradox.

II

The philosopher of a people need not be of that people's blood or born upon its soil, but even more than a people's poet, he must be the authentic voice of the never-to-be-duplicated urge that is its life. The vision he sees, the ideals he formulates, must envisage and give utterance to the drives that are making its history. These drives as a rule will be missed by the official philosophies and theologies of an age. The latter will be concerns of the schools, looking backward, and deriving from the tradition of letters, not from the drama of living. They will be orthodoxies to which the forward look of affairs in the making will always be heretical; and philosophies that express the affairs will be heresies when they first appear; their makers will stand out first by what they reject rather than by what they propose.

So it was in the United States. From the beginning there obtained and there continues to obtain in this broad and abundant land an official philosophy, solidly established and comfortably provided for in the churches and colleges. Deriving from the proud and bitter rigors of the institutes of John Calvin, it was first intensified, and then mitigated by the changing scene of the America of English speech. Riches, ameliorating life, mollified doctrine; new knowledge, extending horizons, diversified perspectives. Calvinism, without altering in principle, took on a new tone: it remained imperious but became better-mannered. Predestination changed from personal fate to cosmic order; original sin from congenital corruption to the natural insufficiency of the individual in the great world he has to struggle for life in; election from pride of dogma to idealistic assurance. The Jehovah of Calvin became in the course of time the Oversoul of Emerson and the Absolute of the idealists. The harshness tended to be forgotten and left behind rather than consciously abandoned; consciously doctrine was what it always had been and in the schools was so taught.

This process of tempering, of toning down and rounding off the national orthodoxy—very uneven, in different parts of the land—constitutes, in Mr. Santayana's admirable phrase, "the genteel tradition" of the national life. The process had, in the more urbane portions of the United States, gathered a significant momentum when Henry James, the father of William James, was a young man; it was the intellectual milieu of his own rejection of it. He himself was in direct communication, often in intimate contact, with the personages who were the leaders in transfusing Calvinism with urbanity; among them, Emerson and Channing, Margaret Fuller, Theodore Parker, Cullen Bryant and many others. Of Scotch-Irish stock, and Presbyterian confession, the scion of a northern New York family of traders, farmers, merchants and lawyers, Henry James the Elder had, at the age of thirteen while heroically putting out a fire, suffered such severe burns of the leg that amputation was required twice within two years. The inference is inevitable that the pang of this prolonged and horrible experience, with the subsequent lifelong handicaps which it imposed, had no little share in leading the father of William James both into the career of speculation he chose, and the rebellion against the established tradition he carried on during his whole lifetime. Family tradition was indifferent or opposed; the social milieu was antagonistic.[1] In fact, his intellectual life had started on the correct lines, for he had graduated from Union College, in Schenectady, New York, and had then gone to the theological seminary in Princeton, with the view of preparing for the Presbyterian ministry. Two years he spent there, from 1835 to 1837; and left without completing his course: all his days thereafter are marked with a scorn of ecclesiastics; his conversation and his writings both coruscate with irony and sarcasm upon them

---

[1] "I remember well," writes William's brother, Henry, "how when we were all young together we had, under the pressure of the American ideal in that matter, then so rigid, felt it tasteless and even humiliating that the head of our little family was *not* in business. . . . Such had never been the case with the father of any boy of our acquaintance; the business in which the boy's father gloriously *was* stood forth inveterately as the very first note of our comrade's impressiveness. . . . Business alone was respectable. . . . 'What shall we tell them that you *are*, don't you see?' could but become on our lips at home a more constant appeal . . . his 'Say I'm a philosopher, say I'm a lover of my kind, say I'm an author of books if you like; or best of all, just say I'm a Student' saw us so very little further." *Notes of a Son and Brother*, pp. 68, 69.

and upon all conventually successful and accepted authority.

Partly, no doubt, this was due to the inherent deficiency of the genteel tradition, whether in its rigorous or urbane form. Partly, one cannot help believing, it was provoked by the failure to win for his own system interest and acceptance. For a system of his own Henry James, Senior, did work out, and the walls of the intellectual Jericho refused so much as to tremble before its horn.[1]

Restless, in his early life, both of mind and body, but the heir of a twelfth share of a considerable fortune (three million dollars, Henry, his son, suggests), and therefore without the arresting necessity to earn a living for himself and his family, the elder Henry James's upset organic idiosyncrasy, hungry, no doubt, for equilibration, for completion, kept him and his family in somewhat the intensities of a migratory state. Shortly after the birth of his second son, he took them to Europe. In England, as he records in his autobiographical confession, "Stephen Dewhurst," he was overcome by a depression from which he was lifted by the impact of the teachings of Immanuel Swedenborg, then luckily called to his attention by a friend. That was in 1844; till the end of his so wandering life the works of Swedenborg stayed his inseparable companions, on his every journey and every lodgment. Not that he be-

[1] See *The Literary Remains of Henry James*, with an Introduction by William James, Boston, 1885.

came a Swedenborgian. The barrier of his idiosyncrasy was too hard and the urge of his need too great for any authority either to pierce or to satisfy: rather, Swedenborg supplied an imaginative material which he could rework into patterns of assurance adequate to correct the mutilation of his accident; his God, his Kosmos, is always a "Perfect Man." He seems never to have attained to the complete expression his system; but he did rework the Swedenborgian matter.

That he did, that he moved out at last into a generosity and calmness of soul which many contemporaries, among them Emerson,[1] testify to, cannot but be regarded a rare spiritual achievement. His tone became one, in Henry James's filial phrasing, of an "almost solely self-nourished equanimity, or in other words insuperable gaiety." This is the tone of all who feel that they have won to saving Vision from the depths. Such spirits cannot do with authority. Feeling themselves possessed of the wellspring of all authority in their own hearts, they move out into the intellectual world either as paranoid prophets of a new dispensation, or as patient warders of The Secret, serenely tolerant in their own assurance of the doubts or assurances of other men. The father of William James came well over the

[1] "I have made no note of these long weary absences at New York and Philadelphia. . . . The people . . . oppress me with their excessive virility, and would soon become intolerable if it were not for a few friends. . . . Henry James was true comfort—wise, gentle, polished, with heroic manners and a serenity like the sun." Quoted from Emerson's Diary in *Notes of a Son and Brother*, pp. 203, 204, by Henry James.

border of this latter class. His son Henry[1] tells how, importuned to say what church they "went" to, "it was colder than any criticism . . . to hear our father reply that we could plead nothing less than the whole privilege of Christendom and that there was no communion, even that of the Catholics, even that of the Jews, even that of the Swedenborgians, from which we need find ourselves excluded."

This generosity toward the sects was repeated in the other reaches of life which Henry James the elder and his family touched. It was, as families go nowadays, a large family—William James had three brothers and one sister—and unique in that the father maintained with his children an intimacy of contact hard to parallel, at the same time allowing them a freedom which only recently has been approved as pedagogical correctness. In his family, as in his community, in a word, Henry James lived his philosophy. The "spiritual world" which was its sole theme was a familiar conversational presence, a part of the habit of communication of the daily life, fringe and aura of whatever visible and solid realities the household might be engaged with. What it most counted for to its promulgator, what it could not have helped meaning in the far deep of his heart, was that inversion of earthly by heavenly significations which is compensation for the ineluctable deficiency of this, our life. As he wrote to Emerson on one occasion: "to the angels, says Swedenborg, death means

[1] *A Small Boy and Others*, p. 234.

resurrection to life; by that necessary rule of inversion which keeps them separate from us and us from them, and so prevents our being mutual nuisances. Let us then accept political and all other distractions that choose to come; because what is disorder and wrath and contention on the surface is sure to be the greatest peace at the center, working its way thus to a surface that shall never be disorderly." [1] And as he wrote to another friend,[2] apropos of spiritualism, "What I deny is that spiritual existence can be directly known on earth, known otherwise than by correspondence or inversely. The letter of every revelation must be directly hostile to its spirit, and only inversely accordant, because the very pretension of revelation is that it is a descent, an absolute coming down of truth, a humiliation of it from its own elevated and habitual plane to a lower one." He was keen for the movement outward of the central peace, and his heart and mind were filled with the monition of an imminent millennium, a spiritual revolution which should culminate in a paradisal "scientific society," a "society of the redeemed form of man"; to his sympathetic eye, Fourier and his phalansteries were charged with revolutionary metaphysical intention.

A Secret like this is not one to be kept. The father of William James was naturally eager for audience and following. He wrote books—and paid to print them;

---

[1] *Notes of a Son and Brother*, p. 209.
[2] *Ibid.*, p. 235.

he lectured, he carried on a varied and voluminous correspondence; he took his Secret from America to Europe and back again. But the world was deaf to him. Its mind was on quite other things—on science and industry—not on salvation. Even if it had been concerned about salvation, there is good reason to doubt whether Henry James the elder's scheme of it could have been a map of life for many: its emotional reference was too specified and personal; its patterns were too much arabesques. Though, however, it failed of public regard, it achieved undying public significance through the influence it can be observed to have exercised as constant permeating atmosphere of the home-life of William James's childhood. Thence it carries over into the latter's own philosophy. But not as American. No one would dream of calling Henry James the elder's mutations of Swedenborg in any way typical of America, whether of its intellectual conventions or intellectual rebellions.

III

Certainly toward the making of William James's philosophy there is nothing else in his childhood and youth that contributes so much as does his father's ways of thought and feeling. "Father's ideas," as the household called its head's philosophy, together with the interests and diversions of playtime, counted for a great deal more than anything attained in the formal disciplines of the many schools it was this American philosopher's lot to be bored in.

"William James," writes his son, Henry,[1] "never acknowledged himself as feeling particularly indebted to any of the numerous schools and tutors to whom his father's oscillations between New York, Europe, and Newport confided him. He was sent first to private schools in New York City; but they seem to have been considered inadequate to his needs, for he was not allowed to remain long in any one. Nor were the changes any less frequent after the family moved to Europe (for the second time since his birth) in 1855. He was then thirteen years old. The exact sequence of events during the next five years of restless movements cannot be determined now, but the important points are clear. The family, including by this time three younger brothers and a younger sister as well as a devoted maternal aunt, remained abroad from 1855 to 1858. London, Paris, Boulogne-sur-Mer, and Geneva harbored them for differing periods. In London and Paris governesses, tutors, and a private school of the sort that admits the irregularly educated children of strangers visiting the Continent, administered what must have been a completely discontinuous instruction. In Boulogne, William and his younger brother Henry attended the *Collège* through the winter of 1857-58. This term at the *Collège de Boulogne*, during which he passed his sixteenth birthday, was his earliest experience of thor-

[1] *The Letters of William James*, vol. i, p. 19.

ough teaching, and he once said that it gave him his first conception of earnest work. Then, after a year at Newport, there was another European migration—this time to Geneva for the winter of 1859-60. There William was entered at the 'Academy,' as the present University was still called. He subsequently described himself as having reached Geneva 'a miserable, home-bred, obscure little ignoramus.' During the following summer he was sent for a while to Bonn-am-Rhein, to learn German. Some Latin, mathematics to the extent of the usual school algebra and trigonometry, a smat-tering of German and an excellent familiarity with French—such, in conventional terms, was the net result of his education in 1859. He tried to make up for the deficiencies in his schooling, and as occasion offered he picked up a few words of Greek, attained to a moderate reading knowledge of Italian, and a quite complete command of German. . . .

"He seldom referred to his schooling with anything but contempt, and usually dismissed all reference to it by saying that he 'never had any'."

Among the interests and diversions of playtime, drawing and science began to figure early. His mind was eager, his perceptions keen, specific and precise. There is nothing in the early record, so far as available, apart from the domestic climate, to indicate any dis-position toward philosophy. He seems to have been the usual normal, healthy youngster, with the trends and propensities appropriate to his years. Toughness was not lacking. His brother Henry tells how, having once offered to join some planned excursion, he, Henry, was rebuffed with "I play with boys who curse and swear." Otherwise, his most articulate youthful recollection of William is "at seated play with his pencil under the lamp . . . intently, though summarily, rapidly drawing." More and more, drawing became an overruling interest. It was finally chosen as a career: "I have fully decided," wrote William to his Genevese fellow student, Charles Ritter, "to try being a painter. I shall know in a year or two whether I am made to be one. If not, it will be easy to retreat. There's nothing in the world so despicable as a bad artist." [1] Paternal consent to being a painter was not, however, so easily forthcoming; the father objected to it—later he objected similarly to Henry's being a writer—as *narrowing*. He wanted his children simply, says Henry, "to *be* something unconnected with specific doing, something free and uncommitted, something finer in short than being *that*, whatever it was, might consist of." In the end he gave in. The serious study of art which was begun in Paris was completed in the United States. Paris, France, the father announced, was to be abandoned for Newport, Rhode Island, in order that William James might study with William Hunt, most distinguished of American painters of the time, he having said he would welcome William James as a pupil.

So, toward the end of 1860, after five and a half

[1] *The Letters of William James*, vol. i, p. 23, note.

years in Europe, Henry James and his family returned to America, making a home in Newport, Rhode Island. There William James, in the company of John La Farge, and more or less of his brother Henry, took himself seriously to the study of painting. That it looked like a promising career for him all declare who have been lucky enough to have seen his studies; but after a year he decided that painting wasn't his vocation after all. In the summer of 1861, being then nineteen years of age, he gave up Art for Science. It was arranged that he should enter the Lawrence Scientific School at Harvard. Among his teachers were Charles William Eliot and Louis Agassiz.

His experience shows how excellent is the reason to believe that the artistic and scientific interests are far from being alien to one another. The sensibilities and skill developed in the studio, with its demands upon fine discriminations of outline and tint, upon ordered arrangement of sharply yet not obviously distinguished items and upon centered wholes, found themselves brought into play in the observation and reproduction of biological specimens or chemical mixtures. James's training in art became the fertile apperceptive background for his discipline in science and of a sudden he assimilated the one to the other. "I had a long talk with one of A.'s [Agassiz's] students the other night, and saw for the first time how a naturalist may feel about his trade exactly as an artist does about his. For instance Agassiz would rather take wholly uninstructed people—'for he has to unteach them all they have learned.' He doesn't let them so much as look into a book for a long while; what they learn they must learn for themselves and be *masters* of it all. The consequence is he makes Naturalists of them—doesn't merely cram them; and this student (he had been there two years) said he felt ready to go anywhere in the world now with nothing but his notebook and study out anything quite alone. A. must be a great teacher."

For the eight years following, William James continued his study of science, at Harvard and in Europe. In 1863 he entered the Harvard Medical School, having given some consideration to the practice of medicine as a career offering distinction and an income. But his theoretic interest was too intense. When, in 1865, Agassiz organized his expedition to the Amazon, James joined it, but the experience signified less to him than he had hoped: "if there is anything I hate," he wrote home toward its end, "it is collecting. I don't think it is suited to my genius at all." It served to turn James's face definitely away from natural history toward medicine. He came back to resume his studies in the Harvard Medical School. From there he went in 1867 to Germany, partly to continue his studies, partly in search of health.

IV

The search for health is a central fact in the life of William James. He seems from adolescence on to have suffered from a constitutional frailness, a nervousness, that for long periods sharply limited his activities. President Eliot, then Professor Eliot, whose pupil in chemistry James became in 1861, takes note of a certain instability of attention, and that "his work was much interfered with by ill-health, or rather by something which I imagined to be a delicacy of nervous constitution." This delicacy took many forms, and in Germany became intensified. "Insomnia, digestive disorders, eye troubles, weakness of the back, and sometimes deep depression of spirits followed each other or afflicted him simultaneously." He kept growing worse and worse, to the point of suicidal mania. "I think," he wrote his father from Berlin in the fall of 1867, "it will be just as well for you not to say anything to any of the others about what I shall tell you of my condition hitherto, as it will only give them useless pain. . . . My confinement to my room and inability to indulge in any social intercourse drove me necessarily into reading a great deal, which in my half-starved and weak condition was very bad for me, making me irritable and tremulous in a way I have never before experienced. Two evenings which I spent out, one at Gerlach's, the other at Thies's, aggravated my dorsal symptoms very much, and as I still clung to the hope of amelioration from repose, I avoided going out to the houses where it was possible. Although I cannot exactly say that I got low-spirited, yet thoughts of the pistol, the dagger and the bowl began to usurp an unduly large part of my attention, and I began to think that some change, even if a hazardous one, was necessary. It was at that time that Dr. Carus advised Teplitz. While there, owing to the weakening effects of the baths, both back and stomach got worse if anything; but the beautiful country and a number of drives which I thought myself justified in taking made me happy as a king. . . . I have purposely hitherto written fallacious accounts of my state home, to produce a pleasant impression on you all —but you may rely on the present one as literally certain, and as it makes the others after all only *premature*, I don't see what will be the use of impairing the family confidence in my letters by saying anything about it to them." . . .

But Teplitz was a temporary assuagement. Until November, 1868, James wandered about Germany, in Switzerland, and in France, hearing lectures, reading voluminously in philosophy as well as physiology and trying new cures. When, after eighteen months in Europe, he returned home, his health was no better than when he had left it. For four years he remained practically invalided in Cambridge, doing very little (although he had easily taken his medical degree in 1869) beyond reading—in philosophy chiefly—and writing an occasional review. At some time during this period he plumbed the lowest depth of mood a sensitive and civilized soul can fall to. Here is the record that his son Henry makes of it, and of how he rose out of it.[1]

---

[1] *The Letters of William James*, vol. i, pp. 145-148.

"No reader of the 'Varieties of Religious Experience' can have doubted that he had known religious despondency himself as well as observed the distress of it in others. The problem of the moral constitution of things, the question of man's relation to the Universe,—whether significant or impotent and meaningless,—these had clearly come home to him as more than questions of metaphysical discourse. It was during that period that such doubts invaded his consciousness in a way that was personal and intimate and, for the time being, oppressive. He was tormented by misgivings which almost paralyzed his naturally buoyant spirit. Bad health, a feeling of the purposelessness of his own particular existence, his philosophic doubts and his constant preoccupation with them, all these combined to plunge him into a state of morbid depression. He seems to have hidden the depth of it from those who were about him. He even had an experience of that kind of melancholy 'which takes the form of panic fear.' When he wrote the chapter on the 'sick soul' thirty years later, he put into it an account of this experience. He still disguised it as the report of an anonymous 'French correspondent.' Subsequently he admitted to M. Abauzit that the passage was really the story of his own case,[1] and it may be repeated here, for the words of the fictitious French correspondent, who was really James, are the most authentic

[1] *William James*, by Theodore Flournoy (Geneva, 1911), p. 149, note.

statement that could be given. They will be found at page 160 of the 'Varieties of Religious Experience.'

'Whilst in this state of philosophic pessimism and general depression of spirits about my prospects, I went one evening into a dressing-room in the twilight, to procure some article that was there; when suddenly there fell upon me without any warning, just as if it came out of the darkness, a horrible fear of my own existence. Simultaneously there arose in my mind the image of an epileptic patient whom I had seen in the asylum, a black-haired youth with greenish skin, entirely idiotic, who used to sit all day on one of the benches, or rather shelves, against the wall, with his knees drawn up against his chin, and the coarse gray undershirt, which was his only garment, drawn over them, inclosing his entire figure. He sat there like a sort of sculptured Egyptian cat or Peruvian mummy, moving nothing but his black eyes and looking absolutely non-human. This image and my fear entered into a species of combination with each other. *That shape am I*, I felt, potentially. Nothing that I possess can defend me against that fate, if the hour for it should strike for me as it struck for him. There was such a horror of him, and such a perception of my own merely momentary discrepancy from him, that it was as if something hitherto solid within my breast gave way entirely, and I became a mass of quivering fear. After this the universe was changed for me altogether. I awoke morning after morning with a horrible dread at the pit of my stomach, and with a sense of the in-security of life that I never knew before, and that I have never felt since. It was like a revelation; and although the immediate feelings passed away, the experience has made me sympathetic with the morbid feelings of others ever since. It gradually faded, but for months I was unable to go out into the dark alone.

'In general I dreaded to be left alone. I remember wondering how other people could live, how I myself had ever lived, so unconscious of that pit of insecurity beneath the surface of life. My mother in particular, a very cheerful person, seemed to me a perfect paradox in her unconsciousness of danger, which you may well believe I was very careful not to disturb by revelations of my own state of mind. I have always thought that this experience of melancholia of mind had a religious bearing. . . . I mean that the fear was so invasive and powerful that, if I had not clung to scripture-texts like *The eternal God is my refuge,* etc., *Come unto me all ye that labor and are heavy-laden,* etc., *I am the Resurrection and the Life,* etc., I think I should have grown really insane.'

"The date of this experience cannot and need not be fixed exactly. It was undoubtedly later than the Berlin winter and after the return to Cambridge. Perhaps it was during the winter of 1869-70, for one of the notebooks contains an entry dated April 30, 1870, in which James's resolution and self-confidence appear to be reasserting themselves. This entry must be quoted too. It is not only illuminating with respect to 1870, but suggests parts of the 'Psychology' and of the philosophic essays that later gave comfort and courage to unnumbered readers.

'I think that yesterday was a crisis in my life. I finished the first part of Renouvier's second "Essais" and see no reason why his definition of Free Will— "the sustaining of a thought *because I choose to* when I might have other thoughts"—need be the definition of an illusion. At any rate, I will assume for the present —until next year—that it is no illusion. My first act of free will shall be to believe in free will. For the remainder of the year, I will abstain from the mere speculation and contemplative *Grüblei*[1] in which my nature takes most delight, and voluntarily cultivate the feeling of moral freedom, by reading books favorable to it, as well as by acting. After the first of January, my callow skin being somewhat fledged, I may perhaps return to metaphysical study and skepticism without danger to my powers of action. For the present then remember: care little for speculation; much for the *form* of my action; recollect that only when habits of order are formed can we advance to really interesting fields of action—and consequently accumulate grain on grain of willful choice like a very miser; never forgetting how one link dropped undoes an indefinite number. *Principiis obsta*—Today has furnished the exceptionally passionate initiative which Bain posits

[1] Grubbing among subtleties.

as needful for the acquisition of habits. I will see to the sequel. Not in maxims, not in *Anschauungen,* but in accumulated *acts* of thought lies salvation. *Passet outre.* Hitherto, when I have felt like taking a free initiative, like daring to act originally, without carefully waiting for contemplation of the external world to determine all for me, suicide seemed the most manly form to put my daring into; now, I will go a step further with my will, not only act with it, but believe as well; believe in my individual reality and creative power. My belief, to be sure, *can't* be optimistic—but I will posit life (the real, the good) in the self-governing *resistance* of the ego to the world. Life shall [be built in] doing and suffering and creating.'"

And he built it so. It was a long, hard drag, but by the winter of 1873, he was quite out of the woods, "[William]," wrote Henry James, Senior, to Henry James, . . . "gets on greatly with his teaching; his students—fifty-seven of them—are elated with their luck in having him, and I feel sure he will have next year a still larger number by his fame. He came in the other afternoon while I was sitting alone, and after walking the floor in an animated way for a moment, broke out: 'Bless my soul, what a difference between me as I am now and as I was last spring at this time! Then so hypochondriacal'—he used that word, though perhaps less in substance than form—'and now with my mind so cleared up and restored to sanity. It's the difference between death and life.'

"He had a great effusion. I was afraid of interfering with it, or possibly checking it, but I ventured to ask what especially in his opinion had produced the change. He said several things: the reading of Renouvier (particularly his vindication of the freedom of the will) and of Wordsworth, whom he has been feeding on now for a good while; but more than anything else, his having given up the notion that all mental disorder requires to have a physical basis. This had become perfectly untrue to him. He saw that the mind does act irrespectively of material coercion, and could be dealt with therefore at first hand, and this was health to his bones. It was a splendid declaration, and though I had known from unerring signs of the fact of the change, I never had been more delighted than by hearing of it so unreservedly from his own lips. He has been shaking off his respect for men of mere science as such, and is even more universal and impartial in his mental judgments than I have known him before. . . ."

What healed William James was then not medicine, nor the altered social scene. What healed him was a self-accomplished psychological reintegration, a new sense of his place in the world and the significance of his attitude toward it. What healed him was the attainment of his philosophy. The most enduring and characteristic points of it are what he won to as victor over his own crisis of spirit, as the reorganizer of his own scattering powers. The sense of the resistance

against which he worked, the gigantic effort the work
was, the uncertainty of the outcome, and yet its in-
vincible hopefulness and its validation by the outcome,[1] these are the deepest things that remained with
him. "Fear of life," he writes nearly a score of years
later to Benjamin Paul Blood, "in one form or another
is the great thing to exorcise; but it isn't reason that
will ever do it. Impulse without reason is enough,
and reason without impulse is a poor makeshift. I
take it that no man is educated who has never dallied
with the thought of suicide." Writing of himself to
Mrs. James in the year of their marriage—1878—he
says that the attitude in which he feels most characteristically himself "always involves an element of active
tension, of holding my own, as it were, and trusting
outward things to perform their part so as to make
it a full harmony, but without any *guaranty* that they
will. Make it a guaranty—and the attitude immediately becomes to my consciousness stagnant and stingless. Take away the guaranty, and I feel . . . a
sort of deep enthusiastic bliss, of bitter willingness to
do and to suffer anything, which translates itself physically by a kind of stinging pain inside my breast-bone
(. . . to me an essential element of the whole thing!)
and which . . . authenticates itself to me as the deep-

---

[1] Ever after, the meaning of ideas gets explicated and fulfilled as
their consequences; Religion, for example, now signifies a survival-
value. "God," he writes in *Some Problems*, "God means that you
can dismiss certain kinds of fear."

est principle of all active and theoretic determination which I possess. . . ."

v

Between the utter inwardness and poignancy of the foregoing personal record and the free responses of the American people to the American scene, there is a certain similarity. I say free responses, to distinguish them from the preëstablished ones; from those that had been fixed beforehand by social custom and private habit brought over from Europe. The free responses have to do with the unprecedented, the hazardous, the unpredictable in the adventure of the white man on the American continent. To the free responses, the genteel tradition, though remaining precious, becomes tangential or compensatory. They are most in play in the effort of the pioneer; the will to believe at one's own risk in the outcome of an enterprise the success of which is not guaranteed in advance is what they sum up to. [Freedom, risk, effort, novelty and an indeterminate future are all involved in them. The genteel tradition is their opposite; it underwrites a foregone conclusion, shutting a man into a finished world where his history is foreordained to its last event: "guaranty" is its essence, predestination its method; and guaranty and predestination are the burdens James, in coming to himself, threw off.]

Now neither in the character of his crisis nor in the materials of his healing is there anything American.

The crisis is such as may come to any man anywhere; and the sages of China or the saints of India as well as the wise men of Europe can repeat its like. And as for the materials—no one will claim Renouvier and Wordsworth for America: or even Agassiz, with his science of classification merely, and description, and his opposition to evolution. Agassiz, if he is to be assimilated to anything in America, is to be assimilated to the genteel tradition. Thus far, then, the persons and stuffs in James's intellectual life have been overwhelmingly European; Charles Peirce has only shown himself "as in a glass darkly"; the impact of his genius is still to come. The rest is European. With so many of his most impressionable years spent abroad, James's attitude toward the American scene must have been different from that of one who had grown to young manhood in it—Henry James speaks in one of his autobiographical volumes of his own and his brother's *detachment* of view. Together, these things make the kind of difference in perspectives and appreciations that a sensitive and highly cultured immigrant's might have.

It is of these aliencies and this detachment, concentrated and transfused in William James, that the philosophy of America, the philosophy, indeed, of what is most inwardly untraditional and modern in the whole of white civilization, comes to be. By one of those curious rhymes of which history is full, the private experience of William James and the public experience

of Europeans making a home in the American wilderness, so coincide that the statement of the one becomes
an adequate symbol, a motto and *panache* and complete
surrogate for the adventure of the other. Each comes
to be as the slow throwing-off of traditional conventions, conventions of the habit of thought and conventions of the habit of life. Each is an assertion of
the autonomy and naturalness of the individual; of
his freedom to win to such success or excellence as
is within his scope on his own belief, in his own
way, by his own effort, at his own risk during his
unending struggle to live in this changing world which
was not made for him, this altogether *un*guaranteed
world. The struggle, the initiative, the courage, the
élan and the inventiveness of the pioneer are the
qualities, and not those of the keepers of the genteel
tradition, to which the "self-evident" propositions of
the Declaration of Independence apply; it is because
of the perduration of pioneer attitudes through the
industrial and intellectual transformations of the nineteenth century that the endeavor persists to embody
them in the going institutions of the land.[1] The
genteel tradition being, as I have already observed,
inoperative, being either irrelevant or compensatory to
the qualities of the pioneer and the natural wilderness
which elicited and established them as ways of life, was
preserved intact and held in otiose honor as the content

[1] Cf. Gustavus Myers, *History of American Idealism.*

of the culture of the fathers.[1]   Ultimately, it also must either be penetrated and transformed by the living forces whose thrust is the story of the American commonwealth.   Meanwhile, its forms provided American emotions with a conventional speech and gave rise to that sharp contrast between American practices and American professions that foreign observers love to dwell on.

Now William James was, in a certain sense, brought up amid the genteel tradition; it not only imparted tone and color to the atmosphere in which he lived; it was a strand in his inheritance.   His inward conflict had been, terminally, a conflict with its implications, and he had found freedom for himself and had become in his own domain a pioneer, when he denied those implications to be valid, and, denying, *made* them invalid.   In his lifelong polemic against the "block-universe" of the idealist, against the laws and determinations of the materialist, he extends and perpetuates his own liberation for mankind.

For he had begun, as the record shows, with complete acquiescence in both.   Indeed, the acquiescence survived late in his mind after his heart had said No. James himself testifies for how long a time the idealistic argument of Royce had seemed coercive.   His psychological studies are punctilious in their deference to the teachings and implications of physiology: what in the then state of that science can be reduced to a

[1] Cf. H. M. Kallen, *Culture and Democracy in the United States*

condition of the body gets so reduced, until emotion becomes visceral tonus, the very innermost Self gets identified as the act of breathing and the Word *I* becomes a noun of position merely. You might be a scientific materialist; you might be a pious idealist; but whatever you were, your argument reduced the multitudinous individualities and *quales* of your experience to a single undifferentiated One,—One matter, One idea, One law, One spirit, One energy, One nature, One god, One anything, but One. In that homogeneous and irresistible unity the variety of appearances live and move and have their being, changing and perishing all, while It remains. Unless the varieties of the world are so through and through *one*, the argument runs, there can't be any world at all.

Many years James struggled with the problem which this argument of science and theology opposed to his deepest feelings and most delicate sensibilities. He sought to establish and to vindicate in the context of science the power of the individual active within his group. He sought in the context of science justification for the finite individual divinities of pagan experience and for what is alive in traditional religion. He applied the Darwinian postulates of spontaneous variation, the struggle for survival, the survival of the fit, not only to great men, but to states of mind and to the "laws of thought" themselves. He signalized the importance of the *functions* of things, and how their structures varied with those. He stressed the limitations of science; its value as a method of knowing rather than a content of knowledge. He underscored its basic character as belief and experiment; he threw its omissions into the foreground even while celebrating its powers. But still there remained the problem of how the world could be at all, and not be through and through one. How to pass free of the Scylla of Zeno or Berkeley or Haeckel and the Charybdis of Hume?

The solution that grew upon him with the years was as simple as Columbus's egg.

Monism is inevitable only when you assume that in order for one thing to become another, or to be related to another, it must be the same as the other. Then there is no change, there are no relations; difference is mere appearance; there is only identity without difference, and that is all. But why, asked James, do you make this assumption? Rather, the record shows, because it is convenient for you, than because your experience with the world imposes it on you. On the contrary, suppose you take the world as it comes. Suppose you take the world at its face value. Suppose you don't look for a substance behind experience but accept your experiences for what they declare themselves to be when they arrive. Then reality is what you know it as. You find the substantive parts of it connected by relations as truly present and existent as the parts themselves. You find transition and change, continuity and discontinuity, routine and surprise, multiple unities of manifold kinds, realities of various stuffs and powers, all connected with one another by transitions from next to next, and each standing away, alone, unmitigated, unincludable, now from some things, now from others. You find movement. You find beginnings. You find endings. You find continuity and you find transformation. In a word, the world of the daily life which we touch and see and smell and hear and taste, which we struggle against and work together with, need be none other than we experience it to be. There are onenesses in it, but there are also endless discontinuities; and these *appear;* they *are* what they appear; they do not require dialectic explication. Freedom and chance are just what they are felt to be. Activity, effort, struggle— they are what they are known as.

Likewise the individual; he counts. Be he ever so humble, he counts; his effort counts, his initiative counts. He is, at least, the captain of his own soul. Count him out, and you count out one of the conditions each of which must come together with the others before this or that aggregate change can be. His faith and his endeavor enter into the texture of the things they work on. The faith itself may be just that added difference in the compounding of events which makes them finally over according to his need. Like his intelligence and his other traits, it is an instrument in his struggle for survival, an engine of his fitness—the item that makes his life significant. . .

VI

So in fleeing the genteel tradition, James found America. The instruments of his flight were Renouvier, Darwinism, and the principle of Peirce. The first established freedom for him. The second enabled him to assimilate this freedom, the reality of change and novelty, to the stuffs and textures of science. The last enabled him to round out his envisagement of science as a method and to vindicate his artist's sense of perceptual reality against the words and abstractions which figure so almost exclusively in all that is usually called thinking. Pragmatism and Radical Empiricism are the ripened fruit of the assimilation of these to his own personal struggle and salvation, and thence to the more general struggle and salvation of the European evangelical in the American pioneer.

For the pioneer and his faith in his adventure dominated what was living in the America wherein James had come to a fullness of his powers. The pioneer adventured along three interests—science, the wilderness and industry.

Of these three science was the nearest to James's own enterprise. The period between the publication of Darwin's "Origin of Species," when James was seventeen years old, and his own "Principles of Psychology," when James was forty-eight—the much-scorned mid-Victorian period, in a word—was one of immense ferment and creation in both the natural sciences and the sciences of man. Many of them had their birth in this period; many were transformed. Physics, chemistry, geology, the various branches of biology and physiology underwent tremendous development. Psychology—largely at the hands of James—was transformed from a "mental philosophy" to a natural science. There appeared the social sciences—anthropology, sociology, their branches and variants. It was the period of the liberal because it was a period of genuine liberation. In every dimension of life new ways opened up over which the individual went, free at last from ancient coercions of the folkway of thought or of action. In every direction, from the core of mid-Victorian conventions of mind and conduct, new and surprising roads of intellectual adventure led out into unmapped regions where any man of courage might stake his belief at his own risk and create new sciences of new matters.

The methodological postulates and the basic assumptions of these sciences were, however, to an unsuspected degree, those derived from an earlier age. Their material observations did not for a generation react upon their conclusions and procedure. They retained the traditional absolutisms, and where they could not hold to them so easily, they sought them. James was still in his observational and polemical mood; Mach was making slow way in methodology; logistics was just beginning; Einstein was unborn or a child in arms; Charles Peirce, destined as time goes on to count more and more as a discoverer and innovator, was making his adventures with the geodetic survey, and formulating his observations on the nature of belief and the relations of symbols to reality. Beside James's, Peirce's is the one—for all practical purposes the only one [1]— American name of high significance in the whole mid-Victorian intellectual pioneering. The rest of the company is European. The adventure is European.

For the pioneering of America was not toward a vision of nature; but toward a conquest. The wilderness was too present and too compelling. The struggle to win a livelihood from nature was too absorbing. The North Atlantic seaboard had just been exhausted by the great Civil War. The settled and humanized areas of the continent were in a post-war depression. Their face was set toward Europe, anyhow, and at that, they were not homogeneously given over to the amenities of cultured living. At points the pioneer was on the very doorstep of the genteel.

And to the west and south was the wilderness untamed and calling for domestication. James himself celebrates the inward beauty of the pioneer's visible ugly triumphs over that wilderness, the translumination of its squalid substance by his ideal. James tells in the essay, "On a Certain Blindness in Human Beings," how he had come upon man-made ugliness while journeying in the mountains of North Carolina;

[1] There was, of course, Willard Gibbs, but his work enters late into the stream of public thought.

his civilized self had revolted; he asked the mountaineer who was driving him, "What sort of people are they who have to make these new clearings?" and the mountaineer answered, "All of us. Why, we ain't happy here unless we are getting one of these coves under cultivation." James saw at once that what to him had been denudation was to them personal victory. What was to him a sickening picture on the retina was to them an inspiriting symbol of duty, struggle and success.

His contact with the other, non-competitive, secure and smug phase of American life, with the very quintessence and dead level of the genteel tradition, the Chautauqua, led him to no such swift revision! The security, intelligence and order he saw there gave him the sense of a thing flat and stale. He missed, he says, "the element of precipitousness . . . of strength and strenuousness, intensity and danger. . . . Sweat and effort, human nature strained to its uttermost on the rack, yet getting through alive, and then turning its back on its success to pursue another more rare and arduous still. . . . Heroism, reduced to its bare chance yet ever and anon snatching victory from the jaws of death." And still, he recognized, these qualities might be found distributively among the Chautauquans no less than among the pioneers. A human being is significant through both "his inner virtue *and* his outer place,—neither taken singly, but both conjoined," and the inner virtue *might* be there, even in

Chautauqua.   But it was the pioneer who touched and quickened him most swiftly.

The other direction of pioneering that dominated the period of James's ripening was industry. The young men who had fought the Civil War out of devotion to an ideal set themselves to the conquest of the continent not alone by converting the wilderness into planted fields, but by binding it with railroads and telephones and telegraphs and pipelines, risking life and property on their faith in the prosperous outcome of their enterprise.   Among these young men were many of James's friends and acquaintances.   Their temper, the urge of their endeavor, the element of precipitousness and struggle they carried with them, could not help, even in the Boston-Cambridge atmosphere where James came to maturity, finding some deep congruity with his own old never-to-be-forgotten inward struggle with himself and his victory over madness and despair. His appeal on their behalf in "What Makes a Life Significant" against the Tolstoian blindness, his admonition there to both labor and capital, show the sympathy with the emotion, if not with the conditions and materials, of the entrepreneur's adventure as well as the worker's.

Not that he was blind to the concomitant vices of this adventure—now grown cancerous and crying aloud for excision.   The swindling, the cant, the adroitness, the corruption, the callousness to justice, the toleration and even the gratulation they win especially when they

lead to "success"—these revolted him. He is emphatic
in his repeated denunciations of the worship of this external "success," of the love of size, of the betrayal of
the inward ideal by this or that tyranny of mind or
body. "Live and let live" he sums up, in "What Makes
a Life Significant." His appearances in affairs are appearances always in behalf of the oppressed or exploited
minority. The cause may be mental healing, Christian
Science, psychical research, universal peace, anti-im-
perialism. He does not always embrace it. He is
ever aware of the nearness and not less righteous urge
of its alternatives. As a pacifist, for example, he has
provided the best defense of the military virtues; as
a religionist, of scientific method; as a scientist, of religion; as a democrat, of the importance of great men;
as an individualist, of the claims of the group. He
is concerned chiefly that they shall each have a free
field to make good their claims; that each shall win
or lose by merit, not by favor or by prejudice.

If he has a particular devotion, a most precious
value, it is individuality: it is novelty and variation and
difference of whatever kind. For he saw in those the
living font of nature and the very core of self, where we
are most at home, the firing line of existence. Here
reality *is* made and freedom *is* felt, and novelties *do*
appear, beyond any nay. Take care, then, he urged of
the individual, of the variant, and society will take
care of itself.

In sum, thus, James is a metaphysical democrat. His

philosophy admits everything that can be named to establish its status and make good its claim on a place in the stream of change we call the universe. There, in all-generating and none-favoring nature, no one thing has greater right or more virtue than any other: every item is tentative, adventurous, experimental, unfinished; nothing is; each thing becomes; change and growth are all in each. Whether in the life of man or the infinitesimal item of matter, the incalculable inhabits all; it invalidates all human conclusions and dissolves all natural laws. The latter, indeed, are to be thought, not any longer as the eternal forms of the structure of nature, but as habits of living together, as patterns of behavior that things have acquired through endless time. The laws of nature, like its stuffs, have also a history. Time was when they were not; the time may come when they will again not be. Though together they make a cosmos, there is an infinitude that their unstable and variant self-inclosed system excludes, whence novelties may break through even to us, to touch us and pass, or perhaps to adjust themselves and win to station in the system, warping it out of its first equilibrium into another . . . again and again . . . endlessly. "There is no conclusion; what has concluded that we might conclude in regard to it?"

But though there are no conclusions, there are stoppings, there are cuttings-off, there are decisions. The inward temporal flow of our biography is checked and blocked and crossed and ever and again wrecked by impact of another stream. Sometimes the two compenetrate and mingle their lights yet still the sources and centers remain external and alien to one another. They may enslave or kill one another but they can never be identical with one another. [Identification, harmony, agreement are peripheral; they take place on the margin, not at the center; they are attributes of the fringes of a being's life.] Existences often overlap, but they coincide never. This observation holds alike of universes immeasurable even by light years and divided by endless spaces, of electrons and protons circling in an infinitesimal ring, of men and women in the complicated disorderly growth of their civilizations. An impregnable, a never-to-be-stormed aliency cuts off each individual from every other, keeps each in ultimate oppugnance to every other, forces them to try conclusions upon each other in the struggle to live. Living is all between alternatives. *Either-or* disjoins the push and pull of the impulses, wishes, appetitions, ideas, imaginations and visions within as well as without; also personality is a matter of decision, a matter of constant selection and rejection, of conclusion and cutting off. All your life you keep taking in from among the environmental multitudes pressing for place against you and about you those you feel available for the precarious, fluctuating equilibrium of your existence and rejecting those that will not serve. Perceptions and their variants and derivatives consequently, originating as responses to the multitudinous impact, survive in the variable constellations or patterns of attitudes and things which is your personality as instruments of adjustment. They compose equally the institutions of society and the shrines and withdrawals of the individual. They become true or good or beautiful as they serve to maintain or advance this or that interest as a going concern. Their value *is* their consequences either in the way of knowing or of doing or of being.

Thus, not nature alone is a flux or a transition. Human nature that is spindrift on the face of her is so no less. Values are relations; and that they accrue to this thing or that is an event. Goodness and truth and beauty and rationality are thus not primary: they are neither given nor begged; they are consequential; they eventuate; they are made.[1]

Because of this relativity of ends and instruments, because they can be interchanged in various contexts, progress is possible; the rule of all or nothing, which produces absolutism in metaphysics or science and unmitigated optimism and pessimism in ethics, turns out to be an empty abstraction. Things improve or deteriorate piecemeal; here a little, there a little. With free initiative, faith and due attention and effort, excellences can be and *are* made to accumulate, evils to wear down; life *can* be given direction and can be hab-

---

[1] It is not, you will see, an accident that the phrase *make good* is aboriginal to America.

ituated therein. By our taking consciously with open eyes and firm heart that risk which is the true inwardness of our being, the risk involving "courage weighted with responsibility—such courage as the Nelsons and Washingtons never failed to show after they had taken everything into account that might tell against their success and made every provision to minimize disaster," Nature does get humanized and we do build a home for ourselves in this heedless and antagonistic world.

VII

The generation which was the generation of William James is gone. The world they lived in is gone, and gone because they lived in it. The days of the pioneer are over. "The great open spaces where men are men" is a cliché for ridiculing the romanticism of small-town rubes and city-dudes. It is a phrase put by a journalistic humorist in the mouth of a simple yokel aspiring to be a hero of the type of motion-picture known as "western." It is the most pregnant commentary of all current on the character of the old generation and the outlook of the new. The realities of yesteryear have become the romance of this. Such a transformation is perennial in the life of the generations, to which the old times are always preëminently the good times; never, however, has the gap between the times been so little. Usually the glorious past is far past—its figures are medieval knights, or Roman consuls or Greek athletes: here the original of the heroic image lives next door, writes his autobiography, and takes his ease in a new astounding world his wildest youthful dreams could not have forefigured.

Indeed, between the man as he was in his youth and the medieval knight and the Roman consul and the Greek athlete there is a greater kinship of feeling and setting than between him and the grandson wriggling in the seat alongside in the dark movie-palace. He and his generation have crowded the world with novelties and transformed its very face and figure. Machinery plows the fields and milks the cows; machinery spins the cloth and sews the clothes. Machinery sets up the framework and bakes the bricks and builds the house. It digs the coal and the ore; it smelts the iron, the steel and the copper. It carries him and his grandson over the ground in the automobile or the train, over the sea and under in ships, through the air in the Zeppelin and the plane. It lights and warms his house, it bakes his bread and cooks his meat. It provides his music through the phonograph, brings his entertainment over astounding spaces through the radio; it enables him to converse with however distant friends through the telephone. It prints his newspapers and his books. The goods of life it provides him with, at their poorest, are a far, far cry from those of that newly cut and newly planted Carolinian clearing which "improved" the forest out of existence.

For this comfort beyond the power of kings of art

earlier time, which the pioneer of the nineteenth century created by his initiative, his science, his inventiveness, his courage and his endeavor, his son of the twentieth pays a price. The price is just those qualities of heart and mind which brought the comfort into existence. Machinery standardizes. It takes from the individual his initiative and his individuality. It calls upon conformity far more than on intelligence. It sets a high price upon passive adjustment. It minimizes creative effort. It imposes upon men and women the necessity of doing the same things in the same way at the same time. Their amusements, their opinions, their ideas, are cut by it to a single pattern and a single measure. New York and San Francisco, Chicago and New Orleans, get the same news at the same hour in precisely the same language; they hear the same jokes, and they are exposed to the same exhortations and admonitions and advice. The telegraph, the syndicated boiler-plate, the radio, the telephone and the phonograph overlay the inward variations of human quality and the outward differences of climatic and topographical setting with a uniformity, a centralization, appalling in its flatness, its stupidity, and monotony. They render it nearly impossible for any variant to take root and ripen. They level out and down. Mind and body are regimented at their hands as thoroughly as ever Prussianized army discipline converted a trustful recruit from a human being into a military automaton.

Within the larger mechanization of the common life which reaches adults and children alike, is the lesser one of the public school system. This tends on the whole and in the long run to concentrate the leveling of individuality out and down at its very source, in the child itself. Its mass instruction by means of standardized lessons imparted in standardized ways provide a subsoil on which the larger regimentations of the community feed and thrive.

And this subsoil is itself nourished and strengthened by the intellectual air. Although at the firing line of science, at the line of advance and growth, the relativity of the basic assumptions of all the sciences of matter and space and time and motion and rest wins a gathering recognition; at its core, where it carries most weight and influence, where it compenetrates with the tradition of thought in the western world, science shows itself as increasingly centralized, monistic, determinist, necessitarian, as industry. The inevitable is the only trail it hunts; the formal equivalences and identities of mathematics are its goal. The biological sciences, consequently, look structurally backward toward the formal simplifications of chemistry and physics; psychology retreats into physiology; the social sciences into statistical averages. Quantification is the rule of all their thought. So that the imaginative extension of them to the universe, which is metaphysics or philosophy, replaces the perceptual realities they set out from with the fabricated symbols they end in; radical empiricism is precipitated into materialism or crystallized into neo-realism.

In both cases, variety and fluidity are lost; the individual is assimilated to the mass, his intrinsic value is rejected; his operative significance is ignored. Whatever effect this may have in philosophy, it tends in the social sciences to verify itself. For in his social relations, in the behavior and habituations of a mind among the personages, customs and traditions and ideals of his community, as a man thinks so he is. A society whose sciences belittle or nullify individuality will repress possibly significant individuals; a society that thinks of itself as made up of averages and masses and glorifies them will overlook the distributive individualities that are in fact operative and efficacious in human life and will resign itself to acquiescence in the "social process" instead of aspiring to conscious control of it. When war is treated as a phase of "human nature" instead of the impact and clash of individuals and interests upon one another whose unprevented conflicts, gathering momentum, culminate in war; when the business cycle is regarded as an economic law, instead of the impact and clash of business men upon one another whose unprevented greed makes inflation and depression, of course there will be war, of course there will be unemployment! When all sequences of the conduct of men in groups are treated as abstractions and averages and uncontrollable inevitables, of course they will be what they are treated as: nationalism or crime

or religion, science or art or "morality"—it is all the
same. The attitude toward them, beginning in the high
places, among men and women of prestige and authority, trickles down, trickles down, with its formulations,
to the masses. Now this, now that individual is deflected in their direction. Soon a group has formed
definable by the attitude. Then the attitude generates
habits. The habits, distributive at first, integrate into a
common way of life which is now the custom of the
group. A tradition grows up, centering on the custom
and accounting for it. Both become sacrosanct and are
hedged about with reverence and taboos; opposition
becomes criminal, and variation blasphemous. It is
the established order now; a new set of folkways, holy,
authoritative, beyond challenge or denial. . . . Yet
with alternatives pressing always on the verge.

The folkways of a society regimented by scientific
generalization and machine-made uniformities in its
work, its play, its arts, its religion, are upon us. They
are ominous of coercions more thoroughgoing, more
drastic, than any a primitive community ever grew into.
Their very complexity and sophistication is their own
menace. For in both the life of man and the life of
nature, individuality remains the irreducible surd.
Kept from free development on the highways of life,
it will break out byways for itself: if it cannot come to
its freedom in the natural contexts of its setting, it will
in the perverse. The heart will find compensations
against all coercions, if not in fact, then in dreams or

drugs or crimes or religions; it will win to its dangers
from all Chautauquas, to its securities from all battle-
fields and abysses. Its sentiment of rationality will not
be denied. A new world of our imaginings is always
redressing the balance of an old world of our experiences. No one who looks at modern life with an impersonal eye can fail to note in the growing cumulus of
the perverse compensation for the regimenting of the
natural.

For both this regimentation and perversity, the
teaching of William James is an anodyne and a cor-
rection. It restores proportions. It shows how coercions may be dissolved into consent and perversities
harmonized toward health. It insists on the reality and
due reverence of the individual, but it acknowledges
the many ways in which individuality enters into group-
ings and the larger wholes it there forms. It points out
the genuineness of freedom and initiative and novelty,
but it pays due deference to the dynamic continuities
of experience. It demonstrates the significance of our
freedom, and the power of belief, but it recognizes the
weight of the environment and renders its due to the
inexorable qualities of the perceptually real. It shows
how personality, with its inward variety, its multiplic-
ity and instability, can install this or that one of its interests amid the stream of being and turn the latter
in the desired direction. Because of the continuity
and consubstantiality of thoughts and things, thoughts
are *of* things and efficacious in changing them. Civ-

ilization is the fruit of the compenetration and mutual transformation of thoughts by things and things by thoughts. Its values are *made* values, and themselves alter as we go. In this going there is room for all natures and all ways of being. Each has an excellence proper and luminously obvious to itself, opaque and ineffable to its neighbors. Each lives by struggle, not by status. For each its unique best is to be found in its appropriate courage, weighted with responsibility, and sustained by the sympathetic insight which is tolerance. An expression of what was noblest in the life and labor of the pioneer generation that in the nineteenth century brought into growth the arts and sciences of industrial civilization, the philosophy of William James opens for the children and victims of this civilization in the twentieth century, a clear way out of its levelings and enslavements. It is a map of life for us modern men, a lamp to light our steps upon the hillroad of freedom, courage, and creative endeavor. It expresses what is most deeply inward in our nature, and shows us how to meet the untoward event in hope without illusion.

HORACE M. KALLEN.

THE PHILOSOPHY OF
WILLIAM JAMES

CHAPTER I

PHILOSOPHY AND THE PHILOSOPHER

Philosophy and Philosophical Teaching in the United States [1]

The philosophical teaching, as a rule, in our higher seminaries is in the hands of the president, who is usually a minister of the Gospel, and, as he more often owes his position to general excellence of character and administrative faculty than to any speculative gifts or propensities, it usually follows that "safeness" becomes the main characteristic of his tuition; that his classes are edified rather than awakened, and leave college with the generous youthful impulse, to reflect on the world and our position in it, rather dampened and discouraged than stimulated by the lifeless discussions and flabby formulas they have had to commit to memory. . . .

Let it not be supposed that we are prejudging the

[1] From a letter printed anonymously in the *Nation* for September 21, 1876.

question whether the final results of speculation will be friendly or hostile to the formulas of Christian thought. All we contend for is that we, like the Greeks and the Germans, should now attack things as if there were no official answer preoccupying the field. At present we are bribed beforehand by our reverence or dislike for the official answer. We work with one eye on our problem, and with the other on the consequences to our enemy or to our lawgiver, as the case may be; the result in both cases is mediocrity.

If the best use of our colleges is to give young men a wider openness of mind and a more flexible way of thinking than special technical training can generate, then we hold that philosophy (taken in the broad sense in which our correspondent uses the word) is the most important of all college studies. - However skeptical one may be of the attainment of universal truths (and to make our position more emphatic, we are willing here to concede the extreme Positivistic position), one can never deny that philosophic study means the habit of always seeing an alternative, of not taking the usual for granted, of making conventionalities fluid again, of imagining foreign states of mind. In a word, it means the possession of mental perspective. Touchstone's question, "Hast any philosophy in thee, shepherd?" will never cease to be one of the tests of a well-born nature. It says, Is there space and air in your mind, or must your companions gasp for breath whenever they talk with you? And if our colleges are to make men, and not machines, they should look, above all things, to this aspect for their influence. . . .

As for philosophy, technically so called, or the reflection of man on his relations with the universe, its educational essence lies in the quickening of the spirit to its *problems*. What doctrines students take from their teachers are of little consequence provided they catch from them the living, philosophic attitude of mind, the independent, personal look at all the data of life, and the eagerness to harmonize them. . . .

In short, philosophy, like Molière, claims her own where she finds it. She finds much of it today in physics and natural history, and must and will educate herself accordingly.

Radical Empiricism as a Philosophic Attitude [1]

At most of our American Colleges there are Clubs formed by the students devoted to particular branches of learning; and these clubs have the laudable custom of inviting once or twice a year some maturer scholar to address them, the occasion often being made a public one. I have from time to time accepted such invitations, and afterwards had my discourse printed in one or other of the Reviews. . . . They [2] shed explanatory light upon each other, and taken together express a tolerably definite philosophic attitude in a very untechnical way.

[1] From the Preface to *The Will to Believe,* pp. vii-ix.
[2] The collection of discourses printed in *The Will to Believe.—Ed.*

Were I obliged to give a short name to the attitude in question, I should call it that of *radical empiricism*, in spite of the fact that such brief nicknames are nowhere more misleading than in philosophy. I say "empiricism," because it is contented to regard its most assured conclusions concerning matters of fact as hypotheses liable to modification in the course of future experience; and I say "radical," because it treats the doctrine of monism itself as an hypothesis, and, unlike so much of the half-way empiricism that is current under the name of positivism or agnosticism or scientific naturalism, it does not dogmatically affirm monism as something with which all experience has got to square. The difference between monism and pluralism is perhaps the most pregnant of all the differences in philosophy. *Primâ facie* the world is a pluralism; as we find it, its unity seems to be that of any collection; and our higher thinking consists chiefly of an effort to redeem it from that first crude form. Postulating more unity than the first experiences yield, we also discover more. But absolute unity, in spite of brilliant dashes in its direction, still remains undiscovered, still remains a *Grenzbegriff*. "Ever not quite" must be the rationalistic philosopher's last confession concerning it. After all that reason can do has been done, there still remains the opacity of the finite facts as merely given, with most of their peculiarities mutually unmediated and unexplained. To the very last, there are the various "points of view" which the philosopher must distinguish in discussing the world; and what is inwardly clear from one point remains a bare externality and datum to the other. The negative, the alogical, is never wholly banished. Something—"call it fate, chance, freedom, spontaneity, the devil, what you will" —is still wrong and other and outside and unincluded, from *your* point of view, even though you be the greatest of philosophers. Something is always mere fact and *givenness;* and there may be in the whole universe no one point of view extant from which this would not be found to be the case. "Reason," as a gifted writer says, "is but one item in the mystery; and behind the proudest consciousness that ever reigned, reason and wonder blushed face to face. The inevitable stales, while doubt and hope are sisters. Not unfortunately the universe is wild,—game-flavored as a hawk's wing. Nature is miracle all; the same returns not save to bring the different. The slow round of the engraver's lathe gains but the breadth of a hair, but the difference is distributed back over the whole curve, never an instant true,—ever not quite."

This is pluralism, somewhat rhapsodically expressed. He who takes for his hypothesis the notion that it is the permanent form of the world is what I call a radical empiricist. For him the crudity of experience remains an eternal element thereof. There is no possible point of view from which the world can appear an absolutely single fact. Real possibilities, real indeterminations, real beginnings, real ends, real evil, real crises, catastrophes, and escapes, a real God, and a real moral life, just as common-sense conceives these things, may remain in empiricism as conceptions which that philosophy gives up the attempt either to "overcome" or to reinterpret in monistic form.

Why Men Philosophize [1]

What is the task which philosophers set themselves to perform; and why do they philosophize at all? Almost every one will immediately reply: They desire to attain a conception of the frame of things which shall on the whole be more rational than that somewhat chaotic view which every one by nature carries about with him under his hat. But suppose this rational conception attained, how is the philosopher to recognize it for what it is, and not let it slip through ignorance? The only answer can be that he will recognize its rationality as he recognizes everything else, by certain subjective marks with which it affects him. When he gets the marks, he may know that he has got the rationality.

What, then, are the marks? A strong feeling of ease, peace, rest, is one of them. The transition from a state of puzzle and perplexity to rational comprehension is full of lively relief and pleasure.

But this relief seems to be a negative rather than a positive character. Shall we then say that the feeling

[1] From "The Sentiment of Rationality," in *The Will to Believe*, pp. 63 seq.

of rationality is constituted merely by the absence of any feeling of irrationality? I think there are very good grounds for upholding such a view. All feeling whatever, in the light of certain recent psychological speculations, seems to depend for its physical condition not on simple discharge of nerve-currents, but on their discharge under arrest, impediment, or resistance. Just as we feel no particular pleasure when we breathe freely, but a very intense feeling of distress when the respiratory motions are prevented,—so any unobstructed tendency to action discharges itself without the production of much cogitative accompaniment, and any perfectly fluent course of thought awakens but little feeling; but when the movement is inhibited, or when the thought meets with difficulties, we experience distress. It is only when the distress is upon us that we can be said to strive, to crave, or to aspire. When enjoying plenary freedom either in the way of motion or of thought, we are in a sort of anæsthetic state in which we might say with Walt Whitman, if we cared to say anything about ourselves at such times, "I am sufficient as I am." This feeling of the sufficiency of the present moment, of its absoluteness,—this absence of all need to explain it, account for it, or justify it,— is what I call the Sentiment of Rationality. As soon, in short, as we are enabled from any cause whatever to think with perfect fluency, the thing we think of seems to us *pro tanto* rational.

Whatever modes of conceiving the cosmos facilitate

this fluency, produce the sentiment of rationality. Conceived in such modes, being vouches for itself and needs no further philosophic formulation. . . .

To sum up: No philosophy will permanently be deemed rational by all men which (in addition to meeting logical demands) does not to some degree pretend to determine expectancy, and in a still greater degree make a direct appeal to all those powers of our nature which we hold in highest esteem. Faith, being one of these powers, will always remain a factor not to be banished from philosophic constructions, the more so since in many ways it brings forth its own verification. In these points, then, it is hopeless to look for literal agreement among mankind.

The ultimate philosophy, we may therefore conclude, must not be too strait-laced in form, must not in all its parts divide heresy from orthodoxy by too sharp a line. There must be left over and above the propositions to be subscribed, *ubique, semper, et ab omnibus,* another realm into which the stifled soul may escape from pedantic scruples and indulge its own faith at its own risks; and all that can here be done will be to mark out distinctly the questions which fall within faith's sphere.

The Meaning of Radical Empiricism [1]

I

I give the name of "radical empiricism" to my *Weltanschauung*. Empiricism is known as the opposite of rationalism. Rationalism tends to emphasize universals and to make wholes prior to parts in the order of logic as well as in that of being. Empiricism, on the contrary, lays the explanatory stress upon the part, the element, the individual, and treats the whole as a collection and the universal as an abstraction. My description of things, accordingly, starts with the parts and makes of the whole a being of the second order. It is essentially a mosaic philosophy, a philosophy of plural facts, like that of Hume and his descendants, who refer these facts neither to Substances in which they inhere nor to an Absolute Mind that creates them as its objects. But it differs from the Humian type of empiricism in one particular which makes me add the epithet radical.

To be radical, an empiricism must neither admit into its constructions any element that is not directly experienced, nor exclude from them any element that is directly experienced. For such a philosophy, *the relations that connect experiences must themselves be experienced relations, and any kind of relation experienced must be accounted as "real" as anything else in the system*. Elements may indeed be redistributed, the

[1] From "A World of Pure Experience," in *Essays in Radical Empiricism*, pp. 41-42.

original placing of things getting corrected, but a real place must be found for every kind of thing experienced, whether term or relation, in the final philosophic arrangement.

II [1]

I am interested in another doctrine in philosophy to which I give the name of radical empiricism, and it seems to me that the establishment of the pragmatist theory of truth is a step of first-rate importance in making radical empiricism prevail. Radical empiricism consists first of a postulate, next of a statement of fact, and finally of a generalized conclusion.

The postulate is that the only things that shall be debatable among philosophers shall be things definable in terms drawn from experience. (Things of an unexperienceable nature may exist *ad libitum,* but they form no part of the material for philosophic debate.)

The statement of fact is that the relations between things, conjunctive as well as disjunctive, are just as much matters of direct particular experience, neither more so nor less so, than the things themselves.

The generalized conclusion is that therefore the parts of experience hold together from next to next by relations that are themselves parts of experience. The directly apprehended universe needs, in short, no extraneous trans-empirical connective support, but possesses in its own right a concatenated or continuous structure.

[1] From *The Meaning of Truth*, Preface, pp. xi-xii.

CHAPTER II

THE WORLD WE LIVE IN

The Original Chaos [1]

The world's contents are *given* to each of us in an order so foreign to our subjective interests that we can hardly by an effort of the imagination picture to ourselves what it is like. We have to break that order altogether,—and by picking out from it the items which concern us, and connecting them with others far away, which we say "belong" with them, we are able to make out definite threads of sequence and tendency; to foresee particular liabilities and get ready for them; and to enjoy simplicity and harmony in place of what was chaos. Is not the sum of your actual experience taken at this moment and impartially added together an utter chaos? The strains of my voice, the lights and shades inside the room and out, the murmur of the wind, the ticking of the clock, the various organic feelings you may happen individually to possess, do these make a whole at all? Is it not the only condition of your mental sanity in the midst of them that most of them should become non-existent for you, and that a few

[1] From "Reflex Action and Theism," in *The Will to Believe*, pp. 118-120.

others—the sounds, I hope, which I am uttering—
should evoke from places in your memory that have
nothing to do with this scene associates fitted to combine with them in what we call a rational train of
thought,—rational, because it leads to a conclusion
which we have some organ to appreciate? We have
no organ or faculty to appreciate the simply given
order. The real world as it is given objectively at
this moment is the sum total of all its beings and
events now. But can we think of such a sum? Can
we realize for an instant what a cross-section of all
existence at a definite point of time would be? While
I talk and the flies buzz, a sea-gull catches a fish at
the mouth of the Amazon, a tree falls in the Adiron-
dack wilderness, a man sneezes in Germany, a horse
dies in Tartary, and twins are born in France. What
does that mean? Does the contemporaneity of these
events with one another, and with a million others as
disjointed, form a rational bond between them, and
unite them into anything that means for us a world?
Yet just such a collateral contemporaneity, and nothing else, is the real order of the world. It is an order
with which we have nothing to do but to get away
from it as fast as possible. As I said, we break it:
we break it into histories, and we break it into arts,
and we break it into sciences; and then we begin to
feel at home. We make ten thousand separate serial
orders of it, and on any one of these we react as
though the others did not exist. We discover among

its various parts relations that were never given to sense at all (mathematical relations, tangents, squares, and roots and logarithmic functions), and out of an infinite number of these we call certain ones essential and lawgiving, and ignore the rest. Essential these relations are, but only *for our purpose,* the other relations being just as real and present as they; and our purpose is to *conceive simply* and to *foresee.* Are not simple conception and prevision subjective ends pure and simple? They are the ends of what we call science and the miracle of miracles, a miracle not yet exhaustively cleared up by any philosophy, is that the given order lends itself to the remodeling. It shows itself plastic to many of our scientific, to many of our æsthetic, to many of our practical purposes and ends.

Determinism and Chance [1]

What does determinism profess?

It professes that those parts of the universe already laid down absolutely appoint and decree what the other parts shall be. The future has no ambiguous possibilities hidden in its womb: the part we call the present is compatible with only one totality. Any other future complement than the one fixed from eternity is impossible. The whole is in each and every part, and welds it with the rest into an absolute unity, an iron block,

[1] From "The Dilemma of Determinism," in *The Will to Believe,* pp. 150-154.

in which there can be no equivocation or shadow of
turning.

> "With earth's first clay they did the last man knead,
> And there of the last harvest sowed the seed.
> And the first morning of creation wrote
> What the last dawn of reckoning shall read."

Indeterminism, on the contrary, says that the parts
have a certain amount of loose play on one another, so
that the laying down of one of them does not necessarily determine what the others shall be. It admits
that possibilities may be in excess of actualities, and
that things not yet revealed to our knowledge may
really in themselves be ambiguous. Of two alternative futures which we conceive, both may now be
really possible; and the one become impossible only
at the very moment when the other excludes it by
becoming real itself. Indeterminism thus denies the
world to be one unbending unit of fact. It says there
is a certain ultimate pluralism in it; and, so saying,
it corroborates our ordinary unsophisticated view of
things. To that view, actualities seem to float in a
wider sea of possibilities from out of which they are
chosen; and, *somewhere,* indeterminism says, such possibilities exist, and form a part of truth.

Determinism, on the contrary, says they exist *nowhere,* and that necessity on the one hand and impossibility on the other are the sole categories of the
real. Possibilities that fail to get realized are, for
determinism, pure illusions: they never were possibili-

ties at all. There is nothing inchoate, it says, about this universe of ours, all that was or is or shall be actual in it having been from eternity virtually there. The cloud of alternatives our minds escort this mass of actuality withal is a cloud of sheer deceptions, to which "impossibilities" is the only name that rightfully belongs.

The issue, it will be seen, is a perfectly sharp one, which no eulogistic terminology can smear over or wipe out. The truth *must* lie with one side or the other, and its lying with one side makes the other side false.

The question relates solely to the existence of possibilities, in the strict sense of the term, as things that may, but need not, be. Both sides admit that a volition, for instance, has occurred. The indeterminists say another volition might have occurred in its place: the determinists swear that nothing could possibly have occurred in its place. Now, can science be called in to tell us which of these two point-blank contradictions of each other is right? Science professes to draw no conclusions but such as are based on matters of fact, things that have actually happened; but how can any amount of assurance that something actually happened give us the least grain of information as to whether another thing might or might not have happened in its place? Only facts can be proved by other facts. With things that are possibilities and not facts, facts have no concern. If we have no other evidence than the evidence of existing facts, the possibility-question must remain a mystery never to be cleared up.

And the truth is that facts practically have hardly anything to do with making us either determinists or indeterminists. Sure enough, we make a flourish of quoting facts this way or that; and if we are determinists, we talk about the infallibility with which we can predict one another's conduct; while if we are indeterminists, we lay great stress on the fact that it is just because we cannot foretell one another's conduct, either in war or statecraft or in any of the great and small intrigues and businesses of men, that life is so intensively anxious and hazardous a game. But who does not see the wretched insufficiency of this so-called objective testimony on both sides? What fills up the gaps in our minds is something not objective, not external. What divides us into possibility men and anti-possibility men is different faiths or postulates,—postulates of rationality. To this man the world seems more rational with possibilities in it,—to that man more rational with possibilities excluded; and talk as we will about having to yield to evidence, what makes us monists and pluralists, determinists or indeterminists, is at bottom always some sentiment like this.

The stronghold of the deterministic sentiment is the antipathy to the idea of chance. As soon as we begin to talk indeterminism to our friends, we find a number of them shaking their heads. This notion of alternative possibility, they say, this admission that any one of several things may come to pass, is, after all, only a roundabout name for chance; and chance is something the notion of which no sane mind can for an instant tolerate in the world. What is it, they ask, but barefaced crazy unreason, the negation of intelligibility and law? And if the slightest particle of it exist anywhere, what is to prevent the whole fabric from falling together, the stars from going out, and chaos from recommencing her topsy-turvy reign?

Remarks of this sort about chance will put an end to discussion as quickly as anything one can find. I have already told you that "chance" was a word I wished to keep and use. Let us then examine exactly what it means, and see whether it ought to be such a terrible bugbear to us. I fancy that squeezing the thistle boldly will rob it of its sting.

The sting of the word "chance" seems to lie in the assumption that it means something positive, and that if anything happens by chance, it must needs be something of an intrinsically irrational and preposterous sort. Now, chance means nothing of the kind. It is a purely negative and relative term,[1] giving us no information about that of which it is predicated,

---

[1] Speaking technically, it is a word with a positive denotation, but a connotation that is negative. Other things must be silent about *what* it is: it alone can decide that point at the moment in which it reveals itself.

except that it happens to be disconnected with something else,—not controlled, secured, or necessitated
by other things in advance of its own actual presence.
What I say is that it tells us nothing about what a thing
may be in itself to call it "chance." It may be a bad
thing, it may be a good thing. It may be lucidity, trans-
parency, fitness incarnate, matching the whole system
of other things, when it has once befallen, in an unim-
aginably perfect way. All you mean by calling it
"chance" is that this is not guaranteed, that it may
also fall out otherwise. For the system of other things
has no positive hold on the chance-thing. Its origin
is in a certain fashion negative: it escapes, and says,
Hands off! coming, when it comes, as a free gift, or
not at all.

Thoughts and Things [1]

The problem convenient to take up next in order
will be that of the difference between thoughts and
things. "Things" are known to us by our senses,
and are called "presentations" by some authors, to
distinguish them from the ideas or "representa-
tions" which we may have when our senses are closed.
I myself have grown accustomed to the words "percept"
and "concept" in treating of the contrast, but concepts
flow out of percepts and into them again, they are so
interlaced, and our life rests on them so interchange-

[1] From "Percept and Concept—The Import of Concepts," in *Some
Problems of Philosophy,* pp. 47-74.

ably and undiscriminatingly, that it is often difficult to impart quickly to beginners a clear notion of the difference meant. Sensation and thought in man are mingled, but they vary independently. In our quadrupedal relatives thought proper is at a minimum, but we have no reason to suppose that their immediate life of feeling is either less or more copious than ours. Feeling must have been originally self-sufficing; and thought appears as a superadded function, adapting us to a wider environment than that of which brutes take account. Some parts of the stream of feeling must be more intense, emphatic, and exciting than others in animals as well as in ourselves; but whereas lower animals simply react upon these more salient sensations by appropriate movements, higher animals remember them, and men react on them intellectually, by using nouns, adjectives, and verbs to identify them when they meet them elsewhere.

The great difference between percepts and concepts [1] is that percepts are continuous and concepts are discrete. Not discrete in their *being*, for conception as an *act* is part of the flux of feeling, but discrete from each other in their several *meanings*. Each concept means just what it singly means, and nothing else;

[1] In what follows I shall freely use synonyms for these two terms "Idea," "thought," and "intellection" are synonymous with "concept." Instead of "percept" I shall often speak of "sensation," "feeling," "intuition," and sometimes of "sensible experience" or of the "immediate flow" of conscious life. Since Hegel's time what is simply perceived has been called the "immediate," while the "mediated" is synonymous with what is conceived.

and if the conceiver does not know whether he means this or means that, it shows that his concept is imperfectly formed. The perceptual flux as such, on the contrary, *means* nothing, and is but what it immediately is. No matter how small a tract of it be taken, it is always a much-at-once, and contains innumerable aspects and characters which conception can pick out, isolate, and thereafter always intend. It shows duration, intensity, complexity or simplicity, interestingness, excitingness, pleasantness or their opposites. Data from all our senses enter into it, merged in a general extensiveness of which each occupies a big or little share. Yet all these parts leave its unity unbroken. Its boundaries are no more distinct than are those of the field of vision. Boundaries are things that intervene; but here nothing intervenes save parts of the perceptual flux itself, and these are overflowed by what they separate, so that whatever we distinguish and isolate conceptually is found perceptually to telescope and compenetrate and diffuse into its neighbors. The cuts we make are purely ideal. If my reader can succeed in abstracting from all conceptual interpretation and lapse back into his immediate sensible life at this very moment, he will find it to be what some one has called a big blooming buzzing confusion, as free from contradiction in its "much-at-onceness" as it is all alive and evidently there.

Out of this aboriginal sensible muchness attention carves out objects, which conception then names and identifies forever—in the sky "constellations," on the earth "beach," "sea," "cliff," "bushes," "grass." Out of time we cut "days" and "nights," "summers" and "winters." We say *what* each part of the sensible continuum is, and all these abstracted *whats* are concepts.

The intellectual life of man consists almost wholly in his substitution of a conceptual order for the perceptual order in which his experience originally comes. But before tracing the consequences of the substitution, I must say something about the conceptual order itself.

Trains of concepts unmixed with percepts grow frequently in the adult mind; and parts of these conceptual trains arrest our attention just as parts of the perceptual flow did, giving rise to concepts of a higher order of abstractness. So subtle is the discernment of man, and so great the power of some men to single out the most fugitive elements of what passes before them, that these new formations have no limit. Aspect within aspect, quality after quality, relation upon relation, absences and negations as well as present features, end by being noted and their names added to the store of nouns, verbs, adjectives, conjunctions, and prepositions by which the human mind interprets life. Every new book verbalizes some new concept, which becomes important in proportion to the use that can be made of it. Different universes of thought thus arise, with specific sorts of relation among their ingredients. The world of common-sense "things"; the world of material tasks to be done; the mathematical world of pure forms; the world of ethical propositions; the worlds of logic, of music, etc., all abstracted and generalized from long forgotten perceptual instances, from which they have as it were flowed out, return and merge themselves again in the particulars of our present and future perception. By those *whats* we apperceive all our *thises*. Percepts and concepts interpenetrate and melt together, impregnate and fertilize each other. Neither, taken alone, knows reality in its completeness. We need them both, as we need both our legs to walk with.

From Aristotle downwards philosophers have frankly admitted the indispensability, for complete knowledge of fact, of both the sensational and the intellectual contribution. For complete knowledge of fact, I say; but facts are particulars and connect themselves with practical necessities and the arts; and Greek philosophers soon formed the notion that a knowledge of so-called "universals," consisting of concepts of abstract forms, qualities, numbers, and relations was the only knowledge worthy of the truly philosophic mind. Particular facts decay and our perceptions of them vary. A concept never varies; and between such unvarying terms the relations must be constant and express eternal verities. Hence there arose a tendency, which has lasted all through philosophy, to contrast the knowledge of universals and intelligibles, as godlike, dignified, and honorable to the knower, with that of particulars and sensibles as something relatively base which more allies us with the beasts.

For rationalistic writers conceptual knowledge was not only the more noble knowledge, but it originated independently of all perceptual particulars. Such concepts as God, perfection, eternity, infinity, immutability, identity, absolute beauty, truth, justice, necessity, freedom, duty, worth, etc., and the part they play in our mind, are, it was supposed, impossible to explain as results of practical experience. The empiricist view, and probably the true view, is that they do result from practical experience. But a more important question than that as to the origin of our concepts is that as to their functional use and value;—is *that* tied down to perceptual experience, or out of all relation to it? Is conceptual knowledge self-sufficing and a revelation all by itself, quite apart from its uses in helping to a better understanding of the world of sense?

Rationalists say, Yes. For, as we shall see in later places . . . the various conceptual universes referred to . . . can be considered in complete abstraction from perceptual reality, and when they are so considered, all sorts of fixed relations can be discovered among their parts. From these the *a priori* sciences of logic, mathematics, ethics, and æsthetics (so far as the last two can be called sciences at all) result. Conceptual knowledge must thus be called a self-sufficing revelation; and by rationalistic writers it has always been treated as admitting us to a diviner world, the world of universal rather than that of perishing facts, of essential qualities, immutable relations, eternal principles of truth and right. Emerson writes: "Generalization is always a new influx of divinity into the mind: hence the thrill that attends it." And a disciple of Hegel, after exalting the knowledge of "the General, Unchangeable, and alone Valuable" above that of "the Particular, Sensible, and Transient," adds that if you reproach philosophy with being unable to make a single grass-blade grow, or even to know how it does grow, the reply is that since such a particular "how" stands not above but below knowledge, strictly so-called, such an ignorance argues no defect.

To this ultra-rationalistic opinion the empiricist contention that *the significance of concepts consists always in their relation to perceptual particulars* has been poposed. Made of percepts, or distilled from parts of percepts, their essential office, it has been said, is to coalesce with percepts again, bringing the mind back into the perceptual world with a better command of the situation there. Certainly whenever we *can* do this with our concepts, we do *more* with them than when we leave them flocking with their abstract and motionless companions. It is possible, therefore, to join the rationalists in allowing conceptual knowledge to be self-sufficing, while at the same time one joins the empiricists in maintaining that the full *value* of such knowledge is got only by combining it with perceptual reality again. This mediating attitude is that which this book must adopt. But to understand the nature of concepts better we must now go on to distinguish their *function* from their *content*.

The concept "man," to take an example, is three things: 1, the word itself; 2, a vague picture of the human form which has its own value in the way of beauty or not; and 3, an instrument for symbolizing certain objects from which we may expect human treatment when occasion arrives. Similarly of "triangle," "cosine,"—they have their substantive value both as words and as images suggested, but they also have a functional value whenever they lead us elsewhere in discourse.

There are concepts, however, the image-part of which is so faint that their whole value seems to be functional. "God," "cause," "number," "substance," "soul," for example, suggest no definite picture; and their significance seems to consist entirely in their *tendency*, in the further turn which they may give to our action or our thought. We cannot rest in the contemplation of their form, as we can in that of a "circle" or a "man"; we must pass beyond.

Now however beautiful or otherwise worthy of stationary contemplation the substantive part of a concept may be, the more important part of its significance may naturally be held to be the consequences to which it leads. These may lie either in the way of making us think, or in the way of making us act. Whoever has a clear idea of these knows effectively what the concept practically signifies, whether its substantive content be interesting in its own right or not.

This consideration has led to a method of interpreting concepts to which I shall give the name of *the Pragmatic Rule*.[1]

The pragmatic rule is that the meaning of a concept may always be found, if not in some sensible particular which it directly designates, then in some particular difference in the course of human experience which its being true will make. Test every concept by the question "What sensible difference to anybody will its truth make?" and you are in the best possible position for understanding what it means and for discussing its importance. If, questioning whether a certain concept be true or false, you can think of absolutely nothing that would practically differ in the two cases, you may assume that the alternative is meaningless and that your concept is no distinct idea. If two concepts lead you to infer the same particular consequence, then you may assume that they embody the same meaning under different names.

This rule applies to concepts of every order of complexity from simple terms to propositions uniting many terms.

So many disputes in philosophy hinge upon ill-defined

---

[1] Compare W. James, *Pragmatism*, chap. ii and *passim;* also Baldwin's *Dictionary of Philosophy*, article "Pragmatism," by C. S. Peirce.

words and ideas, each side claiming its own word or idea to be true, that any accepted method of making meanings clear must be of great utility. No method can be handier of application than our pragmatic rule. If you claim that any idea is true, assign at the same time some difference that its being true will make in some possible person's history, and we shall know not only just what you are really claiming but also how important an issue it is, and how to go to work to verify the claim. In obeying this rule we neglect the substantive content of the concept, and follow its function only. This neglect might seem at first sight to need excuse, for the content often has a value of its own which might conceivably add luster to reality, if it existed, apart from any modification wrought by it in the other parts of reality. Thus it is often supposed that "Idealism" is a theory precious in itself, even though no definite change in the details of our experience can be deduced from it. Later discussion will show that this is a superficial view, and that particular consequences are the only criterion of a concept's meaning, and the only test of its truth.

Instances are hardly called for, they are so obvious. That A and B are "equal," for example, means either that "you will find no difference" when you pass from one to the other, or that in substituting one for the other in certain operations "you will get the same result both times." "Substance" means that "a definite group of sensations will recur." "Incommensurable" means that "you are always confronted with a remainder." "Infinite" means either that, or that "you can count as many units in a part as you can in the whole." "More" and "less" mean certain sensations, varying according to the matter. "Freedom" means "no feeling of sensible restraint." "Necessity" means that "your way is blocked in all directions save one." "God" means that "you can dismiss certain kinds of fear," "cause" that "you may expect certain sequences," etc., etc. We shall find plenty of examples in the rest of this book; so I go back now to the more general question of whether the whole import of the world of concepts lies in its relation to perceptual experience, or whether it be also an independent revelation of reality. Great ambiguity is possible in answering this question, so we must mind our Ps and Qs.

The first thing to notice is that in the earliest stages of human intelligence, so far as we can guess at them, thought proper must have had an exclusively practical use. Men classed their sensations, substituting concepts for them, in order to "work them for what they were worth," and to prepare for what might lie ahead. Class-names suggest consequences that have attached themselves on other occasions to other members of the class—consequences which the present percept will also probably or certainly show.[1] The present percept in

---

[1] For practical uses of conception compare W. James, *Principles of Psychology*, chap. xxii; J. E. Miller, "The Psychology of Thinking," 1909, *passim,* but especially chaps. xv, xvi, xvii.

its immediacy may thus often sink to the status of a bare sign of the consequences which the substituted concept suggests.

The substitution of concepts and their connections, of a whole conceptual order, in short, for the immediate perceptual flow, thus widens enormously our mental panorama. Had we no concepts we should live simply "getting" each successive moment of experience, as the sessile sea-anemone on its rock receives whatever nourishment the wash of the waves may bring. With concepts we go in quest of the absent, meet the remote, actively turn this way or that, bend our experience, and make it tell us whither it is bound. We change its order, run it backwards, bring far bits together and separate near bits, jump about over its surface instead of plowing through its continuity, string its items on as many ideal diagrams as our mind can frame. All these are ways of *handling* the perceptual flux and *meeting* distant parts of it; and as far as this primary function of conception goes, we can only conclude it to be what I began by calling it, a faculty superadded to our barely perceptual consciousness for its use in practically adapting us to a larger environment than that of which brutes take account.[1] We *harness* perceptual reality in concepts in order to drive it better to our ends.

Does our conceptual translation of the perceptual

[1] Herbert Spencer in his *Psychology*, parts iii and iv, has at great length tried to show that such adaptation is the sole meaning of our intellect.

flux enable us also to understand the latter better? What do we mean by making us "understand"? Applying our pragmatic rule to the interpretation of the word, we see that the better we understand anything the more we are able to *tell about it*. Judged by this test, concepts do make us understand our percepts better: knowing *what* these are, we can tell all sorts of farther truths about them, based on the relation of those whats to other whats. The whole system of relations, spatial, temporal, and logical, of our fact, gets plotted out. An ancient philosophical opinion, inherited from Aristotle, is that we do not understand a thing until we know it by its causes. When the maidservant says that "the cat" broke the tea-cup, she would have us conceive the fracture in a causally explanatory way. No otherwise when Clerk-Maxwell asks us to conceive of gas-electricity as due to molecular bombardment. An imaginary agent out of sight becomes in each case a part of the cosmic context in which we now place the percept to be explained; and the explanation is valid in so far as the new causal *that* is itself conceived in a context that makes its existence probable, and with a nature agreeable to the effects it is imagined to produce. All our scientific explanations would seem to conform to this simple type of the "necessary cat." The conceived order of nature built round the perceived order and explaining it theoretically, as we say, is only a system of hypothetically imagined *thats*, the *whats* of which harmoniously connect themselves with the *what* of any *that* which we immediately perceive.

The system is essentially a topographic system, a system of the distribution of things. It tells us what's what, and where's where. In so far forth it merely prolongs that opening up of the perspective of practical consequences which we found to be the primordial utility of the conceiving faculty: it adapts us to an immense environment. Working by the causes of things we gain advantages which we never should have compassed had we worked by the things alone.

But in order to reach such results the concepts in the explanatory system must, I said, "harmoniously connect." What does that mean? Is this also only a practical advantage, or is it something more? It seems something more, for it points to the fact that when concepts of various sorts are once abstracted or constructed, new relations are then found between them, connecting them in peculiarly intimate, "rational," and unchangeable ways. In another book [1] I have tried to show that these rational relations are all products of our faculty of comparison and of our sense of "more."

The sciences which exhibit these relations are the so-called *a priori* sciences of mathematics and logic. But these sciences express relations of comparison and identification exclusively. Geometry and algebra, for example, first define certain conceptual objects, and

[1] *Principles of Psychology,* 1890, chap. xxviii.

then establish equations between them, substituting
equals for equals. Logic has been defined as the "substitution of similars"; and in general one may say that
the perception of likeness and unlikeness generates the
whole of "rational" or "necessary" truth. Nothing
happens in the worlds of logic, mathematics or moral
and æsthetic preference. The static nature of the relations in these worlds is what gives to the propositions
that express them their "eternal" character: The bi-
nomial theorem, e. g., expresses the value of any power
of any sum of two terms, to the end of time.

These vast unmoving systems of universal terms
form the new worlds of thought of which I spoke.
. . . The terms are elements (or are framed of
elements) abstracted from the perceptual flux; but in
their abstract shape we note relations between them
(and again between these relations) which enable us
to set up various schemes of fixed serial orders or of
"more and more." The terms are indeed man-made,
but the order, being established solely by comparison,
is fixed by the nature of the terms on the one hand
and by our power of perceiving relations on the other.
Thus two abstract twos are always the same as an abstract four; what contains the container contains the
contained of whatever material either be made; equals
added to equals always give equal results, in the world
in which abstract equality is the only property the
terms are supposed to possess; the more than the more
is more than the less, no matter in what direction of

moreness we advance; if you dot off a term in one series every time you dot one off in another, the two series will either never end, or will come to an end together, or one will be exhausted first, etc., etc.; the result being those skeletons of "rational" or "necessary" truth in which our logic- and mathematic-books (sometimes our philosophy-books) arrange their universal terms.

The "rationalization" of any mass of perceptual fact consists in assimilating its concrete terms, one by one, to so many terms of the conceptual series, and then in assuming that the relations intuitively found among the latter are what connect the former too. Thus we rationalize gas-pressure by identifying it with the blows of hypothetic molecules; then we see that the more closely the molecules are crowded the more frequent the blows upon the containing walls will become; then we discern the exact proportionality of the crowding with the number of blows; so that finally Mariotte's empirical law gets rationally explained. All our transformations of the sense-order into a more rational equivalent are similar to this one. We interrogate the beautiful apparition, as Emerson calls it, which our senses ceaselessly raise upon our path, and the items there refer us to their interpretants in the shape of ideal constructions in some static arrangement which our mind has already made out of its concepts alone. The interpretants are then substituted for the sensations, which thus get rationally conceived. To "explain" means to coördinate, one to one, the *thises* of the perceptual flow with the *whats* of the ideal manifold, whichever it be.

We may well call this a theoretic conquest over the order in which nature originally comes. The conceptual order into which we translate our experience seems not only a means of practical adaptation, but the revelation of a deeper level of reality in things. Being more constant, it is *truer,* less illusory than the perceptual order, and ought to command our attention more.

There is still another reason why conception appears such an exalted function. Concepts not only guide us over the map of life, but we *revalue* life by their use. Their relation to percepts is like that of sight to touch. Sight indeed helps us by preparing us for contacts while they are yet far off, but it endows us in addition with a new world of optical splendor, interesting enough all by itself to occupy a busy life. Just so do concepts bring their proper splendor. The mere possession of such vast and simple pictures is an inspiring good: they arouse new feelings of sublimity, power, and admiration, new interests and motivations.

Ideality often clings to things only when they are taken thus abstractly. "Causes, as anti-slavery, democracy, etc., dwindle when realized in their sordid particulars. Abstractions will touch us when we are callous to the concrete instances in which they lie embodied. Loyal in our measure to particular ideals, we soon set up abstract loyalty as something of a superior

order, to be infinitely loyal to; and truth at large becomes a 'momentous issue' compared with which truths
in detail are 'poor scraps, mere crumbling successes.' "
So strongly do objects that come as universal and eternal arouse our sensibilities, so greatly do life's values
deepen when we translate percepts into ideas! The
translation appears as far more than the original's
equivalent.

Concepts thus play three distinct parts in human
life.

1. They steer us practically every day, and provide
an immense map of relations among the elements of
things, which, though not now, yet on some possible
future occasion, may help to steer us practically;

2. They bring new values into our perceptual life,
they reanimate our wills, and make our action turn
upon new points of emphasis;

3. The map which the mind frames out of them is
an object which possesses, when once it has been
framed, an independent existence. It suffices all by
itself for purposes of study. The "eternal" truths it
contains would have to be acknowledged even were
the world of sense annihilated.

We thus see clearly what is gained and what is lost
when percepts are translated into concepts. Perception
is solely of the here and now; conception is of the
like and unlike, of the future, of the past, and of the
far away. But this map of what surrounds the present,
like all maps, is only a surface; its features are but

abstract signs and symbols of things that in themselves are concrete bits of sensible experience. We have but to weigh extent against content, thickness against spread, and we see that for some purposes the one, for other purposes the other, has the higher value. Who can decide offhand which is absolutely better, to live or to understand life? We must do both alternately, and a man can no more limit himself to either than a pair of scissors can cut with a single one of its blades.

What Is It to Be Real? [1]

What is it to be "real"? The best definition I know is that which the pragmatist rule gives: "anything is real of which we find ourselves obliged to take account in any way." Concepts are thus as real as percepts, for we cannot live a moment without taking account of them. But the "eternal" kind of being which they enjoy is inferior to the temporal kind, because it is so static and schematic and lacks so many characters which temporal reality possesses. Philosophy must thus recognize many realms of reality which mutually interpenetrate. The conceptual systems of mathematics, logic, æsthetics, ethics, are such realms, each strung upon some peculiar form of relation, and each differing from perceptual reality in that in no one of them is history or happening displayed. Perceptual reality involves and contains all these ideal systems, and vastly more besides.

[1] From *Some Problems of Philosophy*, pp. 101-108.

A concept, it was said above, means always the same thing: Change means always change, white always white, a circle always a circle. On this self-sameness of conceptual objects the static and "eternal" character of our systems of ideal truth is based; for a relation, once perceived to obtain, must obtain always, between terms that do not alter. But many persons find difficulty in admitting that a concept used in different contexts can be intrinsically the same. When we call both snow and paper "white" it is supposed by these thinkers that there must be two predicates in the field. As James Mill says:[1] "Every colour is an individual colour, every size is an individual size, every shape is an individual shape. But things have no individual colour in common, no individual shape in common; no individual size in common; that is to say, they have neither shape, colour, nor size in common. What, then, is it which they have in common which the mind can take into view? Those who affirmed that it was something, could by no means tell. They substituted words for things; using vague and mystical phrases, which, when examined, meant nothing." The truth, according to this nominalist author, is that the only thing that can be possessed in common by two objects is the same *name*. Black in the coat and black in the shoe are the same in so far forth as both shoe and coat are called black—the fact that on this view the name can never twice be the "same" being quite overlooked.

[1] *Analysis of the Human Mind.* 1869, i, 249.

What now does the concept "same" signify? Applying, as usual, the pragmatic rule, we find that when we call two objects the same we mean either (a) that no difference can be found between them when compared, or (b) that we can substitute the one for the other in certain operations without changing the result. If we are to discuss sameness profitably we must bear these pragmatic meanings in mind.

Do then the snow and the paper show no difference in color? And can we use them indifferently in operations? They may certainly replace each other for reflecting light, or be used indifferently as backgrounds to set off anything dark, or serve as equally good samples of what the word "white" signifies. But the snow may be dirty, and the paper pinkish or yellowish without ceasing to be called "white"; or both snow and paper in one light may differ from their own selves in another and still be "white,"—so the no-difference criterion seems to be at fault. This physical difficulty (which all house painters know) of matching two tints so exactly as to show no difference seems to be the sort of fact that nominalists have in mind when they say that our ideal meanings are never twice the same. Must we therefore admit that such a concept as "white" can never keep exactly the same meaning?

It would be absurd to say so, for we know that under all the modifications wrought by changing light, dirt, impurity in pigment, etc., there is an element of color-quality, different from other color-qualities, which we mean that our word *shall* inalterably signify. The impossibility of isolating and fixing this quality physically is irrelevant, so long as we can isolate and fix it mentally, and decide that whenever we say "white," that identical quality, whether applied rightly or wrongly, is what we shall be held to mean. Our meanings can be the same as often as we intend to have them so, quite irrespective of whether what is meant be a physical possibility or not. Half the ideas we make use of are of impossible or problematic things—zeros, infinites, fourth dimensions, limits of ideal perfection, forces, relations sundered from their terms, or terms defined only conceptually, by their relations to other terms which may be equally fictitious. "White" means a color quality of which the mind appoints the standard, and which it can decree to be there under all physical disguises. *That* white is always the same white. What sense can there be in insisting that although we ourselves have fixed it as the same, it cannot be the same twice over? It works perfectly for us on the supposition that it is there self-identically; so the nominalist doctrine is false of things of that conceptual sort, and true only of things in the perceptual flux.

What I am affirming here is the platonic doctrine that concepts are singulars, that concept-stuff is inalterable, and that physical realities are constituted by the various concept-stuffs of which they "partake." It is known as "logical realism" in the history of philosophy; and has usually been more favored by rationalistic than by empiricist minds. For rationalism, concept-stuff is primordial and perceptual things are secondary in nature. The present book, which treats concrete percepts as primordial and concepts as of secondary origin, may be regarded as somewhat eccentric in its attempt to combine logical realism with an otherwise empiricist mode of thought.

I mean by this that they are made of the same kind of stuff, and melt into each other when we handle them together. How could it be otherwise when the concepts are like evaporations out of the bosom of perception, into which they condense again whenever practical service summons them? No one can tell, of the things he now holds in his hand and reads, how much comes in through his eyes and fingers, and how much, from his apperceiving intellect, unites with that and makes of it this particular "book"? The universal and the particular parts of the experience are literally immersed in each other, and both are indispensable. Conception is not like a painted hook, on which no real chain can be hung; for we hang concepts upon percepts, and percepts upon concepts interchangeably and indefinitely; and the relation of the two is much more like what we find in those cylindrical "panoramas" in which a painted background continues a real foreground so cunningly that one fails to detect the joint. The world we practically live in is one in which it is impossible, except by theoretic retrospection, to disentangle the contributions of intellect from those of sense. They are wrapt and rolled together as a gunshot in the mountains is wrapt and rolled in fold on fold of echo and reverberative clamor. Even so do intellectual reverberations enlarge and prolong the perceptual experience which they envelop, associating it with remoter parts of existence. And the ideas of these in turn work like those resonators that pick out partial tones in complex sounds. They help us to decompose our percept into parts and to abstract and isolate its elements.

The Stuffs of Experience [1]

First of all, this will be asked: "If experience has not 'conscious' existence, if it be not partly made of 'consciousness,' of what then is it made? Matter we know, and thought we know, and conscious content we know, but neutral and simple 'pure experience' is something we know not at all. Say *what* it consists of—for it must consist of something—or be willing to give it up!"

To this challenge the reply is easy. Although for fluency's sake I myself spoke early in this article of a stuff of pure experience, I have now to say that there is no *general* stuff of which experience at large is made. There are as many stuffs as there are "natures" in the things experienced. If you ask what any one bit of

[1] From "Does 'Consciousness' Exist?" in *Essays on Radical Empiricism*, pp. 26-30.

pure experience is made of, the answer is always the same: "It is made of *that,* of just what appears, of space, of intensity, of flatness, brownness, heaviness, or what not." Shadworth Hodgson's analysis here leaves nothing to be desired. Experience is only a collective name for all these sensible natures, and save for time and space (and, if you like, for "being") there appears no universal element of which all things are made.

The next objection is more formidable, in fact it sounds quite crushing when one hears it first.

"If it be the self-same piece of pure experience, taken twice over, that serves now as thought and now as thing"—so the objection runs—"how comes it that its attributes should differ so fundamentally in the two takings? As thing, the experience is extended; as thought, it occupies no space or place. As thing, it is red, hard, heavy; but who ever heard of a red, hard or heavy thought? Yet even now you said that an experience is made of just what appears, and what appears is just such adjectives. How can the one experience in its thing-function be made of them, consist of them, carry them as its own attributes, while in its thought-function it disowns them and attributes them elsewhere? There is a self-contradiction here from which the radical dualism of thought and thing is the only truth that can save us. Only if the thought is one kind of being can the adjectives exist in it 'intentionally' (to use the scholastic term); only if the thing is another kind, can they exist in it constitutively and energetically. No simple subject can take the same adjectives and at one time be qualified by it, and at another time be merely 'of' it, as of something only meant or known."

The solution insisted on by this objector, like many other common-sense solutions, grows the less satisfactory the more one turns it in one's mind. To begin with, *are* thought and thing as heterogeneous as is commonly said?

No one denies that they have some categories in common. Their relations to time are identical. Both, moreover, may have parts (for psychologists in general treat thoughts as having them); and both may be complex or simple. Both are of kinds, can be compared, added and subtracted and arranged in serial orders. All sorts of adjectives qualify our thoughts which appear incompatible with consciousness, being as such a bare diaphaneity. For instance, they are natural and easy, or laborious. They are beautiful, happy, intense, interesting, wise, idiotic, focal, marginal, insipid, confused, vague, precise, rational, casual, general, particular, and many things besides. Moreover, the chapters on "Perception" in the psychology-books are full of facts that make for the essential homogeneity of thought with thing. How, if "subject" and "object" were separated "by the whole diameter of being," and had no attributes in common, could it be so hard to tell, in a presented and recognized material object, what part comes in through the sense-organs and what part comes "out of one's own head"? Sensations and apperceptive ideas fuse here so intimately that you can no more tell where one begins and the other ends, than you can tell, in those cunning circular panoramas that have lately been exhibited, where the real foreground and the painted canvas join together.

The Reality of Novelty [1]

The impotence to explain being which we have attributed to all philosophers is, it will be recollected, a conceptual impotence. It is when thinking abstractly of the whole of being at once, as it confronts us ready-made, that we feel our powerlessness so acutely. Possibly, if we followed the empiricist method, considering the parts rather than the whole, and imagining ourselves inside of them perceptually, the subject might defy us less provokingly. We are thus brought back to the problem with which Chapter VII left off. When perceptible amounts of new phenomenal being come to birth, must we hold them to be in all points predetermined and necessary outgrowths of the being already there, or shall we rather admit the possibility that originality may thus instil itself into reality?

If we take concrete perceptual experience, the question can be answered in only one way. "The same returns not, save to bring the different." Time keeps budding into new moments, every one of which presents

[1] From Some Problems of Philosophy, pp. 147-157.

a content which in its individuality never was before and will never be again. Of no concrete bit of experience was an exact duplicate ever framed. "My youth," writes Delbœuf, "has it not taken flight, carrying away with it love, illusion, poetry, and freedom from care, and leaving with me instead science, austere always, often sad and morose, which sometimes I would willingly forget, which repeats to me hour by hour its grave lessons, or chills me by its threats? Will time, which untiringly piles deaths on births, and births on deaths, ever remake an Aristotle or an Archimedes, a Newton or a Descartes? Can our earth ever cover itself again with those gigantic ferns, those immense equisetaceans, in the midst of which the same antediluvian monsters will crawl and wallow as they did of yore? . . . No, what has been will not, cannot, be again. Time moves on with an unfaltering tread, and never strikes twice an identical hour. The instants of which the existence of the world is composed are all dissimilar—and whatever may be done, something remains that can never be reversed." [1]

The everlasting coming of concrete novelty into being is so obvious that the rationalizing intellect, bent ever on explaining what is by what was, and having no logical principle but identity to explain by, treats the perceptual flux as a phenomenal illusion, resulting from

[1] J. Delbœuf: *Revue Philosophique*, vol. ix, p. 138 (1880). On the infinite variety of reality, compare also W. T. Marvin: *An Introduction to Systematic Philosophy*, New York, 1903, pp. 22-30.

the unceasing re-combination in new forms of mixture, of unalterable elements, coeval with the world. These elements are supposed to be the only real beings; and, for the intellect once grasped by the vision of them, there can be nothing genuinely new under the sun. The world's history, according to molecular science, signifies only the "redistribution" of the unchanged atoms of the primal firemist, parting and meeting so as to appear to us spectators in the infinitely diversified configurations which we name as processes and things.

So far as physical nature goes few of us experience any temptation to postulate real novelty. The notion of eternal elements and their mixture serves us in so many ways, that we adopt unhesitatingly the theory that primordial being is inalterable in its attributes as well as in its quantity, and that the laws by which we describe its habits are uniform in strictest mathematical sense. These are the absolute conceptual foundations, we think, spread beneath the surface of perceptual variety. It is when we come to human lives, that our point of view changes. It is hard to imagine that "really" our own subjective experiences are only molecular arrangements, even though the molecules be conceived as beings of a psychic kind. A material fact may indeed be different from what we feel it to be, but what sense is there in saying that a feeling, which has no other nature than to be felt, is not as it *is* felt? Psychologically considered, our experiences resist conceptual reduction, and our fields of consciousness, taken simply as such, remain just what they appear, even though facts of a molecular order should prove to be the signals of the appearance. Biography is the concrete form in which all that is is immediately given; the perceptual flux is the authentic stuff of each of our biographies, and yields a perfect effervescence of novelty all the time. New men and women, books, accidents, events, inventions, enterprises, burst unceasingly upon the world. It is vain to resolve these into ancient elements, or to say that they belong to ancient kinds, so long as no one of them in its full individuality ever was here before or will ever come again. Men of science and philosophy, the moment they forget their theoretic abstractions, live in their biographies as much as any one else, and believe as naïvely that fact even now is making, and that they themselves, by doing "original work," help to determine what the future shall become.

Novelty and Causation [1]

If reality changes by finite sensible steps, the question whether the bits of it that come are radically new, remains unsettled still. Remember our situation at the end of Chapter III. Being *überhaupt* or at large, we there found to be undeduceable. For our *intellect* it remains a casual and contingent quantum that is simply found or begged. May it be begged bit by bit,

[1] From *Some Problems of Philosophy*, pp. 189-190; 208-215.

as it adds itself? Or must we beg it only once, by assuming it either to be eternal or to have come in an instant that co-implicated all the rest of time? Did or did not "the first morning of creation write what the last dawn of reckoning shall read"? With these questions monism and pluralism stand face to face again. The classic obstacle to pluralism has always been what is known as the "principle of causality." This principle has been taken to mean that the effect in some way already exists in the cause. If this be so, the effect cannot be absolutely novel, and in no radical sense can pluralism be true.

Most persons remain quite incredulous when they are told that the rational principle of causality has exploded our native belief in naïf activity as something real, and our assumption that genuinely new fact can be created by work done. "Le sens de la vie qui s'indigne de tant de discours," awakens in them and snaps its fingers at the "critical" view. The present writer has also just called the critical view an incomplete abstraction. But its "functional laws" and schematisms are splendidly useful, and its negations are true oftener than is commonly supposed. We feel as if our "will" immediately moved our members, and we ignore the brain-cells whose activity that will must first arouse; we think we cause the bell-ring, but we only close a contact and the battery in the cellar rings the bell; we think a certain star's light is the cause of our now seeing it, but ether-waves are the causes, and the star may have been extinguished long ago. We call the "draft," the cause of our "cold"; but without co-operant microbes the draft could do no harm. Mill says that causes must be unconditional antecedents, and Venn that they must be "close" ones. In nature's numerous successions so many links are hidden, that we seldom know exactly which antecedent is unconditional or which is close. Often the cause which we name only fits some other cause for producing the phenomenon; and things, as Mill says, are frequently then most active when we assume them to be acted upon.

This vast amount of error in our instinctive perceptions of causal activity encourages the conceptualist view. A step farther, and we suspect that to suppose causal activity anywhere may be a blunder, and that only consecutions and juxtapositions can be real. Such sweeping skepticism is, however, quite uncalled for. Other parts of experience expose us to error, yet we do not say that in them is no truth. We see trains moving at stations, when they are really standing still, or falsely we feel ourselves to be moving, when we are giddy, without such errors leading us to deny that motion anywhere exists. It exists elsewhere; and the problem is to place it rightly. It is the same with all other illusions of sense.

There is doubtless somewhere an original perceptual experience of the kind of thing we mean by causation, and that kind of thing we locate in various other places, rightly or wrongly as the case may be. Where now is the typical experience originally got?

Evidently it is got in our own personal activity-situations. In all of these what we feel is that a previous field of "consciousness" containing (in the midst of its complexity) the idea of a result, develops gradually into another field in which that result either appears as accomplished, or else is prevented by obstacles against which we still feel ourselves to press. As I now write, I am in one of these activity situations. I "strive" after words, which I only half prefigure, but which, when they shall have come, must satisfactorily complete the nascent sense I have of what they ought to be. The words are to run out of my pen, which I find that my hand actuates so obediently to desire that I am hardly conscious either of resistance or of effort. Some of the words come wrong, and then I do feel a resistance, not muscular but mental, which instigates a new installment of my activity, accompanied by more or less feeling of exertion. If the resistance were to my muscles, the exertion would contain an element of strain or squeeze which is less present where the resistance is only mental. If it proves considerable in either kind I may leave off trying to overcome it; or, on the other hand, I may sustain my effort till I have succeeded in my aim.

It seems to me that in such a continuously developing experiential series our concrete perception of causality is found in operation. If the word have any meaning at all it must mean what there we live through. What "efficacy" and "activity" are *known-as* is what these appear.

The experiencer of such a situation feels the push, the obstacle, the will, the strain, the triumph, or the passive giving up, just as he feels the time, the space, the swiftness of intensity, the movement, the weight and color, the pain and pleasure, the complexity, or whatever remaining characters the situation may involve. He goes through all that can ever be imagined where activity is supposed. The word "activity" has no content save these experiences of process, obstruction, striving, strain, or release, ultimate *qualia* as they are of the life given us to be known. No matter what "efficacies" there may really be in this extraordinary universe it is impossible to conceive of any one of them being either lived through or authentically known otherwise than in this dramatic shape of something sustaining a felt purpose against felt obstacles, and overcoming or being overcome. What "sustaining" means here is clear to any one who has lived through the experience, but to no one else; just as "loud," "red," "sweet," mean something only to beings with ears, eyes, and tongues. The *percipi* in these originals of experience is the *esse;* the curtain is the picture. If there is anything hiding in the background, it ought not to be called causal agency, but should get itself another name.

The way in which we feel that our successive fields

continue each other in these cases is evidently what
the orthodox doctrine means when it vaguely says that
"in some way" the cause "contains" the effect. It
contains it by proposing it as the end pursued. Since
the desire of that end is the efficient cause, we see that
in the total fact of personal activity final and efficient
causes coalesce. Yet the effect is oftenest contained
aliquo modo only, and seldom explicitly foreseen. The
activity sets up more effects than it proposes literally.
The end is defined beforehand in most cases only as a
general direction, along which all sorts of novelties and
surprises lie in wait. These words I write even now
surprise me; yet I adopt them as effects of my scrip-
torial causality. Their being "contained" means only
their harmony and continuity with my general aim.
They "fill the bill" and I accept them, but the exact
shape of them seems determined by something outside
of my explicit will.

If we look at the general mass of things in the midst
of which the life of men is passed, and ask "How came
they here?" the only broad answer is that man's desires
preceded and produced them. If not all-sufficient
causes, desire and will were at any rate what John
Mill calls unconditional causes, indispensable causes
namely, without which the effects could not have come
at all. Human causal activity is the only known unconditional antecedent of the works of civilization; so
've find, as Edward Carpenter says,[1] something like a

[1] *The Art of Creation,* 1894, chap. i.

law of nature, the law that a movement from feeling to thought and thence to action, from the world of dreams to the world of things, is everywhere going on. Since at each phase of this movement novelties turn up, we may fairly ask, with Carpenter, whether we are not here witnessing in our own personal experience what is really the essential process of creation. Is not the world really growing in these activities of ours? And where we predicate activities elsewhere, have we a right to suppose aught different in kind from this?

To some such vague vision are we brought by taking our perceptual experience of action at its face-value, and following the analogies which it suggests.

Activity as a Stuff of Experience [1]

Activity is, for example, attributed either to a physical or to a mental agent, and is either aimless or directed. If directed, it shows tendency. The tendency may or may not be resisted. If not, we call the activity immanent, as when a body moves in empty space by its momentum, or our thoughts wander at their own sweet will. If resistance is met, *its* agent complicates the situation. If now, in spite of resistance, the original tendency continues, effort makes its appearance, and along with effort, strain or squeeze. Will, in the narrower sense of the word, then comes upon the scene, whenever, along with the tendency, the strain and

[1] From "The Experience of Activity," in *A Pluralistic Universe.* pp. 375-377; 390-392.

squeeze are sustained. But the resistance may be great enough to check the tendency, or even to reverse its path. In that case, we (if "we" were the original agents or subjects of the tendency) are overpowered. The phenomenon turns into one of tension simply, or of necessity succumbed-to, according as the opposing power is only equal, or is superior to ourselves.

Whosoever describes an experience in such terms as these, describes an experience *of* activity. If the word have any meaning, it must denote what there is found. *There* is complete activity in its original and first intention. What it is "known-as" is what there appears. The experiencer of such a situation possesses all that the idea contains. He feels the tendency, the obstacle, the will, the strain, the triumph, or the passive giving up, just as he feels the time, the space, the swiftness or intensity, the movement, the weight and color, the pain and pleasure, the complexity, or whatever remaining characters the situation may involve. He goes through all that ever can be imagined where activity is supposed. If we suppose activities to go on outside of our experience, it is in forms like these that we must suppose them, or else give them some other name; for the word "activity" has no imaginable content whatever save these experiences of process, obstruction, striving, strain, or release, ultimate *qualia* as they are of the life given us to be known. . . .

Wherever the seat of real causality *is,* as ultimately known "for true" (in nerve-processes, if you will, that cause our feelings of activity as well as the movements which these seem to prompt), a philosophy of pure experience can consider the real causation as no other *nature* of thing than that which even in our most erroneous experiences appears to be at work. Exactly what appears there is what we *mean* by working, though we may later come to learn that working was not exactly *there*. Sustaining, persevering, striving, paying with effort as we go, hanging on, and finally achieving our intention—this *is* action, this *is* effectuation in the only shape in which, by a pure experience-philosophy, the whereabouts of it anywhere can be discussed. Here is creation in its first intention, here is causality at work. To treat this offhand as the bare illusory surface of a world whose real causality is an unimaginable ontological principle hidden in the cubic deeps, is, for the more empirical way of thinking, only animism in another shape. You explain your given fact by your "principle," but the principle itself, when you look clearly at it, turns out to be nothing but a previous little spiritual copy of the fact. Away from that one and only kind of fact your mind, considering causality, can never get.[1]

I conclude, then, that real effectual causation as an

[1] . . . The only "free will" I have ever thought of defending is the character of novelty in fresh activity-situations. If an activity-process is the form of a whole "field of consciousness," and if each field of consciousness is not only in its totality unique (as is now commonly admitted), but has its elements unique (since in that situation they are all dyed in the total), then novelty is perpetually entering the world and what happens there is not pure *repetition*, as

ultimate nature, as a "category," if you like, of reality, is *just what we feel it to be,* just that kind of conjunction which our own activity-series reveal. We have the whole butt and being of it in our hands; and the healthy thing for philosophy is to leave off grubbing underground for what effects effectuation, or what makes action act, and to try to solve the concrete questions of where effectuation in this world is located, of which things are the true causal agents there, and of what the more remote effects consist.

On the Notion of Reality as Changing [1]

In my "Principles of Psychology" (vol. ii, p. 646) I gave the name of the "axiom of skipped intermediaries and transferred relations" to a serial principle of which the foundation of logic, the *dictum de omni et nullo* (or, as I expressed it, the rule that what is of a kind is of that kind's kind), is the most familiar instance. More than the more is more than the less, equals of equals are equal, sames of the same are the same, the cause of a cause is the cause of its effects, are other examples of this serial law. Although it applies infallibly and without restriction throughout certain ab-

the dogma of the literal uniformity of nature requires. Activity-situations come, in short, each with an original touch. A "principle" of free will, if there were one, would doubtless manifest itself in such phenomena, but I never saw, nor do I now see, what the principle could do except rehearse the phenomenon beforehand, or why it ever should be invoked.

[1] From *A Pluralistic Universe,* pp. 395-400.

stract series, where the "sames," "causes," etc., spoken of, are "pure," and have no properties save their sameness, causality, etc., it cannot be applied offhand to concrete objects with numerous properties and relations, for it is hard to trace a straight line of sameness, causation, or whatever it may be, through a series of such objects without swerving into some "respect" where the relation, as pursued originally, no longer holds: the objects have so many "aspects" that we are constantly deflected from our original direction, and find, we know not why, that we are following something different from what we started with. Thus a cat is in a sense the same as a mouse-trap, and a mouse-trap the same as a bird-cage; but in no valuable or easily intelligible sense is a cat the same as a bird-cage. Commodore Perry was in a sense the cause of the new régime in Japan, and the new régime was the cause of the russian Douma; but it would hardly profit us to insist on holding to Perry as the cause of the Douma: the terms have grown too remote to have any real or practical relation to each other. In every series of real terms, not only do the terms themselves and their associates and environments change, but we change, and their *meaning* for us changes, so that new kinds of sameness and types of causation continually come into view and appeal to our interest. Our earlier lines, having grown irrelevant, are then dropped. The old terms can no longer be substituted nor the relations "transferred," because of so many new dimensions into which experience has opened. Instead of a straight line, it now follows a zigzag; and to keep it straight, one must do violence to its spontaneous development. Not that one might not possibly, by careful seeking (though I doubt it), *find* some line in nature along which terms literally the same, or causes causal in the same way, might be serially strung without limit, if one's interest lay in such finding. Within such lines our axioms might hold, causes might cause their effect's effects, etc.; but such lines themselves would, if found, only be partial members of a vast natural network, within the other lines of which you could not say, in any sense that a wise man or a sane man would ever think of, in any sense that would not be concretely *silly*, that the principle of skipped intermediaries still held good. In the *practical* world, the world whose significances we follow, sames of the same are certainly not sames of one another; and things constantly cause other things without being held responsible for everything of which those other things are causes.

Professor Bergson, believing as he does in a heraclitean "devenir réel," ought, if I rightly understand him, positively to deny that in the actual world the logical axioms hold good without qualification. Not only, according to him, do terms change, so that after a certain time the very elements of things are no longer what they were, but relations also change, so as no longer to obtain in the same identical way between the new things that have succeeded upon the old ones.

If this were really so, then however indefinitely sames might still be substituted for sames in the logical world of nothing but pure sameness, in the world of real operations every line of sameness actually started and followed up would eventually give out, and cease to be traceable any farther. Sames of the same, in such a world, will not always (or rather, in a strict sense will never) be the same as one another, for in such a world there *is* no literal or ideal sameness among numerical differents. Nor in such a world will it be true that the cause of the cause is unreservedly the cause of the effect; for if we follow lines of real causation, instead of contenting ourselves with Hume's and Kant's eviscerated schematism, we find that remoter effects are seldom aimed at by causal intentions,[1] that no one kind of causal activity continues indefinitely, and that that principle of skipped intermediaries can be talked of only *in abstracto*.

Both philosophers [2] believe that the appearance of novelty in things is genuine. To an observer standing outside of its generating causes, novelty can appear only as so much "chance"; to one who stands inside it is the expression of "free creative activity." . . . Novelty, as empirically found, doesn't arrive by jumps and jolts, it leaks in insensibly, for adjacents in experience are always interfused, the smallest real datum

[1] Compare the Douma with what Perry aimed at.
[2] Bergson and C. S. Peirce, referred to in the omitted sentences —*Ed.*

being both a coming and a going, and even numerical distinctness being realized effectively only after a concrete interval has passed. The intervals also deflect us from the original paths of direction, and all the old identities at last give out, for the fatally continuous infiltration of otherness warps things out of every original rut. Just so, in a curve, the same direction is *never* followed, and the conception of it as a myriad-sided polygon falsifies it by supposing it to do so for however short a time. Peirce speaks of an "infinitesinal" tendency to diversification. The mathematical notion of an infinitesimal contains, in truth, the whole paradox of the same and yet the nascent other, of an identity that won't *keep* except so far as it keeps *failing,* that won't *transfer,* any more than the serial relations in question transfer, when you apply them to reality instead of applying them to concepts alone.

A friend of mine has an idea, which illustrates on such a magnified scale the impossibility of tracing the same line through reality, that I will mention it here. He thinks that nothing more is needed to make history "scientific" than to get the content of any two epochs (say the end of the thirteenth and the end of the nineteenth century) accurately defined, then accurately to define the direction of the change that led from the one epoch into the other, and finally to prolong the line of that direction into the future. So prolonging the line, he thinks, we ought to be able to define the actual state of things at any future date we please. We all feel the essential unreality of such a conception of "history" as this; but if such a synechistic pluralism as I believe in, be what really exists, every phenomenon of development, even the simplest, would prove equally rebellious to our science should the latter pretend to give us literally accurate instead of approximate, or statistically generalized, pictures of the development of reality.

Pluriverse or Universe [1]

No matter what the content of the universe may be, if you only allow that it is *many* everywhere and always, that *nothing* real escapes from having an environment; so far from defeating its rationality, as the absolutists so unanimously pretend, you leave it in possession of the maximum amount of rationality practically attainable by our minds. Your relations with it, intellectual, emotional, and active, remain fluent and congruous with your own nature's chief demands.

It would be a pity if the word "rationality" were allowed to give us trouble here. It is one of those eulogistic words that both sides claim—for almost no one is willing to advertise his philosophy as a system of irrationality. But like most of the words which people used eulogistically, the word "rational" carries too many meanings. The most objective one is that of the older logic—the connection between two things is rational when you can infer one from the other, mortal from Socrates, e. g.; and you can do that only

1 From *A Pluralistic Universe*, pp. 319-327.

when they have a quality in common. But this kind
of rationality is just that logic of identity which all
disciples of Hegel find insufficient. They supersede
it by the higher rationality of negation and contradiction and make the notion vague again. Then you
get the æsthetic or teleologic kinds of rationality, saying that whatever fits in any way, whatever is beautiful
or good, whatever is purposive or gratifies desire, is
rational in so far forth. Then again, according to
Hegel, whatever is "real" is rational. I myself said
a while ago that whatever lets loose any action which
we are fond of exerting seems rational. It would be
better to give up the word "rational" altogether than
to get into a merely verbal fight about who has the
best right to keep it.

Perhaps the words "foreignness" and "intimacy,"
which I put forward in my first lecture, express the
contrast I insist on better than the words "rationality"
and "irrationality"—let us stick to them, then. I now
say that the notion of the "one" breeds foreignness
and that of the "many" intimacy, for reasons which
I have urged at only too great length, and with which,
whether they convince you or not, I may suppose that
you are now well acquainted. But what at bottom
is meant by calling the universe many or by calling
it one?

Pragmatically interpreted, pluralism or the doctrine
that it is many means only that the sundry parts of
reality *may be externally related*. Everything you can

think of, however vast or inclusive, has on the pluralis‹ tic view a genuinely "external" environment of some sort or amount. Things are "with" one another in many ways, but nothing includes everything, or domi‹ nates over everything. The word "and" trails along after every sentence. Something always escapes. "Ever not quite" has to be said of the best attempts made anywhere in the universe at attaining all-inclu- siveness. The pluralistic world is thus more like a federal republic than like an empire or a kingdom. However much may be collected, however much may report itself as present at any effective center of con- sciousness or action, something else is self-governed and absent and unreduced to unity.

Monism, on the other hand, insists that when you come down to reality as such, to the reality of realities, everything is present to *everything* else in one vast instantaneous co-implicated completeness—nothing can in *any* sense, functional or substantial, be really absent from anything else, all things interpenetrate and tele- scope together in the great total conflux.

For pluralism, all that we are required to admit as the constitution of reality is what we ourselves find empirically realized in every minimum of finite life. Briefly it is this, that nothing real is absolutely simple, that every smallest bit of experience is a *multum in parvo* plurally related, that each relation is one aspect, character, or function, way of its being taken, or way of its taking something else; and that a bit of reality when actively engaged in one of these relations is not *by that very fact* engaged in all the other relations simultaneously. The relations are not *all* what the French call *solidaires* with one another. Without losing its identity a thing can either take up or drop another thing, like the log I spoke of, which by taking up new carriers and dropping old ones can travel anywhere with a light escort.

For monism, on the contrary, everything, whether we realize it or not, drags the whole universe along with itself and drops nothing. The log starts and arrives with all its carriers supporting it. If a thing were once disconnected, it could never be connected again, according to monism. The pragmatic difference between the two systems is thus a definite one. It is just thus, that if *a* is once out of sight of *b* or out of touch with it, or, more briefly, "out" of it at all, then, according to monism, it must always remain so, they can never get together; whereas pluralism admits that on another occasion they may work together, or in some way be connected again. Monism allows for no such things as "other occasions" in reality—in *real* or absolute reality, that is.

The difference I try to describe amounts, you see, to nothing more than the difference between what I formerly called the each-form and the all-form of reality. Pluralism lets things really exist in the each-form or distributively. Monism thinks that the all-form or collective-unit form is the only form that is rational.   The all-form allows of no taking up and dropping of connexions, for in the all the parts are essentially and eternally co-implicated.   In the each-form, on the contrary, a thing may be connected by intermediary things, with a thing with which it has no immediate or essential connection.   It is thus at all times in many possible connections which are not necessarily actualized at the moment.   They depend on which actual path of intermediation it may functionally strike into: the word "or" names a genuine reality. Thus, as I speak here, I may look ahead *or* to the right *or* to the left, and in either case the intervening space and air and ether enable me to see the faces of a different portion of this audience.   My being here is independent of any one set of these faces.

If the each-form be the eternal form of reality no less than it is the form of temporal appearance, we still have a coherent world, and not an incarnate incoherence, as is charged by so many absolutists.   Our "multiverse" still makes a "universe"; for every part, though it may not be in actual or immediate connection, is nevertheless in some possible or mediated connection, with every other part however remote, through the fact that each part hangs together with its very next neighbors in inextricable interfusion.   The type of union, it is true, is different here from the monistic type of *alleinheit*.   It is not a universal co-implication, or integration of all things *durcheinander*.   It is what I call the strung-along type, the type of continuity, contiguity, or concatenation. If you prefer Greek words, you may call it the synechistic type. At all events, you see that it forms a definitely conceivable alternative to the through-and-through unity of all things at once, which is the type opposed to it by monism. You see also that it stands or falls with the notion I have taken such pains to defend, of the through-and-through union of adjacent minima of experience, of the confluence of every passing moment of concretely felt experience with its immediately next neighbors. The recognition of this fact of coalescence of next with next in concrete experience, so that all the insulating cuts we make there are artificial products of the conceptualizing faculty, is what distinguishes the empiricism which I call "radical," from the bugaboo empiricism of the traditional rationalist critics, which (rightly or wrongly) is accused of chopping up experience into atomistic sensations, incapable of union with one another until a purely intellectual principle has swooped down upon them from on high and folded them in its own conjunctive categories.

Here, then, you have the plain alternative, and the full mystery of the difference between pluralism and monism, as clearly as I can set it forth on this occasion. It packs up into a nutshell:—Is the manyness in oneness that indubitably characterizes the world we inhabit, a property only of the absolute whole of things, so that you must postulate that one-enormous whole indivisibly as the *prius* of there being any many at all—

in other words, start with the rationalistic block-universe, entire, unmitigated, and complete?—or can the finite elements have their own aboriginal forms of manyness in oneness, and where they have no immediate oneness still be continued into one another by intermediary terms—each one of these terms being one with its next neighbors, and yet the total "oneness" never getting absolutely complete? . . .

CHAPTER III

THE SELF [1]

Let us begin with the Self in its widest acceptation, and follow it up to its most delicate and subtle form, advancing from the study of the empirical, as the Germans call it, to that of the pure, Ego.

The Empirical Self or Me

The Empirical Self of each of us is all that he is tempted to call by the name of *me*. But it is clear that between what a man calls *me* and what he simply calls *mine* the line is difficult to draw. We feel and act about certain things that are ours very much as we feel and act about ourselves. Our fame, our children, the work of our hands, may be as dear to us as our bodies are, and arouse the same feelings and the same acts of reprisal if attacked. And our bodies themselves, are they simply ours, or are they *us*? Certainly men have been ready to disown their very bodies and to regard them as mere vestures, or even as prisons of clay from which they should some day be glad to escape.

We see then that we are dealing with a fluctuating material. The same object being sometimes treated as

[1] From *The Principles of Psychology*, pp. 291-305; 309-317; 400-401.

a part of me, at other times as simply mine, and then again as if I had nothing to do with it at all. *In its widest possible sense,* however, *a man's Self is the sum total of all that he* CAN *call his,* not only his body and his psychic powers, but his clothes and his house, his wife and children, his ancestors and friends, his reputation and works, his lands and horses, and yacht and bank-account. All these things give him the same emotions. If they wax and prosper, he feels triumphant; if they dwindle and die away, he feels cast down,—not necessarily in the same degree for each thing, but in much the same way for all. Understanding the Self in this widest sense, we may begin by dividing the history of it into three parts, relating respectively to—

1. Its constituents;

2. The feelings and emotions they arouse,—*Self-feelings;*

3. The actions to which they prompt,—*Self-seeking and Self-preservation.*

1. *The constituents of the Self* may be divided into two classes, those which make up respectively—

   (*a*) The material Self;

   (*b*) The social Self;

   (*c*) The spiritual Self; and

   (*d*) The pure Ego.

   (*a*) The body is the innermost part of *the material Self* in each of us; and certain parts of the body seem more intimately ours than the rest. The clothes come next. The old saying that the human person is composed of three parts—soul, body and clothes—is more than a joke. We so appropriate our clothes and identify ourselves with them that there are few of us who, if asked to choose between having a beautiful body clad in raiment perpetually shabby and unclean, and having an ugly and blemished form always spotlessly attired, would not hesitate a moment before making a decisive reply.[1]   Next, our immediate family is a part of ourselves. Our father and mother, our wife and babes, are bone of our bone and flesh of our flesh. When they die, a part of our very selves is gone. If they do anything wrong, it is our shame. If they are insulted, our anger flashes forth as readily as if we stood in their place. Our home comes next. Its scenes are part of our life; its aspects awaken the tenderest feelings of affection; and we do not easily forgive the stranger who, in visiting it, finds fault with its arrangements or treats it with contempt. All these different things are the objects of instinctive preferences coupled with the most important practical interests of life. We all have a blind impulse to watch over our body, to deck it with clothing of an ornamental sort, to cherish parents, wife and babes, and to find for ourselves a home of our own which we may live in and "improve."

An equally instinctive impulse drives us to collect

[1] See, for a charming passage on the Philosophy of Dress, H. Lotze's *Microcosmus*. Eng. tr., vol i, p. 592 ff.

property; and the collections thus made become, with different degrees of intimacy, parts of our empirical selves. The parts of our wealth most intimately ours are those which are saturated with our labor. There are few men who would not feel personally annihilated if a life-long construction of their hands or brains— say an entomological collection or an extensive work in manuscript—were suddenly swept away. The miser feels similarly towards his gold, and although it is true that a part of our depression at the loss of possessions is due to our feeling that we must now go without certain goods that we expected the possessions to bring in their train, yet in every case there remains, over and above this, a sense of the shrinkage of our personality, a partial conversion of ourselves to nothingness, which is a psychological phenomenon by itself. We are all at once assimilated to the tramps and poor devils whom we so despise, and at the same time removed farther than ever away from the happy sons of earth who lord it over land and sea and men in the full-blown lustihood that wealth and power can give, and before whom, stiffen ourselves as we will by appealing to 'anti-snobbish first principles, we cannot escape an emotion, open or sneaking, of respect and dread.

(b) *A man's Social Self* is the recognition which he gets from his mates. We are not only gregarious animals, liking to be in sight of our fellows, but we have an innate propensity to get ourselves noticed, and noticed favorably, by our kind. No more fiendish punishment could be devised, were such a thing physically possible, than that one should be turned loose in society and remain absolutely unnoticed by all the members thereof. If no one turned round when we entered, answered when we spoke, or minded what we did, but if every person we met "cut us dead," and acted as if we were non-existing things, a kind of rage and impotent despair would ere long well up in us, from which the cruelest bodily tortures would be a relief; for these would make us feel that, however bad might be our plight, we had not sunk to such a depth as to be unworthy of attention at all.

Properly speaking, *a man has as many social selves as there are individuals who recognize him* and carry an image of him in their mind. To wound any one of these his images is to wound him.[1] But as the individuals who carry the images fall naturally into classes, we may practically say that he has as many different social selves as there are distinct *groups* of persons about whose opinion he cares. He generally shows a different side of himself to each of these different groups. Many a youth who is demure enough before his parents and teachers, swears and swaggers like a pirate among his "tough" young friends. We do not show ourselves to our children as to our club companions, to our customers as to the laborers we employ, to our own masters and employers as to our intimate

[1] "Who filches from me my good name," etc.

friends. From this there results what practically is a division of the man into several selves; and this may be a discordant splitting, as where one is afraid to let one set of his acquaintances know him as he is elsewhere; or it may be a perfectly harmonious division of labor, as where one tender to his children is stern to the soldiers or prisoners under his command.

The most peculiar social self which one is apt to have is in the mind of the person one is in love with. The good or bad fortunes of this self cause the most intense elation and dejection—unreasonable enough as measured by every other standard than that of the organic feeling of the individual. To his own consciousness he *is* not, so long as this particular social self fails to get recognition, and when it is recognized his contentment passes all bounds.

A man's *fame*, good or bad, and his *honor* or dishonor, are names for one of his social selves. The particular social self of a man called his honor is usually the result of one of those splittings of which we have spoken. It is his image in the eyes of his own "set," which exalts or condemns him as he conforms or not to certain requirements that may not be made of one in another walk of life. Thus a layman may abandon a city infected with cholera; but a priest or a doctor would think such an act incompatible with his honor. A soldier's honor requires him to fight or to die under circumstances where another man can apologize or run away with no stain upon his social self. A judge, a statesman, are in like manner debarred by the honor of their cloth from entering into pecuniary relations perfectly honorable to persons in private life. Nothing is commoner than to hear people discriminate between their different selves of this sort: "As a man I pity you, but as an official I must show you no mercy; as a politician I regard him as an ally, but as a moralist I loathe him"; etc., etc. What may be called "club-opinion" is one of the very strongest forces in life. The thief must not steal from other thieves; the gambler must pay his gambling-debts, though he pay no other debts in the world. The code of honor of fashionable society has throughout history been full of permissions as well as of vetoes, the only reason for following either of which is that so we best serve one of our social selves. You must not lie in general, but you may lie as much as you please if asked about your relations with a lady; you must accept a challenge from an equal, but if challenged by an inferior you may laugh him to scorn: these are examples of what is meant.

(c) By *the Spiritual Self,* so far as it belongs to the Empirical Me, I mean a man's inner or subjective being, his psychic faculties or dispositions, taken concretely; not the bare principle of personal Unity, or "pure" Ego, which remains still to be discussed. These psychic dispositions are the most enduring and intimate part of the self, that which we most verily seem to be.

We take a purer self-satisfaction when we think of our ability to argue and discriminate, of our moral sensibility and conscience, of our indomitable will, than when we survey any of our other possessions. Only when these are altered is a man said to be *alienatus a se*.

Now this spiritual self may be considered in various ways. We may divide it into faculties, as just instanced, isolating them one from another, and identifying ourselves with either in turn. This is an *abstract* way of dealing with consciousness, in which, as it actually presents itself, a plurality of such faculties are always to be simultaneously found; or we may insist on a concrete view, and then the spiritual self in us will be either the entire stream of our personal consciousness, or the present "segment" or "section" of that stream, according as we take a broader or a narrower view—both the stream and the section being concrete existences in time, and each being a unity after its own peculiar kind. But whether we take it abstractly or concretely, our considering the spiritual self at all is a reflective process, is the result of our abandoning the outward-looking point of view, and of our having become able to think of subjectivity as such, *to think ourselves as thinkers*.

This attention to thought as such, and the identification of ourselves with it rather than with any of the objects which it reveals, is a momentous and in some respects a rather mysterious operation, of which we need here only say that as a matter of fact it exists;

and that in every one, at an early age, the distinction between thought as such, and what it is "of" or "about," has become familiar to the mind. The deeper grounds for this discrimination may possibly be hard to find; but superficial grounds are plenty and near at hand. Almost any one will tell us that thought is a different sort of existence from things, because many sorts of thought are of no things—e.g., pleasures, pains, and emotions; others are of non-existent things—errors and fictions; others again of existent things, but in a form that is symbolic and does not resemble them—abstract ideas and concepts; whilst in the thoughts that do resemble the things they are "of" (percepts, sensations), we can feel, alongside of the thing known, the thought of it going on as an altogether separate act and operation in the mind.

Now this subjective life of ours, distinguished as such so clearly from the objects known by its means, may, as aforesaid, be taken by us in a concrete or in an abstract way. Of the concrete way I will say nothing just now, except that the actual "section" of the stream will ere long, in our discussion of the nature of the principle of *unity* in consciousness, play a very important part. The abstract way claims our attention first. If the stream as a whole is identified with the Self far more than any outward thing, a *certain portion of the stream abstracted from the rest* is so identified in an altogether peculiar degree, and is felt by all men as a sort of innermost center within the circle, of sanctuary within the citadel, constituted by the subjective life as a whole. Compared with this element of the stream, the other parts, even of the subjective life, seem transient external possessions, of which each in turn can be disowned, whilst that which disowns them remains. Now, *what is this self of all the other selves?*

Probably all men would describe it in much the same way up to a certain point. They would call it the *active* element in all consciousness; saying that whatever qualities a man's feelings may possess, or whatever content his thought may include, there is a spiritual something in him which seems to *go out* to meet these qualities and contents, whilst they seem to *come in* to be received by it. It is what welcomes or rejects. It presides over the perception of sensations, and by giving or withholding its assent it influences the movements they tend to arouse. It is the home of interest, —not the pleasant or the painful, not even pleasure or pain, as such, but that within us to which pleasure and pain, the pleasant and the painful, speak. It is the source of effort and attention, and the place from which appear to emanate the fiats of the will. A physiologist who should reflect upon it in his own person could hardly help, I should think, connecting it more or less vaguely with the process by which ideas or incoming sensations are "reflected" or pass over into outward acts. Not necessarily that it should *be* this process or the mere feeling of this process, but that it should be in some close way *related* to this process; for it plays a part analogous to it in the psychic life, being a sort of junction at which sensory ideas terminate and from which motor ideas proceed, and forming a kind of link between the two. Being more incessantly there than any other single element of the mental life, the other elements end by seeming to accrete round it and to belong to it. It becomes opposed to them as the permanent is opposed to the changing and inconstant.

One may, I think, without fear of being upset by any future Galtonian circulars, believe that all men must single out from the rest of what they call themselves some central principle of which each would recognize the foregoing to be a fair general description,—accurate enough, at any rate, to denote what is meant, and keep it unconfused with other things. The moment, however, they came to closer quarters with it, trying to define more accurately its precise nature, we should find opinions beginning to diverge. Some would say that it is a simple active substance, the soul, of which they are thus conscious; others, that it is nothing but a fiction, the imaginary being denoted by the pronoun I; and between these extremes of opinion all sorts of intermediaries would be found.

Later we must ourselves discuss them all, and sufficient to that day will be the evil thereof. *Now*, let us try to settle for ourselves as definitely as we can, just how this central nucleus of the Self may *feel*, no matter whether it be a spiritual substance or only a delusive word.

For this central part of the Self is *felt*. It may be all that Transcendentalists say it is, and all that Empiricists say it is into the bargain, but it is at any rate no *mere ens rationis,* cognized only in an intellectual way, and no *mere* summation of memories or *mere* sound of a word in our ears. It is something with which we also have direct sensible acquaintance, and which is as fully present at any moment of consciousness in which it *is* present, as in a whole lifetime of such moments. When, just now, it was called an abstraction, that did not mean that, like some general notion, it could not be presented in a particular experience. It only meant that in the stream of consciousness it never was found all alone. But when it is found, it is *felt;* just as the body is felt, the feeling of which is also an abstraction, because never is the body felt all alone, but always together with other things. *Now can we tell more precisely in what the feeling of this central active self consists,*— not necessarily as yet what the active self *is,* as a being or principle, but what we *feel* when we become aware of its existence?

I think I can in my own case; and as what I say will be likely to meet with opposition if generalized (as indeed it may be in part inapplicable to other individuals), I had better continue in the first person, leaving my description to be accepted by those to whose introspection it may commend itself as true, and confessing my inability to meet the demands of others, if others there be.

First of all, I am aware of a constant play of furtherances and hindrances in my thinking, of checks and releases, tendencies which run with desire, and tendencies which run the other way. Among the matters I think of, some range themselves on the side of the thought's interests, whilst others play an unfriendly part thereto. The mutual inconsistencies and agreements, reinforcements and obstructions, which obtain amongst these objective matters reverberate backwards and produce what seem to be incessant reactions of my spontaneity upon them, welcoming or opposing, appropriating or disowning, striving with or against, saying yes or no. This palpitating inward life is, in me, that central nucleus which I just tried to describe in terms that all men might use.

But when I forsake such general descriptions and grapple with particulars, coming to the closest possible quarters with the facts, *it is difficult for me to detect in the activity any purely spiritual element at all. Whenever my introspective glance succeeds in turning round quickly enough to catch one of these manifestations of spontaneity in the act, all it can ever feel distinctly is some bodily process, for the most part taking place within the head.* Omitting for a moment what is obscure in these introspective results, let me try to state those particulars which to my own consciousness seem indubitable and distinct.

In the first place, the acts of attending, assenting, negating, making an effort, are felt as movements of something in the head. In many cases it is possible to describe these movements quite exactly. In attending to either an idea or a sensation belonging to a particular sense-sphere, the movement is the adjustment of the sense-organ, felt as it occurs. I cannot think in visual terms, for example, without feeling a fluctuating play of pressures, convergences, divergences, and accommodations in my eyeballs. The direction in which the object is conceived to lie determines the character of these movements, the feeling of which becomes, for my consciousness, identified with the manner in which I make myself ready to receive the visible thing. My brain appears to me as if all shot across with lines of direction, of which I have become conscious as my attention has shifted from one sense-organ to another, in passing to successive outer things, or in following trains of varying sense-ideas.

When I try to remember or reflect, the movements in question, instead of being directed towards the periphery, seem to come from the periphery inwards and feel like a sort of *withdrawal* from the outer world. As far as I can detect, these feelings are due to an actual rolling outwards and upwards of the eyeballs, such as I believe occurs in me in sleep, and is the exact opposite of their action in fixating a physical thing. In reasoning, I find that I am apt to have a kind of vaguely localized diagram in my mind, with the various fractional objects of the thought disposed at particular points thereof; and the oscillations of my attention from one of them to another are most distinctly felt as alternations of direction in movements occurring inside the head.

In consenting and negating, and in making a mental effort, the movements seem more complex, and I find them harder to describe. The opening and closing of the glottis play a great part in these operations, and, less distinctly, the movements of the soft palate, etc., shutting off the posterior nares from the mouth. My glottis is like a sensitive valve, intercepting my breath instantaneously at every mental hesitation or felt aversion to the objects of my thought, and as quickly opening, to let the air pass through my throat and nose, the moment the repugnance is overcome. The feeling of the movement of this air is, in me, one strong ingredient of the feeling of assent. The movements of the muscles of the brow and eyelids also respond very sensitively to every fluctuation in the agreeableness or disagreeableness of what comes before my mind.

In *effort* of any sort, contractions of the jaw-muscles and of those of respiration are added to those of the brow and glottis, and thus the feeling passes out of the head properly so called. It passes out of the head whenever the welcoming or rejecting of the object is *strongly* felt. Then a set of feelings pour in from many bodily parts, all "expressive" of my emotion, and the head-feelings proper are swallowed up in this larger mass.

In a sense, then, it may be truly said that, in one person at least, *the "Self of selves," when carefully examined, is found to consist mainly of the collection of these peculiar motions in the head or between the head and throat.* I do not for a moment say that this is *all* it consists of, for I fully realize how desperately hard is introspection in this field. But I feel quite sure that these cephalic motions are the portions of my innermost activity of which I am *most distinctly aware.* If the dim portions which I cannot yet define should prove to be like unto these distinct portions in me, and I like other men, *it would follow that our entire feeling of spiritual activity, or what commonly passes by that name, is really a feeling of bodily activities whose exact nature is by most men overlooked.*

Now, without pledging ourselves in any way to adopt this hypothesis, let us dally with it for a while to see to what consequences it might lead if it were true.

In the first place, the nuclear part of the Self, intermediary between ideas and overt acts, would be a collection of activities physiologically in no essential way different from the overt acts themselves. If we divide all possible physiological acts into *adjustments* and *executions,* the nuclear self would be the adjustments collectively considered; and the less intimate, more shifting self, so far as it was active, would be the executions. But both adjustments and executions would obey the reflex type. Both would be the result of sensorial and ideational processes discharging either into each other within the brain, or into muscles and other parts outside. The peculiarity of the adjustments would be that they are minimal reflexes, few in number, incessantly repeated, constant amid great fluctuations in the rest of the mind's content, and entirely unimportant and uninteresting except through their uses in furthering or inhibiting the presence of various things, and actions before consciousness. These characters would naturally keep us from introspectively paying much attention to them in detail, whilst they would at the same time make us aware of them as a coherent group of processes, strongly contrasted with all the other things consciousness contained,—even with the other constituents of the "Self," material, social, or spiritual, as the case might be. They are reactions, and they are *primary* reactions. Everything arouses them; for objects which have no other effects will for a moment contract the brow and make the glottis close. It is as if all that visited the mind had to stand an entrance-examination, and just show its face so as to be either approved or sent back. These primary reactions are like the opening or the closing of the door. In the midst of psychic change they are the permanent core of turnings-towards and turnings-from, of yieldings and arrests, which naturally seem central and interior in comparison with the foreign matters, *apropos* to which they occur, and hold a sort of arbitrating, decisive position, quite unlike that held by any of the other constituents of the Me. It would not be surprising, then, if we were to feel them as the birthplace of conclusions and the starting point of acts, or if they came to appear as what we called a while back the "sanctuary within the citadel" of our personal life.

If they really were the innermost sanctuary, the *ulti-mate* one of all the selves whose being we can ever directly experience, it would follow that *all* that is experienced is, strictly considered, *objective;* that this Objective falls asunder into two contrasted parts, one realized as "Self," the other as "not-Self"; and that over and above these parts there *is* nothing save the fact that they are known, the fact of the stream of thought being there as the indispensable subjective *condition* of their being experienced at all. But this *condition* of the experience is not one of the *things experienced* at the moment; this knowing is not immediately *known*. It is only known in subsequent reflection. Instead, then, of the stream of thought being one of *con*sciousness, "thinking its own existence along with whatever else it thinks," (as Ferrier says) it might be better called a stream of *Scious*ness pure and simple, thinking objects of some of which it makes what it calls a "Me," and only aware of its "pure" Self in an abstract, hypothetic or conceptual way. Each "section" of the stream would then be a bit of sciousness or knowledge of this sort, including and contemplating its "me" and its "not-me" as objects which work out their drama together, but not yet including or contemplating its own subjective being. The sciousness in question would be the *Thinker*, and the existence of this thinker would be given to us rather as a logical postulate than as that direct inner perception of spiritual activity which we naturally believe ourselves to have. "Matter," as something behind physical phenomena, is a postulate of this sort. Between the postulated Matter and the postulated Thinker, the sheet of phenomena would then swing, some of them (the "realities") pertaining more to the Matter, others (the fictions, opinions, and errors) pertaining more to the Thinker. But *who* the Thinker would be, or how many distinct Thinkers we ought to suppose in the universe, would all be subjects for an ulterior metaphysical inquiry. . . .

At present, then, the only conclusion I come to is the following: That (in some persons at least) the part of the innermost Self which is most vividly felt turns out to consist for the most part of a collection of cephalic movements of "adjustments" which, for want of attention and reflection, usually fail to be perceived and classed as what they are; that over and above these there is an obscurer feeling of something more; but whether it be of fainter physiological processes, or of nothing objective at all, but rather of subjectivity as such, of thought become "its own object," must at present remain an open question,—like the question whether it be an indivisible active soul-substance, or the question whether it be a personification of the pronoun I, or any other of the guesses as to what its nature may be. . . .

Rivalry and Conflict of the Different Selves

With most objects of desire, physical nature restricts our choice to but one of many represented goods, and even so it is here. I am often confronted by the necessity of standing by one of my empirical selves and relinquishing the rest. Not that I would not, if I could, be both handsome and fat and well dressed, and a great athlete, and make a million a year, be a wit, a *bon-vivant*, a lady-killer, as well as a philosopher; a philanthropist, statesman, warrior, and African explorer, as well as a "tone-poet" and saint. But the thing is simply impossible. The millionaire's work would run counter to the saint's; the *bon-vivant* and the philanthropist would trip each other up; the philosopher and the lady-killer could not well keep house in the same tenement of clay. Such different characters may conceivably at the outset of life be alike *possible* to a man. But to make any one of them actual, the rest must more or less be suppressed. So the seeker of his truest, strongest, deepest self must review the list carefully, and pick out the one on which to stake his salvation. All other selves thereupon become unreal, but the fortunes of this self are real. Its failures are real failures, its triumphs real triumphs, carrying shame and gladness with them. This is as strong an example as there is of that selective industry of the mind on which I insisted some pages back. . . . Our thought, incessantly deciding, among many things of a kind, which ones for it shall be realities, here chooses one of many possible selves or characters, and forthwith reckons it no shame to fail in any of those not adopted expressly as its own.

I, who for the time have staked my all on being a psychologist, am mortified if others know much more psychology than I. But I am contented to wallow in the grossest ignorance of Greek. My deficiencies there give me no sense of personal humiliation at all. Had I "pretensions" to be a linguist, it would have been just the reverse. So we have the paradox of a man shamed to death because he is only the second pugilist or the second oarsman in the world. That he is able to beat the whole population of the globe minus one is nothing; he has "pitted" himself to beat that one; and as long as he doesn't do that nothing else counts. He is to his own regard as if he were not, indeed he *is* not.

Yonder puny fellow, however, whom every one can beat, suffers no chagrin about it, for he has long ago abandoned the attempt to "carry that line," as the merchants say, of self at all. With no attempt there can be no failure; with no failure no humiliation. So our self-feeling in this world depends entirely on what we *back* ourselves to be and do. It is determined by the ratio of our actualities to our supposed potentialities; a fraction of which our pretensions are the denominator and the numerator our success: thus,

$$\text{Self-esteem} = \frac{\text{Success}}{\text{Pretensions}}.$$ Such a fraction may be increased as well by diminishing the denominator as by increasing the numerator.[1] To give up pretensions is as blessed a relief as to get them gratified; and where disappointment is incessant and the struggle unending, this is what men will always do. The history of evangelical theology, with its conviction of sin, its self-despair, and its abandonment of salvation by works, is the deepest of possible examples, but we meet others in every walk of life. There is the strangest lightness about the heart when one's nothingness in a particular line is once accepted in good faith. *All* is not bitterness in the lot of the lover sent away by the final inexorable "No." Many Bostonians, *credo experto* (and inhabitants of other cities, too, I fear), would be happier women and men to-day, if they could once for all abandon the notion of keeping up a Musical Self, and without shame let people hear them call a symphony a nuisance. How pleasant is the day when we give up striving to be young,—or slender! Thank God! we say,

[1] Cf. Carlyle: *Sartor Resartus,* "The Everlasting Yea." "I tell thee, blockhead, it all comes of thy vanity; of what thou fanciest those same deserts of thine to be. Fancy that thou deservest to be hanged (as is most likely), thou wilt feel it happiness to be only shot: fancy that thou deservest to be hanged in a hair halter, it will be a luxury to die in hemp. . . . What act of legislature was there that *thou* shouldst be happy? A little while ago thou hadst no right to *be* at all," etc., etc.

those illusions are gone. Everything added to the Self is a burden as well as a pride. A certain man who lost every penny during our civil war went and actually rolled in the dust, saying he had not felt so free and happy since he was born.

Once more, then, our self-feeling is in our power. As Carlyle says: "Make thy claim of wages a zero, then hast thou the world under thy feet. Well did the wisest of our time write, it is only with *renunciation* that life, properly speaking, can be said to begin."

Neither threats nor pleadings can move a man unless they touch some one of his potential or actual selves. Only thus can we, as a rule, get a "purchase" on another's will. The first care of diplomatists and monarchs and all who wish to rule or influence is, accordingly, to find out their victim's strongest principle of self-regard, so as to make that the fulcrum of all appeals. But if a man has given up those things which are subject to foreign fate, and ceased to regard them as parts of himself at all, we are well-nigh powerless over him. The Stoic receipt for contentment was to dispossess yourself in advance of all that was out of your own power,—then fortune's shocks might rain down unfelt. Epictetus exhorts us, by thus narrowing and at the same time solidifying our Self to make it invulnerable: "I must die; well, but must I die groaning too? I will speak what appears to be right, and if the despot says, then I will put you to death, I will reply, 'When did I ever tell you that I was immortal?

You will do your part and I mine; it is yours to kill and mine to die intrepid; yours to banish, mine to depart untroubled.' How do we act in a voyage? We choose the pilot, the sailors, the hour. Afterwards comes a storm. What have I to care for? My part is performed. This matter belongs to the pilot. But the ship is sinking; what then have I to do? That which alone I can do—submit to being drowned without fear, without clamor or accusing of God, but as one who knows that what is born must likewise die." [1]

This Stoic fashion, though efficacious and heroic enough in its place and time, is, it must be confessed, only possible as an habitual mood of the soul to narrow and unsympathetic characters. It proceeds altogether by exclusion. If I am a Stoic, the goods I cannot appropriate cease to be *my* goods, and the temptation lies very near to deny that they are goods at all. We find this mode of protecting the Self by exclusion and denial very common among people who are in other respects not Stoics. All narrow people *intrench* their Me, they *retract* it,—from the region of what they cannot securely possess. People who don't resemble them, or who treat them with indifference, people over whom they gain no influence, are people on whose existence, however meritorious it may intrinsically be, they look with chill negation, if not with positive hate. Who will not be mine I will exclude from existence altogether; that is, as far as I can make it so, such people

[1] T. W. Higginson's translation (1866), p. 105.

shall be as if they were not.[1]   Thus may a certain absoluteness and definiteness in the outline of my Me console me for the smallness of its content.

Sympathetic people, on the contrary, proceed by the entirely opposite way of expansion and inclusion. The outline of their self often gets uncertain enough, but for this the spread of its content more than atones. *Nil humani a me alienum*. Let them despise this little person of mine, and treat me like a dog. *I* shall not negate *them* so long as I have a soul in my body. They are realities as much as I am. What positive good is in them shall be mine too, etc., etc. The magnanimity of these expansive natures is often touching indeed. Such persons can feel a sort of delicate rapture in thinking that, however sick, ill-favored, mean-conditioned, and generally forsaken they may be, they yet are integral parts of the whole of this brave world, have a fellow's share in the strength of the dray-horses, the happiness of the young people, the wisdom of the wise ones, and are not altogether without part or lot in the good fortunes of the Vanderbilts and the Hohenzollerns themselves. Thus either by negating or by embracing, the Ego may seek to establish itself in reality. He who, with Marcus Aurelius, can truly say, "O Universe, I wish all that thou wishest," has a self from which every

---

[1] "The usual mode of lessening the shock of disappointment or disesteem is to contract, if possible, a low estimate of the persons that inflict it. This is our remedy for the unjust censures of party spirit, as well as of personal malignity." (Bain: *Emotion and Will*, p. 209.)

trace of negativeness and obstructiveness has been removed—no wind can blow except to fill its sails.

A tolerably unanimous opinion ranges the different selves of which a man may be "seized and possessed," and the consequent different orders of his self-regard, in an *hierarchical scale, with the bodily Self at the bottom, the spiritual Self at top, and the extracorporeal material selves and the various social selves between.* Our merely natural self-seeking would lead us to aggrandize all these selves; we give up deliberately only those among them which we find we cannot keep. Our unselfishness is thus apt to be a "virtue of necessity"; and it is not without all show of reason that cynics quote the fable of the fox and the grapes in describing our progress therein. But this is the moral education of the race; and if we agree in the result that on the whole the selves we can keep are the intrinsically best, we need not complain of being led to the knowledge of their superior worth in such a tortuous way.

Of course this is not the only way in which we learn to subordinate our lower selves to our higher. A direct ethical judgment unquestionably also plays its part, and last, not least, we apply to our own persons judgments originally called forth by the acts of others. It is one of the strangest laws of our nature that many things which we are well satisfied with in ourselves disgust us when seen in others. With another man's bodily "hoggishness" hardly any one has any sympathy;—almost as little with his cupidity, his social vanity and eagerness, his jealousy, his despotism, and his pride. Left absolutely to myself I should probably allow all these spontaneous tendencies to luxuriate in me unchecked, and it would be long before I formed a distinct notion of the order of their subordination. But having constantly to pass judgment on my associates, I come ere long to see, as Herr Horwicz says, my own lusts in the mirror of the lusts of others, and to *think* about them in a very different way from that in which I simply *feel*. Of course, the moral generalities which from childhood have been instilled into me accelerate enormously the advent of this reflective judgment on myself.

So it comes to pass that, as aforesaid, men have arranged the various selves which they may seek in an hierarchical scale according to their worth. A certain amount of bodily selfishness is required as a basis for all the other selves. But too much sensuality is despised, or at best condoned on account of the other qualities of the individual. The wider material selves are regarded as higher than the immediate body. He is esteemed a poor creature who is unable to forego a little meat and drink and warmth and sleep for the sake of getting on in the world. The social self as a whole, again, ranks higher than the material self as a whole. We must care more for our honor, our friends, our human ties, than for a sound skin or wealth. And the spiritual self is so supremely precious that, rather than lose it, a man ought to be willing to give up friends and good fame, and property, and life itself.

In each kind of self, material, social, and spiritual, men distinguish between the immediate and actual, and the remote and potential, between the narrower and the wider view, to the detriment of the former and advantage of the latter. One must forego a present bodily enjoyment for the sake of one's general health; one must abandon the dollar in the hand for the sake of the hundred dollars to come; one must make an enemy of his present interlocutor if thereby one makes friends of a more valued circle; one must go without learning and grace, and wit, the better to compass one's soul's salvation.

Of all these wider, more potential selves, *the potential social self* is the most interesting, by reason of certain apparent paradoxes to which it leads in conduct, and by reason of its connection with our moral and religious life. When for motives of honor and conscience I brave the condemnation of my own family, club, and "set"; when, as a Protestant, I turn Catholic; as a Catholic, freethinker; as a "regular practitioner," homœopath, or what not, I am always inwardly strengthened in my course and steeled against the loss of my actual social self by the thought of other and better *possible* social judges than those whose verdict goes against me now. The ideal social self which I thus seek in appealing to their decision may be very remote: it may be represented as barely possible. I may not hope for its realization during my lifetime; I may even expect the future generations, which would approve me if they knew me, to know nothing about me when I am dead and gone. Yet still the emotion that beckons me on is indubitably the pursuit of an ideal social self, of a self that it at least *worthy* of approving recognition by the highest *possible* judging companion, if such companion there be.[1] This self is the true, the intimate, the ultimate, the permanent Me which I seek. This judge is God, the Absolute Mind, the "Great Companion." We hear, in these days of scientific enlightenment, a great deal of discussion about the efficacy of prayer; and many reasons are given us why we should not pray, whilst others are given us why we should. But in all this very little is said of the reason why we *do* pray, which is simply that we cannot *help* praying. It seems probable that, in spite of all that "science" may do to the contrary, men will continue to pray to the end of time, unless their mental nature changes in a manner which nothing we know should lead us to expect. The impulse to pray is a

[1] It must be observed that the qualities of the Self thus ideally constituted are all qualities approved by my actual fellows in the first instance; and that my reason for now appealing from their verdict to that of the ideal judge lies in some outward peculiarity of the immediate case. What once was admired in me as courage has now become in the eyes of men "impertinence"; what was fortitude is obstinacy; what was fidelity is now fanaticism. The ideal judge alone, I now believe, can read my qualities, my willingness, my powers, for what they truly are. My fellows, misled by interest and prejudice, have gone astray.

necessary consequence of the fact that whilst the innermost of the empirical selves of a man is a Self of the *social* sort, it yet can find its only adequate *Socius* in an ideal world.

All progress in the social Self is the substitution of higher tribunals for lower; this ideal tribunal is the highest; and most men, either continually or occasionally, carry a reference to it in their breast. The humblest outcast on this earth can feel himself to be real and valid by means of this higher recognition. And, on the other hand, for most of us, a world with no such inner refuge when the outer social self failed and dropped from us would be the abyss of horror. I say "for most of us," because it is probable that individuals differ a good deal in the degree in which they are haunted by this sense of an ideal spectator. It is a much more essential part of the consciousness of some men than of others. Those who have the most of it are possibly the most *religious* men. But I am sure that even those who say they are altogether without it deceive themselves, and really have it in some degree. Only a non-gregarious animal could be completely without it. Probably no one can make sacrifices for "right," without to some degree personifying the principle of right for which the sacrifice is made, and expecting thanks from it. *Complete* social unselfishness, in other words, can hardly exist; *complete* social suicide hardly occur to a man's mind. Even such texts as Job's, "Though He slay me yet will I trust Him," or Marcus Aurelius's, "If gods hate me and my children, there is a reason for it," can least of all be cited to prove the contrary. For beyond all doubt Job revelled in the thought of Jehovah's recognition of the worship after the slaying should have been done; and the Roman emperor felt sure the Absolute Reason would not be all indifferent to his acquiescence in the gods' dislike. The old test of piety, "Are you willing to be damned for the glory of God?" was probably never answered in the affirmative except by those who felt sure in their heart of hearts that God would "credit" them with their willingness, and set more store by them thus than if in His unfathomable scheme He had not damned them at all.

All this about the impossibility of suicide is said on the supposition of *positive* motives. When possessed by the emotion of *fear*, however, we are in a *negative* state of mind; that is, our desire is limited to the mere banishing of something, without regard to what shall take its place. In this state of mind there can unquestionably be genuine thoughts, and genuine acts, of suicide, spiritual and social, as well as bodily. Anything, *anything*, at such times, so as to escape and not to be! But such conditions of suicidal frenzy are pathological in their nature and run dead against everything that is regular in the life of the Self in man.

The Focal Point of Character [1]

. . . I have often thought that the best way to define a man's character would be to seek out the particular mental or moral attitude in which, when it came upon him, he felt himself most deeply and intensely active and alive. At such moments there is a voice inside which speaks and says: *"This* is the real me!" And afterwards, considering the circumstances in which the man is placed, and noting how some of them are fitted to evoke this attitude, whilst others do not call for it, an outside observer may be able to prophesy where the man may fail, where succeed, where be happy and where miserable. Now as well as I can describe it, this characteristic attitude in me always involves an element of active tension, of holding my own, as it were, and trusting outward things to perform their part so as to make it a full harmony, but without any *guaranty* that they will. Make it a guaranty—and the attitude immediately becomes to my consciousness stagnant and stingless. Take away the guaranty, and I feel (provided I am *überhaupt* in vigorous condition) a sort of deep enthusiastic bliss, of bitter willingness to do and suffer anything, which translates itself physically by a kind of stinging pain inside my breast-bone (don't smile at this—it is to me an essential element of the whole thing!), and

[1] From a letter to Mrs. James, December, 1878, in *The Letters of William James,* vol. i, p. 199.

which, although it is a mere mood or emotion to which
I can give no form in words, authenticates itself to
me as the deepest principle of all active and theoretic
determination which I possess. . . .

W. J.

The Body as the Self [1]

The individualized self, which I believe to be the
only thing properly called self, is a part of the content
of the world experienced. The world experienced
(otherwise called the "field of consciousness") comes
at all times with our body as its center, center of
vision, center of action, center of interest. Where
the body is is "here"; when the body acts is "now";
what the body touches is "this"; all other things are
"there" and "then" and "that." These words of emphasized position imply a systematization of things
with reference to a focus of action and interest which
lies in the body; and the systematization is now so
instinctive (was it ever not so?) that no developed or
active experience exists for us at all except in that
ordered form. So far as "thoughts" and "feelings"
can be active, their activity terminates in the activity of
the body, and only through first arousing its activities
can they begin to change those of the rest of the world.
The body is the storm center, the origin of coördinates,
the constant place of stress in all that experience-train.

[1] From "The Experience of Activity," in *A Pluralistic Universe*,
Note, p. 380.

Everything circles round it, and is felt from its point of view. The word "I," then, is primarily a noun of position, just like "this" and "here." Activities attached to "this" position have prerogative emphasis, and, if activities have feelings, must be felt in a peculiar way. The word "my" designates the kind of emphasis. I see no inconsistency whatever in defending, on the one hand, "my" activities as unique and opposed to those of outer nature, and, on the other hand, in affirming, after introspection, that they consist in movements in the head. The "my" of them is the emphasis, the feeling of perspective-interest in which they are dyed.

CHAPTER IV

HOW WE KNOW

Faith and Hypothesis [1]

Let us give the name of *hypothesis* to anything that may be proposed to our belief; and just as the electricians speak of live and dead wires, let us speak of any hypothesis as either *live* or *dead*. A live hypothesis is one which appeals as a real possibility to him to whom it is proposed. If I ask you to believe in the Mahdi, the notion makes no electric connection with your nature—it refuses to scintillate with any credibility at all. As an hypothesis it is completely dead. To an Arab, however (even if he be not one of the Mahdi's followers), the hypothesis is among the mind's possibilities: it is alive. This shows that deadness and liveness in an hypothesis are not intrinsic properties, but relations to the individual thinker. They are measured by his willingness to act. The maximum of liveness in an hypothesis means willingness to act irrevocably. Practically, that means belief; but there is some believing tendency wherever there is willingness to act at all.

Next, let us call the decision between two hypotheses an *option*. Options may be of several kinds. They

[1] From *The Will to Believe*, pp. 1-4.

may be—1, *living* or *dead;* 2, *forced* or *avoidable;* 3, *momentous* or *trivial;* and for our purposes we may call an option a *genuine* option when it is of the forced, living, and momentous kind.

1. A living option is one in which both hypotheses are live ones. If I say to you: "Be a theosophist or be a Mohammedan," it is probably a dead option, because for you neither hypothesis is likely to be alive. But if I say: "Be an agnostic or be a Christian," it is otherwise: trained as you are, each hypothesis makes some appeal, however small, to your belief.

2. Next, if I say to you: "Choose between going out with your umbrella or without it," I do not offer you a genuine option, for it is not forced. You can easily avoid it by not going out at all. Similarly, if I say, "Either love me or hate me," "Either call my theory true or call it false," your option is avoidable. You may remain indifferent to me, neither loving nor hating, and you may decline to offer any judgment as to my theory. But if I say, "Either accept this truth or go without it," I put on you a forced option, for there is no standing place outside of the alternative. Every dilemma based on a complete logical disjunction, with no possibility of not choosing, is an option of this forced kind.

3. Finally, if I were Dr. Nansen and proposed to you to join my North Pole expedition, your option would be momentous; for this would probably be your only similar opportunity, and your choice now would

either exclude you from the North Pole sort of immortality altogether or put at least the chance of it into your hands. He who refuses to embrace a unique opportunity loses the prize as surely as if he tried and failed. *Per contra,* the option is trivial when the opportunity is not unique, when the stake is insignificant, or when the decision is reversible if it later prove unwise. Such trivial options abound in the scientific life. A chemist finds an hypothesis live enough to spend a year in its verification: he believes in it to that extent. But if his experiments prove inconclusive either way, he is quit for his loss of time, no vital harm being done.

How We Think [1]

Any mind, constructed on the triadic-reflex pattern, must first get its impression from the object which it confronts; then define what that object is, and decide what active measures its presence demands; and finally react. The stage of reaction depends on the stage of definition, and these, of course, on the nature of the impressing object. When the objects are concrete, particular, and familiar, our reactions are firm and certain enough—often instinctive. I see the desk, and lean on it; I see your quiet faces, and I continue to talk. But the objects will not stay concrete and particular: they fuse themselves into general essences, and they sum themselves into a whole—the universe. And

[1] From "Reflex Action and Theism," in *The Will to Believe,* pp. 122-124.

then the object that confronts us, that knocks on our mental door and asks to be let in, and fixed and decided upon and actively met, is just this whole universe itself and its essence.

What are *they*, and how shall I meet *them?*

The whole flood of faiths and systems here rush in. Philosophies and denials of philosophy, religions and atheisms, skepticisms and mysticisms, confirmed emotional moods and habitual practical biases, jostle one another; for all are alike trials, hasty, prolix, or of seemly length, to answer this momentous question. And the function of them all, long or short, that which the moods and the systems alike subserve and pass into, is the third stage—the stage of action. For no one of them itself is final. They form but the middle segment of the mental curve, and not its termination. As the last theoretic pulse dies away, it does not leave the mental process complete: it is but the forerunner of the practical moment, in which alone the cycle of mentality finds its rhythmic pause.

We easily delude ourselves about this middle stage Sometimes we think it final, and sometimes we fail to see, amid the monstrous diversity in the length and complication of the cogitations which may fill it, that it can have but one essential function, and that the one we have pointed out—the function of defining the direction which our activity, immediate or remote, shall take.

If I simply say, "Vanitas vanitatum, omnia vanitas!"

I am defining the total nature of things in a way that carries practical consequences with it as decidedly as if I write a treatise De Natura Rerum in twenty volumes. The treatise may trace its consequences more minutely than the saying; but the only worth of either treatise or saying is that the consequences are there. The long definition can do no more than draw them; the short definition does no less. Indeed, it may be said that if two apparently different definitions of the reality before us should have identical consequences, those two definitions would really be identical definitions, made delusively to appear different merely by the different verbiage in which they are expressed.

Thinking as Selection [1]

The human mind has no . . . power of universal intuition. Its finiteness obliges it to see but two or three things at a time. If it wishes to take wider sweeps it has to use "general ideas," as they are called, and in so doing to drop all concrete truths. . . . The human mind is essentially partial. It can be efficient at all only by *picking out* what to attend to, and ignoring everything else—by narrowing its point of view. Otherwise, what little strength it has is dispersed, and it loses its way altogether. Man always wants his curiosity gratified for a particular purpose.

It is, then, a necessity laid upon us as human beings

[1] From "Great Men and their Environment," in *The Will to Believe*, pp. 219-221.

to limit our view. In mathematics we know how this method of ignoring and neglecting quantities lying outside of a certain range has been adopted in the differential calculus. The calculator throws out all the "infinitesimals" of the quantities he is considering. He treats them (under certain rules) as if they did not exist. In themselves they exist perfectly all the while; but they are as if they did not exist for the purposes of his calculation. Just so an astronomer, in dealing with the tidal movements of the ocean, takes no account of the waves made by the wind, or by the pressure of all the steamers which day and night are moving their thousands of tons upon its surface. Just so the marksman, in sighting his rifle, allows for the motion of the wind, but not for the equally real motion of the earth and solar system. Just so a business man's punctuality may overlook an error of five minutes, while a physicist, measuring the velocity of light, must count each thousandth of a second.

There are, in short, *different cycles of operation* in nature; different departments, so to speak, relatively independent of one another, so that what goes on at any moment in one may be compatible with almost any condition of things at the same time in the next. The mold on the biscuit in the store-room of a man-of-war vegetates in absolute indifference to the nationality of the flag, the direction of the voyage, the weather, and the human dramas that may go on on board; and a mycologist may study it in complete abstraction from all these larger details. Only by so studying it, in fact, is there any chance of the mental concentration by which alone he may hope to learn something of its nature. On the other hand, the captain who in manœuvring the vessel through a naval fight should think it necessary to bring the moldy biscuit into his calculations would very likely lose the battle by reason of the excessive "thoroughness" of his mind.

The causes which operate in these incommensurable cycles are connected with one another only *if we take the whole universe into account*. For all lesser points of view it is lawful—nay, more, it is for human wisdom necessary—to regard them as disconnected and irrelevant to one another.

The Point of Pragmatism [1]

The pivotal part of my book named *Pragmatism* is its account of the relation called "truth" which may obtain between an idea (opinion, belief, statement, or what not) and its object. "Truth," I there say, "is a property of certain of our ideas. It means their agreement, as falsity means their disagreement, with reality. Pragmatists and intellectualists both accept this definition as a matter of course.

"Where our ideas [do] not copy definitely their object, what does agreement with that object mean? . . . Pragmatism asks its usual question. 'Grant an

[1] From the Preface to *The Meaning of Truth*, pp. v-viii.

idea or belief to be true,' it says, 'what concrete difference will its being true make in any one's actual life? What experiences [may] be different from those which would obtain if the belief were false? How will the truth be realized? What, in short, is the truth's cash-value in experiential terms?' The moment pragmatism asks this question, it sees the answer. *True ideas are those that we can assimilate, validate, corroborate, and verify. False ideas are those that we cannot.* That is the practical difference it makes to us to have true ideas; that therefore is the meaning of truth, for it is all that truth is known as.

"The truth of an idea is not a stagnant property inherent in it. Truth *happens* to an idea. It *becomes* true, is *made* true by events. Its verity *is* in fact an event, a process, the process namely of its verifying itself, its veri*fication*. Its validity is the process of its valid*ation*.[1]

"To agree in the widest sense with a reality can only mean to be guided either straight up to it or into its surroundings, or to be put into such working touch with it as to handle either it or something connected with it better than if we disagreed. Better either intellectually or practically. . . . Any idea that helps us to

[1] But *"verifiability,"* I add, "is as good as verification. For one truth-process completed, there are a million in our lives that function in [the] state of nascency. They lead us towards direct verification; lead us into the surroundings of the object they envisage; and then, if everything runs on harmoniously, we are so sure that verification is possible that we omit it, and are usually justified by all that happens."

deal, whether practically or intellectually, with either the reality or its belongings, that doesn't entangle our progress in frustrations, that *fits*, in fact, and adapts our life to the reality's whole setting, will agree sufficiently to meet the requirement. It will be true of that reality.

"The true, to put it very briefly, *is only the expedient in the way of our thinking, just as the right is only the expedient in the way of our behaving.* Expedient in almost any fashion, and expedient in the long run and on the whole, of course; for what meets expediently all the experience in sight won't necessarily meet all farther experiences equally satisfactorily. Experience, as we know, has ways of *boiling over,* and making us correct our present formulas."

This account of truth, following upon the similar ones given by Messrs. Dewey and Schiller, has occasioned the liveliest discussion. Few critics have defended it, most of them have scouted it. It seems evident that the subject is a hard one to understand, under its apparent simplicity; and evident also, I think, that the definitive settlement of it will mark a turning-point in the history of epistemology and consequently in that of general philosophy. . . .

The Cognitive Relation [1]

The first great pitfall from which such a radical standing by experience will save us is an artificial con-

[1] From "A World of Pure Experience," in *Essays in Radical Empiricism,* pp. 52-60.

ception of the *relations between knower and known*. Throughout the history of philosophy the subject and its object have been treated as absolutely discontinuous entities; and thereupon the presence of the latter to the former, or the "apprehension" by the former of the latter, has assumed a paradoxical character which all sorts of theories had to be invented to overcome. Representative theories put a mental "representation," "image," or "content" into the gap, as a sort of intermediary. Common-sense theories left the gap untouched, declaring our mind able to clear it by a self-transcending leap. Transcendentalist theories left it impossible to traverse by finite knowers, and brought an Absolute in to perform the saltatory act. All the while, in the very bosom of the finite experience, every conjunction required to make the relation intelligible is given in full. Either the knower and the known are:

(1) the self-same piece of experience taken twice over in different contexts; or they are

(2) two pieces of *actual* experience belonging to the same subject, with definite tracts of conjunctive transitional experience between them; or

(3) the known is a *possible* experience either of that subject or another, to which the said conjunctive transitions *would* lead, if sufficiently prolonged.

To discuss all the ways in which one experience may function as the knower of another, would be incompatible with the limits of this essay. I have just treated of type 1, the kind of knowledge called perception. This is the type of case in which the mind enjoys direct "acquaintance" with a present object. In the other types the mind has "knowledge-about" an object not immediately there. Of type 2, the simplest sort of conceptual knowledge, I have given some account in two [earlier] articles. Type 3 can always formally and hypothetically be reduced to type 2, so that a brief description of that type will put the present reader sufficiently at my point of view, and make him see what the actual meanings of the mysterious cognitive relation may be.

Suppose me to be sitting here in my library at Cambridge, at ten minutes' walk from "Memorial Hall," and to be thinking truly of the latter object. My mind may have before it only the name, or it may have a clear image, or it may have a very dim image of the hall, but such intrinsic differences in the image make no difference in its cognitive function. Certain *extrinsic* phenomena, special experiences of conjunction, are what impart to the image, be it what it may, its knowing office.

For instance, if you ask me what hall I mean by my image, and I can tell you nothing; or if I fail to point or lead you towards the Harvard Delta; or if, being led by you, I am uncertain whether the Hall I see be what I had in mind or not; you would rightly deny that I had "meant" that particular hall at all, even though my mental image might to some degree have resembled it. The resemblance would count in that case as coincidental merely, for all sorts of things of a kind resemble one another in this world without being held for that reason to take cognizance of one another.

On the other hand, if I can lead you to the hall, and tell you of its history and present uses; if in its presence I feel my idea, however imperfect it may have been, to have led hither and to be now *terminated;* if the associates of the image and of the felt hall run parallel, so that each term of the one context corresponds serially, as I walk, with an answering term of the others; why then my soul was prophetic, and my idea must be, and by common consent would be, called cognizant of reality. That percept was what I *meant,* for into it my idea has passed by conjunctive experiences of sameness and fulfilled intention. Nowhere is there jar, but every later moment continues and corroborates an earlier one.

In this continuing and corroborating, taken in no transcendental sense, but denoting definitely felt transitions, *lies all that the knowing of a percept by an idea can possibly contain or signify*. Wherever such transitions are felt, the first experience *knows* the last one. Where they do not, or where even as possible they cannot, intervene, there can be no pretense of knowing. In this latter case the extremes will be connected, if connected at all, by inferior relations—bare likeness or succession, or by "withness" alone. Knowledge of sensible realities thus comes to life inside the tissue of experience. It is *made;* and made by relations that unroll themselves in time. Whenever certain inter-mediaries are given, such that, as they develop towards their terminus, there is experience from point to point of one direction followed, and finally of one process fulfilled, the result is that *their starting-point thereby becomes a knower and their terminus an object meant or known.* That is all that knowing (in the simple case considered) can be known-as, that is the whole of its nature, put into experiential terms. Whenever such is the sequence of our experiences we may freely say that we had the terminal object "in mind" from the outset, even although *at* the outset nothing was there in us but a flat piece of substantive experience like any other, with no self-transcendency about it, and no mystery save the mystery of coming into existence and of being gradually followed by other pieces of substantive experience, with conjunctively transitional experiences between. That is what we *mean* here by the object's being "in mind." Of any deeper more real way of being in mind we have no positive conception, and we have no right to discredit our actual experience by talking of such a way at all.

I know that many a reader will rebel at this. "Mere intermediaries," he will say, "even though they be feelings of continuously growing fulfillment, only *separate* the knower from the known, whereas what we have in knowledge is a kind of immediate touch of the one by the other, an 'apprehension' in the etymological sense of the word, a leaping of the chasm as by lightning, an act by which two terms are smitten into one, over the head of their distinctness. All these dead intermediaries of yours are out of each other, and outsid/ of their termini still."

But do not such dialectic difficulties remind us of the dog dropping his bone and snapping at its image in the water? If we knew any more real kind of union *aliunde,* we might be entitled to brand all our empirical unions as a sham. But unions by continuous transition are the only ones we know of, whether in this matter of a knowledge-about that terminates in an acquaintance, whether in personal identity, in logical predication through the copula "is," or elsewhere. If anywhere there were more absolute unions realized, they could only reveal themselves to us by just such conjunctive results. These are what the unions are *worth,* these are all that *we can ever practically mean* by union, by continuity. Is it not time to repeat what Lotze said of substances, that to *act like* one is to *be* one? Should we not say here that to be experienced as continuous is to be really continuous, in a world where experience and reality come to the same thing? In a picture gallery a painted hook will serve to hang a painted chain by, a painted cable will hold a painted ship. In a world where both the terms and their distinctions are affairs of experience, conjunctions that are experienced must be at least as real as anything else. They will be "absolutely" real conjunctions, if we have no transphenomenal Absolute ready, to derealize the whole experienced world by, at a stroke. If, on the other hand, we had such an Absolute, not one of our opponents' theories of knowledge could remain standing any better than ours could; for the distinctions as well as the conjunctions of experience would impartially fall its prey. The whole question of how "one" thing can know "another" would cease to be a real one at all in a world where otherness itself was an illusion.

The Pragmatist Account of Truth and Its Misunderstanders [1]

The account of truth given in my volume entitled *Pragmatism,* continues to meet with such persistent misunderstanding that I am tempted to make a final brief reply. My ideas may well deserve refutation, but they can get none till they are conceived of in their proper shape. The fantastic character of the current misconceptions shows how unfamiliar is the concrete point of view which pragmatism assumes. . . . The critics have boggled at every word they could boggle at, and refused to take the spirit rather than the letter of our discourse. . . .

First misunderstanding: Pragmatism is only a re-editing of positivism.

This seems the commonest mistake. Skepticism, positivism, and agnosticism agree with ordinary dogmatic rationalism in presupposing that everybody

[1] From *The Meaning of Truth,* pp. 180-216.

knows what the word "truth" means, without further explanation. But the former doctrines then either suggest or declare that real truth, absolute truth, is inaccessible to us, and that we must fain put up with relative or phenomenal truth as its next best substitute. By skepticism this is treated as an unsatisfactory state of affairs, while positivism and agnosticism are cheerful about it, call real truth sour grapes, and consider phenomenal truth quite sufficient for all our "practical" purposes.

In point of fact, nothing could be farther from all this than what pragmatism has to say of truth. Its thesis is an altogether previous one. It leaves off where these other theories begin, having contented itself with the word truth's *definition*. "No matter whether any mind extant in the universe possess truth or not," it asks, "what does the notion of truth signify *ideally?*" "What kind of things would true judgments be *in case* they existed?" The answer which pragmatism offers is intended to cover the most complete truth that can be conceived of, "absolute" truth if you like, as well as truth of the most relative and imperfect description. This question of what truth would be like if it did exist, belongs obviously to a purely speculative field of inquiry. It is not a theory about any sort of reality, or about what kind of knowledge is actually possible; it abstracts from particular terms altogether, and defines the nature of a possible relation between two of them.

As Kant's question about synthetic judgments had

escaped previous philosophers, so the pragmatist question is not only so subtle as to have escaped attention hitherto, but even so subtle, it would seem, that when openly broached now, dogmatists and skeptics alike fail to apprehend it, and deem the pragmatist to be treating of something wholly different. He insists, they say, (I quote an actual critic), "that the greater problems are insoluble by human intelligence, that our need of knowing truly is artificial and illusory, and that our reason, incapable of reaching the foundations of reality, must turn itself exclusively towards *action.*" There could not be a worse misapprehension.

Second misunderstanding: Pragmatism is primarily an appeal to action.

The name "pragmatism," with its suggestions of action, has been an unfortunate choice, I have to admit, and has played into the hands of this mistake. But no word could protect the doctrine from critics so blind to the nature of the inquiry that, when Dr. Schiller speaks of ideas "working" well, the only thing they think of is their immediate workings in the physical environment, their enabling us to make money, or gain some similar "practical" advantage. Ideas do work thus, of course, immediately or remotely; but they work indefinitely inside of the mental world also. Not crediting us with this rudimentary insight, our critics treat our view as offering itself exclusively to engineers, doctors, financiers, and men of action generally, who need some sort of a rough and ready *weltanschauung,* but have no time or wit to study genuine philosophy. It is usually described as a characteristically American movement, a sort of bobtailed scheme of thought, excellently fitted for the man on the street, who naturally hates theory and wants cash returns immediately.

It is quite true that, when the refined theoretic question that pragmatism begins with is once answered, secondary corollaries of a practical sort follow. Investigation shows that, in the function called truth, previous realities are not the only independent variables. To a certain extent our ideas, being realities, are also independent variables, and, just as they follow other reality and fit it, so, in a measure, does other reality follow and fit them. When they add themselves to being, they partly redetermine the existent, so that reality as a whole appears incompletely definable unless ideas also are kept account of. This pragmatist doctrine, exhibiting our ideas as complemental factors of reality, throws open (since our ideas are instigators of our action) a wide window upon human action, as well as a wide license to originality in thought. But few things could be sillier than to ignore the prior epistemological edifice in which the window is built, or to talk as if pragmatism began and ended at the window. This, nevertheless, is what our critics do almost without exception. They ignore our primary step and its motive, and make the relation to action, which is our secondary achievement, primary.

Third misunderstanding: Pragmatists cut themselves off from the right to believe in ejective realities.

They do so, according to the critics, by making the truth of our beliefs consist in their verifiability, and their verifiability in the way in which they do work for us. Professor Stout, in his otherwise admirable and hopeful review of Schiller in *Mind* for October, 1907, considers that this ought to lead Schiller (could he sincerely realize the effects of his own doctrine) to the absurd consequence of being unable to believe genuinely in another man's headache, even were the headache there. He can only "postulate" it for the sake of the working value of the postulate to himself. The postulate guides certain of his acts and leads to advantageous consequences; but the moment he understands fully that the postulate is true *only* (!) in this sense, it ceases (or should cease) to be true for him that the other man really *has* a headache. All that makes the postulate most precious then evaporates: his interest in his fellow-man "becomes a veiled form of self-interest and his world grows cold, dull, and heartless."

Such an objection makes a curious muddle of the pragmatist's universe of discourse. Within that universe the pragmatist finds some one with a headache or other feeling, and some one else who postulates that feeling. Asking on what condition the postulate is "true," the pragmatist replies that, for the postulator at any rate, it is true just in proportion as to believe in it works in him the fuller sum of satisfactions. What is it that is satisfactory here? Surely to *believe* in the postulated object, namely, in the really existing feeling of the other man. But how (especially if the postulator were himself a thoroughgoing pragmatist) could it ever be satisfactory to him *not* to believe in that feeling, so long as, in Professor Stout's words, disbelief "made the world seem to him cold, dull, and heartless"? Disbelief would seem, on pragmatist principles, quite out of the question under such conditions, unless the heartlessness of the world were made probable already on other grounds. And since the belief in the headache, true for the subject assumed in the pragmatist's universe of discourse, is also true for the pragmatist who for his epistemologizing purposes has assumed that entire universe, why is it not true in that universe absolutely? The headache believed in is a reality there, and no extant mind disbelieves it, neither the critic's mind nor his subject's! Have our opponents any better brand of truth in this real universe of ours that they can show us?

So much for the third misunderstanding, which is but one specification of the following still wider one:

Fourth misunderstanding: No pragmatist can be a realist in his epistemology.

This is supposed to follow from his statement that the truth of our beliefs consists in general in their giving satisfaction. Of course satisfaction *per se* is a subjective condition; so the conclusion is drawn that truth falls wholly inside of the subject, who then may manufacture it at his pleasure. True beliefs become thus wayward affections, severed from all responsibility to other parts of experience.

It is difficult to excuse such a parody of the pragmatist's opinion, ignoring as it does every element but one of his universe of discourse. The terms of which that universe consists positively forbid any non-realistic interpretation of the function of knowledge defined there. The pragmatizing epistemologist posits there a reality and a mind with ideas. What, now, he asks, can make those ideas true of that reality? Ordinary epistemology contents itself with the vague statement that the ideas must "correspond" or "agree"; the pragmatist insists on being more concrete, and asks what such "agreement" may mean in detail. He finds first that the ideas must point to or lead towards *that* reality and no other, and then that the pointings and leadings must yield satisfaction as their result. So far the pragmatist is hardly less abstract than the ordinary slouchy epistemologist; but as he defines himself farther, he grows more concrete. The entire quarrel of the intellectualist with him is over his concreteness, intellectualism contending that the vaguer and more abstract account is here the more profound. The concrete pointing and leading are conceived by the pragmatist to be the work of other portions of the same universe to which the reality and the mind belong, intermediary verifying bits of experience with which the mind at one end, and the reality at the other, are joined. The "satisfaction," in turn, is no abstract satisfaction *überhaupt,* felt by an unspecified being, but is assumed to consist of such satisfactions (in the plural) as concretely existing men actually do find in their beliefs. As we humans are constituted in point of fact, we find that to believe in other men's minds, in independent physical realities, in past events, in eternal logical relations, is satisfactory. We find hope satisfactory. We often find it satisfactory to cease to doubt. Above all we find *consistency* satisfactory, consistency between the present idea and the entire rest of our mental equipment, including the whole order of our sensations, and that of our intuitions of likeness and difference, and our whole stock of previously acquired truths.

The pragmatist, being himself a man, and imagining in general no contrary lines of truer belief than ours about the "reality" which he has laid at the base of his epistemological discussion, is willing to treat our satisfactions as possibly really true guides to it, not as guides true solely for *us.* It would seem here to be the duty of his critics to show with some explicitness why, being our subjective feelings, these satisfactions can *not* yield "objective" truth. The beliefs which they accompany "posit" the assumed reality, "correspond" and "agree" with it, and "fit" it in perfectly definite and assignable ways, through the sequent trains of thought and action which form their verification, so merely to insist on using these words abstractly instead of concretely is no way of driving the pragmatist from the field—his more concrete account virtually includes his critic's. If our critics have any definite idea of a truth more objectively grounded than the kind we propose, why do they not show it more articulately? As they stand, they remind one of Hegel's man who wanted "fruit," but rejected cherries, pears, and grapes, because they were not fruit in the abstract. We offer them the full quart-pot, and they cry for the empty quart-capacity.

But here I think I hear some critic retort as follows: "If satisfactions are all that is needed to make truth, how about the notorious fact that errors are so often satisfactory? And how about the equally notorious fact that certain true beliefs may cause the bitterest dissatisfaction? Isn't it clear that not the satisfaction which it gives, but the relation of the belief *to the reality* is all that makes it true? Suppose there were no such reality, and that the satisfactions yet remained: would they not then effectively work falsehood? Can they consequently be treated distinctively as the truth-builders? It is the *inherent relation to reality* of a belief that gives us that specific *truth*-satisfaction, compared with which all other satisfactions are the hollowest humbug. The satisfaction of *knowing truly* is thus the only one which the pragmatist ought to have considered. As a *psychological sentiment,* the anti-pragmatist gladly concedes it to him, but then only as a concomitant of truth, not as a constituent. What *constitutes* truth is not the sentiment, but the purely logical or objective function of right cognizing the reality, and the pragmatist's failure to reduce this function to lower values is patent."

Such anti-pragmatism as this seems to me a tissue of confusion. To begin with, when the pragmatist says "indispensable," it confounds this with "sufficient." The pragmatist calls satisfactions indispensable for truth-building, but I have everywhere called them insufficient unless reality be also incidentally led to. If the reality assumed were canceled from the pragmatist's universe of discourse, he would straightway give the name of falsehoods to the beliefs remaining, in spite of all their satisfactoriness. For him, as for his critic, there can be no truth if there is nothing to be true about. Ideas are so much flat psychological surface unless some mirrored matter gives them cognitive luster. This is why as a pragmatist I have so carefully posited "reality" *ab initio,* and why, throughout my whole discussion, I remain an epistemological realist.[1]

The anti-pragmatist is guilty of the further confusion of imagining that, in undertaking to give him an account of what truth formally means, we are assuming at the same time to provide a warrant for it, trying to define the occasions when he can be sure of mate-

---

[1] I need hardly remind the reader that both sense-percepts and percepts of ideal relation (comparisons, etc.) should be classed among the realities. The bulk of our mental "stock" consists of truths concerning these terms.

rially possessing it. Our making it hinge on a reality so "independent" that when it comes, truth comes, and when it goes, truth goes with it, dissappoints this *naïve* expectation, so he deems our description unsatisfactory. I suspect that under this confusion lies the still deeper one of not discriminating sufficiently between the two notions, truth and reality. Realities are not *true*, they *are;* and beliefs are true *of* them. But I suspect that in the anti-pragmatist mind the two notions sometimes swap their attributes. The reality itself, I fear, is treated as if "true," and conversely. Whoso tells us of the one, it is then supposed, must also be telling us of the other; and a true idea must in a manner *be*, or at least *yield* without extraneous aid, the reality it cognitively is possessed of.

To this absolute-idealistic demand pragmatism simply opposes its *non possumus*. If there is to be truth, it says, both realities and beliefs about them must conspire to make it; but whether there ever is such a thing, or how any one can be sure that his own beliefs possess it, it never pretends to determine. That truth-satisfaction *par excellence* which may tinge a belief unsatisfactory in other ways, it easily explains as the feeling of consistency with the stock of previous truths, or supposed truths, of which one's whole past experience may have left one in possession.

But are not all pragmatists sure that their own belief is right? their enemies will ask at this point; and this leads me to the

Fifth misunderstanding: What pragmatists say is inconsistent with their saying so.

A correspondent puts this objection as follows: "When you say to your audience, 'pragmatism is the truth concerning truth,' the first truth is different from the second. About the first you and they are not to be at odds; you are not giving them liberty to take or leave it according as it works satisfactorily or not for their private uses. Yet the second truth, which ought to describe and include the first, affirms this liberty. Thus the *intent* of your utterance seems to contradict the *content* of it."

General skepticism has always received this same classic refutation. "You have to dogmatize," the rationalists say to the skeptics, "whenever you express the skeptical position; so your lives keep contradicting your thesis." One would suppose that the impotence of so hoary an argument to abate in the slightest degree the amount of general skepticism in the world might have led some rationalists themselves to doubt whether these instantaneous logical refutations are such fatal ways, after all, of killing off live mental attitudes. General skepticism is the live mental attitude of refusing to conclude. It is a permanent torpor of the will, renewing itself in detail towards each successive thesis that offers, and you can no more kill it off by logic than you can kill off obstinacy or practical joking. This is why it is so irritating. Your consistent skeptic never puts his skepticism into a formal proposition—

he simply chooses it as a habit. He provokingly hangs back when he might so easily join us in saying yes, but he is not illogical or stupid—on the contrary, he often impresses us by his intellectual superiority. This is the *real* skepticism that rationalists have to meet, and their logic does not even touch it.

No more can logic kill the pragmatist's behavior: his act of utterance, so far from contradicting, accurately exemplifies the matter which he utters. What is the matter which he utters? In part, it is this, that truth, concretely considered, is an attribute of our beliefs, and that these are attitudes that follow satisfactions. The ideas around which the satisfactions cluster are primarily only hypotheses that challenge or summon a belief to come and take its stand upon them. The pragmatist's idea of truth is just such a challenge. He finds it ultra-satisfactory to accept it, and takes his own stand accordingly. But, being gregarious as they are, men seek to spread their beliefs, to awaken imitation, to infect others. Why should not *you* also find the same belief satisfactory? thinks the pragmatist, and forthwith endeavors to convert you. You and he will then believe similarly; you will hold up your subject-end of a truth, which will be a truth objective and irreversible if the reality holds up the object-end by being itself present simultaneously. What there is of self-contradiction in all this I confess I cannot discover. The pragmatist's conduct in his own case seems to me on the contrary admirably to illustrate his universal formula; and of all epistemologists, he is perhaps the only one who is irreproachably self-consistent.

Sixth misunderstanding: Pragmatism explains not what truth is, but only how it is arrived at.

In point of fact it tells us both, tells us what it is incidentally to telling us how it is arrived at,—for what *is* arrived at except just what the truth is? If I tell you how to get to the railroad station, don't I implicitly introduce you to the *what,* to the being and nature of that edifice? It is quite true that the abstract *word* "how" hasn't the same meaning as the abstract *word* "what," but in this universe of concrete facts you cannot keep hows and whats asunder. The reasons why I find it satisfactory to believe that any idea is true, the *how* of my arriving at that belief, may be among the very reasons why the idea *is* true in reality. If not, I summon the anti-pragmatist to explain the impossibility articulately.

His trouble seems to me mainly to arise from his fixed inability to understand how a concrete statement can possibly mean as much, or be as valuable, as an abstract one. I said above that the main quarrel between us and our critics was that of concreteness *versus* abstractness. This is the place to develop that point farther.

In the present question, the links of experience sequent upon an idea, which mediate between it and a reality, form and for the pragmatist indeed *are,* the

concrete relation of truth that may obtain between the
idea and that reality. They, he says, are all that we
mean when we speak of the idea "pointing" to the
reality, "fitting" it, "corresponding" with it, or "agree-
ing" with it—they or other similar mediating trains
of verification. Such mediating events *make* the idea
"true." The idea itself, if it exists at all, is also a
concrete event: so pragmatism insists that truth in the
singular is only a collective name for truths in the
plural, these consisting always of series of definite
events; and that what intellectualism calls *the* truth,
the *inherent* truth, of any one such series is only the
abstract name for its truthfulness in act, for the fact
that the ideas there do lead to the supposed reality
in a way that we consider satisfactory.

The pragmatist himself has no objection to abstractions. Elliptically, and "for short," he relies on them
as much as any one, finding upon innumerable occasions
that their comparative emptiness makes of them useful
substitutes for the overfulness of the facts he meets
with. But he never ascribes to them a higher grade
of reality. The full reality of a truth for him is always
some process of verification, in which the abstract property of connecting ideas with objects truly is workingly
embodied. Meanwhile it is endlessly serviceable to be
able to talk of properties abstractly and apart from
their working, to find them the same in innumerable
cases, to take them "out of time," and to treat of their
relations to other similar abstractions. We thus form

whole universes of platonic ideas *ante rem,* universes *in posse,* though none of them exists effectively except *in rebus.* Countless relations obtain there which nobody experiences as obtaining—as, in the eternal universe of musical relations, for example, the notes of Aennchen von Tharau were a lovely melody long ere mortal ears ever heard them. Even so the music of the future sleeps now, to be awakened hereafter. Or, if we take the world of geometrical relations, the thousandth decimal of π sleeps there, though no one may ever try to compute it. Or, if we take the universe of "fitting," countless coats "fit" backs, and countless boots "fit" feet, on which they are not practically *fitted;* countless stones "fit" gaps in walls into which no one seeks to fit them actually. In the same way countless opinions "fit" realities, and countless truths are valid, though no thinker ever thinks them.

For the anti-pragmatist these prior timeless relations are the presupposition of the concrete ones, and possess the profounder dignity and value. The actual workings of our ideas in verification-processes are as naught in comparison with the "obtainings" of this discarnate truth within them.

For the pragmatist, on the contrary, all discarnate truth is static, impotent, and relatively spectral, full truth being the truth that energizes and does battle. Can any one suppose that the sleeping quality of truth would ever have been abstracted or have received a name, if truths had remained forever in that storage-vault of essential timeless "agreements" and had never been embodied in any panting struggle of men's live ideas for verification? Surely no more than the abstract property of "fitting" would have received a name, if in our world there had been no backs or feet or gaps in walls to be actually fitted. *Existential* truth is incidental to the actual competition of opinions. *Essential* truth, the truth of the intellectualists, the truth with no one thinking it, is like the coat that fits though no one has ever tried it on, like the music that no ear has listened to. It is less real, not more real, than the verified article; and to attribute a superior degree of glory to it seems little more than a piece of perverse abstraction-worship. As well might a pencil insist that the outline is the essential thing in all pictorial representation, and chide the paint-brush and the camera for omitting it, forgetting that *their* pictures not only contain the whole outline, but a hundred other things in addition. Pragmatist truth contains the whole of intellectualist truth and a hundred other things in addition. Intellectualist truth is then only pragmatist truth *in posse*. That on innumerable occasions men do substitute truth *in posse* or verifiability, for verification or truth in act, is a fact to which no one attributes more importance than the pragmatist: he emphasizes the practical utility of such a habit. But he does not on that account consider truth *in posse*—truth not alive enough ever to have been asserted or questioned or contradicted—to be the metaphysically prior thing, to which truths in act are tributary and subsidiary. When intellectualists do this, pragmatism charges them with inverting the real relation. Truth in posse *means* only truths in act; and he insists that these latter take precedence in the order of logic as well as in that of being.

Seventh misunderstanding: Pragmatism ignores the theoretic interest.

This would seem to be an absolutely wanton slander, were not a certain excuse to be found in the linguistic affinities of the word "pragmatism," and in certain off-hand habits of speech of ours which assumed too great a generosity on our reader's part. When we spoke of the meaning of ideas consisting in their "practical" consequences, or of the "practical" differences which our beliefs make to us; when we said that the truth of a belief consists in its "working" value, etc.; our language evidently was too careless, for by "practical" we were almost unanimously held to mean *opposed* to theoretical or genuinely cognitive, and the consequence was punctually drawn that a truth in our eyes could have no relation to any independent reality, or to any other truth, or to anything whatever but the acts which we might ground on it or the satisfactions they might bring. The mere existence of the idea, all by itself, if only its results were satisfactory, would give full truth to it, it was charged, in our absurd pragmatist epistemology. The solemn attribution of this rubbish to us was also encouraged by two other circumstances.

First, ideas *are* practically useful in the narrow sense, false ideas sometimes, but most often ideas which we can verify by the sum total of all their leadings, and the reality of whose objects may thus be considered established beyond doubt. That these ideas should be true in advance of and apart from their utility, that, in other words, their objects should be really there, is the very condition of their having that kind of utility —the objects they connect us with are so important that the ideas which serve as the objects' substitutes grow important also. This manner of their practical working was the first thing that made truths good in the eyes of primitive men; and buried among all the other good workings by which true beliefs are characterized, this kind of subsequential utility remains.

The second misleading circumstance was the emphasis laid by Schiller and Dewey on the fact that, unless a truth be relevant to the mind's momentary predicament, unless it be germane to the "practical" situation—meaning by this the quite particular perplexity—it is no good to urge it. It doesn't meet our interests any better than a falsehood would under the same circumstances. But why our predicaments and perplexities might not be theoretical here as well as narrowly practical, I wish that our critics would explain. They simply assume that no pragmatist *can* admit a genuinely theoretic interest. Having used the phrase "cash-value" of an idea, I am implored by one correspondent to alter it, "for every one thinks you mean only pecuniary profit or loss." Having said that the true is "the expedient in our thinking," I am rebuked in this wise by another learned correspondent: "The word expedient has no other meaning than that of self-interest. The pursuit of this has ended by landing a number of officers of national banks in penitentiaries. A philosophy that leads to such results must be unsound."

But the word "practical" is so habitually loosely used that more indulgence might have been expected. When one says that a sick man has now practically recovered, or that an enterprise has practically failed, one usually means just the opposite of practically in the literal sense. One means that, although untrue in strict practice, what one says is true in theory, true virtually, *certain to be* true. Again, by the practical one often means the distinctively concrete, the individual, particular, and effective, as opposed to the abstract, general, and inert. To speak for myself, whenever I have emphasized the practical nature of truth, this is mainly what has been in my mind. "Pragmata" are things in their plurality; and in that early California address, when I described pragmatism as holding that "the meaning of any proposition can always be brought down to some particular consequence in our future practical experience, whether passive or active," I expressly added these qualifying words: "the point lying rather in the fact that the experience must be particular than in the fact that it must be active"—by "active" meaning here "practical" in the narrow literal sense.[1] But particular consequences can perfectly well be of a theoretic nature. Every remote fact which we infer from an idea is a particular theoretic consequence which our mind practically works towards. The loss of every old opinion of ours which we see that we shall have to give up if a new opinion be true, is a particular theoretic as well as a particular practical consequence. After man's interest in breathing freely, the greatest of all his interests (because it never fluctuates or remits, as most of his physical interests do), is his interest in *consistency,* in feeling that what he now thinks goes with what he thinks on other occasions. We tirelessly compare truth with truth for this sole purpose. Is the present candidate for belief perhaps contradicted by principle number one? Is it compatible with fact number two? and so forth. The particular operations here are the purely logical ones of analysis, deduction, comparison, etc.; and although general terms may be used *ad libitum,* the satisfactory *practical working* of

[1] The ambiguity of the word "practical" comes out well in these words of a recent would-be reporter of our views: "Pragmatism is an Anglo-Saxon reaction against the intellectualism and rationalism of the Latin mind. . . . Man, each individual man is the measure of things. He is able to conceive none but relative truths, that is to say, illusions. What these illusions are worth is revealed to him, not by general theory, but by individual practice. Pragmatism, which consists in experiencing these illusions of the mind and obeying them by acting them out, is a *philosophy without words,* a philosophy of *gestures and of acts,* which abandons what is general and holds only to what is *particular."* (Bourdeau, in *Journal des Débats,* October 29, 1907.)

the candidate-idea consists in the consciousness yielded by each successive theoretic consequence in particular. It is therefore simply idiotic to repeat that pragmatism takes no account of purely theoretic interests. All it insists on is that verity in act means *verifications,* and that these are always particulars. Even in exclusively theoretic matters, it insists that vagueness and generality serve to verify nothing.

Eighth misunderstanding: Pragmatism is shut up to solipsism.

I have already said something about this misconception under the third and fourth heads, above, but a little more may be helpful. The objection is apt to clothe itself in words like these: "You make truth to consist in every value except the cognitive value proper; you always leave your knower at many removes (or, at the uttermost, at one remove) from his real object; the best you do is to let his ideas carry him towards it; it remains forever outside of him," etc.

I think that the leaven working here is the rooted intellectual persuasion that, to know a reality, an idea must in some inscrutable fashion possess or be it.[1] For pragmatism this kind of coalescence is inessential. As a rule our cognitions are only processes of mind off

[1] Sensations may, indeed, possess their objects or coalesce with them, as common sense supposes that they do; and intuited differences between concepts may coalesce with the "eternal" objective differences; but to simplify our discussion here we can afford to abstract from these very special cases of knowing.

their balance and in motion towards real termini; and the reality of the termini, believed in by the states of mind in question, can be *guaranteed* only by some wider knower.[1] But if there is no reason extant in the universe why they should be doubted, the beliefs are true in the only sense in which anything can be true anyhow: they are practically and concretely true, namely. True in the mystical mongrel sense of an *Identitätsphilosophie* they need not be; nor is there any intelligible reason why they ever need be true otherwise than verifiably and practically. It is reality's part to possess its own existence; it is thought's part to get into "touch" with it by innumerable paths of verification.

I fear that the "humanistic" developments of pragmatism may cause a certain difficulty here. We get at one truth only through the rest of truth; and the reality, everlastingly postulated as that which all our

---

[1] The transcendental idealist thinks that, in some inexplicable way, the finite states of mind are identical with the transfinite all-knower which he finds himself obliged to postulate in order to supply a *fundamentum* for the relation of knowing, as he apprehends it. Pragmatists can leave the question of identity open; but they cannot do without the wider knower any more than they can do without the reality, if they want to *prove* a case of knowing. They themselves play the part of the absolute knower for the universe of discourse which serves them as material for epistemologizing. They warrant the reality there, and the subject's true knowledge, there, of it. But whether what they themselves say about that whole universe is objectively true, *i.e.*, whether the pragmatic theory of truth is true *really*, they cannot warrant,—they can only believe it. To their hearers they can only *propose* it, as I propose it to my readers, as something to be verified *ambulando*, or by the way in which its consequences may confirm it.

truth must keep in touch with, may never be given to us save in the form of truth other than that which we are now testing. But since Dr. Schiller has shown that all our truths, even the most elemental, are affected by race-inheritance with a human co-efficient, reality *per se* thus may appear only as a sort of limit; it may be held to shrivel to the mere *place* for an object, and what is known may be held to be only matter of our psyche that we fill the place with.

It must be confessed that pragmatism, worked in this humanistic way, is *compatible* with solipsism. It joins friendly hands with the agnostic part of kantism, with contemporary agnosticism, and with idealism generally. But worked thus, it is a metaphysical theory about the matter of reality, and flies far beyond pragmatism's own modest analysis of the nature of the knowing function, which analysis may just as harmoniously be combined with less humanistic accounts of reality. One of pragmatism's merits is that it is so purely epistemological. It must assume realities; but it prejudges nothing as to their constitution, and the most diverse metaphysics can use it as their foundation. It certainly has no special affinity with solipsism.

As I look back over what I have written, much of it gives me a queer impression, as if the obvious were set forth so condescendingly that readers might well laugh at my pomposity. It may be, however, that concreteness as radical as ours is not so obvious. The whole originality of pragmatism, the whole point in it, is its use of the concrete way of seeing. It begins with concreteness, and returns and ends with it. Dr. Schiller, with his two "practical" aspects of truth, (1) relevancy to situation, and (2) subsequential utility, is only filling the cup of concreteness to the brim for us. Once seize that cup, and you cannot misunderstand pragmatism. It seems as if the power of imagining the world concretely *might* have been common enough to let our readers apprehend us better, as if they might have read between our lines, and, in spite of all our infelicities of expression, guessed a little more correctly what our thought was. But alas! this was not on fate's program, so we can only think, with the German ditty:—

> "Es wär' zu schön gewesen,
> Es hat nicht sollen sein."

CHAPTER V

THE POWERS AND LIMITATIONS OF SCIENCE

Scientific Systems and Reality [1]

"The great field for new discoveries," said a scientific friend to me the other day, "is always the unclassified residuum." Round about the accredited and orderly facts of every science there ever floats a sort of dust-cloud of exceptional observations, of occurrences minute and irregular and seldom met with, which it always proves more easy to ignore than to attend to. The ideal of every science is that of a closed and completed system of truth. The charm of most sciences to their more passive disciples consists in their appearing, in fact, to wear just this ideal form. Each one of our various *ologies* seems to offer a definite head of classification for every possible phenomenon of the sort which it professes to cover; and so far from free is most men's fancy, that, when a consistent and organized scheme of this sort has once been comprehended and assimilated, a different scheme is unimaginable. No alternative, whether to whole or parts, can any longer be conceived as possible. Phenomena unclassifiable within the system are therefore paradoxical absurdities, and must be held untrue. When, moreover, as so often happens, the

[1] From "What Psychical Research Has Accomplished," in *The Will to Believe*, pp. 299-302; 319-320; 323-327.

197

reports of them are vague and indirect; when they come as mere marvels and oddities rather than as things of serious moment,—one neglects or denies them with the best of scientific consciences. Only the born geniuses let themselves be worried and fascinated by these outstanding exceptions, and get no peace till they are brought within the fold. Your Galileos, Galvanis, Fresnels, Purkinjes, and Darwins are always getting confounded and troubled by insignificant things. Any one will renovate his science who will steadily look after the irregular phenomena. And when the science is renewed, its new formulas often have more of the voice of the exceptions in them than of what were supposed to be the rules. . . .

To no one type of mind is it given to discern the totality of truth. Something escapes the best of us,—not accidentally, but systematically, and because we have a twist. The scientific-academic mind and the feminine-mystical mind shy from each other's facts, just as they fly from each other's temper and spirit. Facts are there only for those who have a mental affinity with them. When once they are indisputably ascertained and admitted, the academic and critical minds are by far the best fitted ones to interpret and discuss them,—for surely to pass from mystical to scientific speculations is like passing from lunacy to sanity; but on the other hand if there is anything which human history demonstrates, it is the extreme slowness with which the ordinary academic and critical mind acknowledges facts to exist which present themselves as wild facts, with no stall or pigeon-hole, or as facts which threaten to break up the accepted system. In psychology, physiology, and medicine, wherever a debate between the mystics and the scientifics has been once for all decided, it is the mystics who have usually proved to be right about the *facts,* while the scientifics had the better of it in respect to the theories. The most recent and flagrant example of this is "animal magnetism," whose facts were stoutly dismissed as a pack of lies by academic medical science the world over, until the non-mystical theory of "hypnotic suggestion" was found for them,—when they were admitted to be so excessively and dangerously common that special penal laws, forsooth, must be passed to keep all persons unequipped with medical diplomas from taking part in their production. Just so stigmatizations, invulnerabilities, instantaneous cures, inspired discourses, and demoniacal possessions, the records of which were shelved in our libraries but yesterday in the alcove headed "superstitions," now, under the brand-new title of "cases of hystero-epilepsy," are republished, reobserved, and reported with an even too credulous avidity. . . .

Science means, first of all, a certain dispassionate method. To suppose that it means a certain set of results that one should pin one's faith upon and hug forever is sadly to mistake its genius, and degrades the scientific body to the status of a sect.

We all, scientists and non-scientists, live on some inclined plane of credulity. The plane tips one way in one man, another way in another; and may he whose plane tips in no way be the first to cast a stone! . . . Science, like life, feeds on its own decay. New facts burst old rules; then newly divined conceptions bind old and new together into a reconciling law. . . .

Although in its essence science only stands for a method and for no fixed belief, yet as habitually taken, both by its votaries and outsiders, it is identified with a certain fixed belief,—the belief that the hidden order of nature is mechanical exclusively, and that non-mechanical categories are irrational ways of conceiving and explaining even such things as human life. Now, this mechanical rationalism, as one may call it, makes, if it becomes one's only way of thinking, a violent breach with the ways of thinking that have played the greatest part in human history. Religious thinking, ethical thinking, poetical thinking, teleological, emotional, sentimental thinking, what one might call the personal view of life to distinguish it from the impersonal and mechanical, and the romantic view of life to distinguish it from the rationalistic view, have been, and even still are, outside of well-drilled scientific circles, the dominant forms of thought. But for mechanical rationalism, personality is an insubstantial illusion. The chronic belief of mankind, that events may happen for the sake of their personal significance, is an abomination; and the notions of our grandfathers about oracles and omens, divinations and apparitions, miraculous changes of heart and wonders worked by inspired persons, answers to prayer and providential leadings, are a fabric absolutely baseless, a mass of sheer *un*truth.

Now, of course, we must all admit that the excesses to which the romantic and personal view of nature may lead, if wholly unchecked by impersonal rationalism, are direful. Central African Mumbo-jumboism is one of unchecked romanticism's fruits. One ought accordingly to sympathize with that abhorrence of romanticism as a sufficient world-theory; one ought to understand that lively intolerance of the least grain of romanticism in the views of life of other people, which are such characteristic marks of those who follow the scientific professions today. Our debt to science is literally boundless, and our gratitude for what is positive in her teachings must be correspondingly immense. But . . . it seems to me . . . that the verdict of pure insanity, of gratuitous preference for error, of superstition without an excuse, which the scientists of our day are led by their intellectual training to pronounce upon the entire thought of the past, is a most shallow verdict. The personal and romantic view of life has other roots besides wanton exuberance of imagination and perversity of heart. It is perennially fed by *facts of experience*, whatever the ulterior interpretation of those facts may prove to be. . . . These experiences have three characters in common: They are capricious, discontinuous, and not easily controlled;

they require peculiar persons for their production; their significance seems to be wholly for personal life. Those who preferentially attend to them, and still more those who are individually subject to them, not only easily may find, but are logically bound to find, in them valid arguments for their romantic and personal conception of the world's course. . . .

When from our present advanced standpoint we look back upon the past stages of human thought, whether it be scientific thought or theological thought, we are amazed that a universe which appears to us of so vast and mysterious a complication should ever have seemed to any one so little and plain a thing. Whether it be Descartes's world or Newton's, whether it be that of the materialists of the last century or that of the Bridgewater treatises of our own, it always looks the same to us,—incredibly perspectiveless and short. Even Lyell's, Faraday's, Mill's, and Darwin's consciousness of their respective subjects are already beginning to put on an infantile and innocent look. Is it then likely that the science of our own day will escape the common doom; that the minds of its votaries will never look old-fashioned to the grandchildren of the latter? It would be folly to suppose so. Yet if we are to judge by the analogy of the past, when our science once becomes old-fashioned, it will be more for its omissions of fact, for its ignorance of whole ranges and orders of complexity in the phenomena to be explained, than for any fatal lack in its spirit and principles. The spirit and principles of science are mere affairs of method; there is nothing in them that need hinder science from dealing successfully with a world in which personal forces are the starting-point of new effects. The only form of thing that we directly encounter, the only experience that we concretely have, is our own personal life. The only complete category of our thinking, our professors of philosophy tell us, is the category of personality, every other category being one of the abstract elements of that. And this systematic denial on science's part of personality as a condition of events, this rigorous belief that in its own essential and innermost nature our world is a strictly impersonal world, may, conceivably, as the whirligig of time goes round, prove to be the very defect that our descendants will be most surprised at in our own boasted science, the omission that to their eyes will most tend to make it look perspectiveless and short.

Science Is Selective [1]

Certain of our positivists keep chiming to us, that, amid the wreck of every other god and idol, one divinity still stands upright,—that his name is Scientific Truth, and that he has but one commandment, but that one supreme, saying, *Thou shalt not be a theist,* for that would be to satisfy thy subjective propensities, and the satisfaction of those is intellectual damnation. These most conscientious gentlemen think they have jumped

[1] From "Reflex Action and Theism," in *The Will to Believe,* pp. 131-132.

off their own feet,—emancipated their mental operations from the control of their subjective propensities
at large and *in toto*. But they are deluded. They have
simply chosen from among the entire set of propensities at their command those that were certain to con-
struct, out of the materials given, the leanest, lowest,
aridest result,—namely, the bare molecular world,—
and they have sacrificed all the rest.[1]

Man's chief difference from the brutes lies in the
exuberant excess of his subjective propensities,—his
preëminence over them simply and solely in the number
and in the fantastic and unnecessary character of his
wants, physical, moral, æsthetic, and intellectual. Had
his whole life not been a quest for the superfluous, he
would never have established himself as inexpugnably
as he has done in the necessary. And from the consciousness of this he should draw the lesson that his
wants are to be trusted; that even when their gratifica-
tion seems farthest off, the uneasiness they occasion
is still the best guide of his life, and will lead him to
issues entirely beyond his present powers of reckoning.
Prune down his extravagance, sober him, and you undo
him. The appetite for immediate consistency at any

[1] As our ancestors said, *Fiat justitia, pereat mundus*, so we, who
do not believe in justice or any absolute good, must, according to
these prophets, be willing to see the world perish, in order that
scientia fiat. Was there ever a more exquisite idol of the den, or
rather of the *shop?* In the clean sweep to be made of superstitions,
let the idol of stern obligation to be scientific go with the rest, and
people will have a fair chance to understand one another. But
this blowing of hot and of cold makes nothing but confusion.

cost, or what the logicians call the "law of parsimony," —which is nothing but the passion for conceiving the universe in the most labor-saving way,—will, if made the exclusive law of the mind, end by blighting the development of the intellect itself quite as much as that of the feelings or the will. The scientific conception of the world as an army of molecules gratifies this appetite after its fashion most exquisitely. But if the religion of exclusive scientificism should ever succeed in suffocating all other appetites out of a nation's mind, and imbuing a whole race with the persuasion that simplicity and consistency demand a *tabula rasa* to be made of every notion that does not form part of the *soi-disant* scientific synthesis, that nation, that race, will just as surely go to ruin, and fall a prey to their more richly constituted neighbors, as the beasts of the field, as a whole, have fallen a prey to man.

Insufficiency of Scientists [1]

Of all insufficient authorities as to the total nature of reality, give me the "scientists," from Münsterberg up, or down. Their interests are most incomplete and their professional conceit and bigotry immense. I know no narrower sect or club, in spite of their excellent authority in the lines of fact they have explored, and their splendid achievement there. Their only authority *at large* is for *method*—and the pragmatic method completes and enlarges them there.

[1] From a letter to C. A. Strong, in *The Letters of William James* vol. ii, p. 270.

The Genesis of the Natural Sciences [1]

Our "scientific" ways of thinking the outer reality are highly abstract ways. The essence of things for science is not to be what they seem, but to be atoms and molecules moving to and from each other according to strange laws. Nowhere does the account of inner relations produced by outer ones in proportion to the frequency with which the latter have been met, more egregiously break down than in the case of scientific conceptions. The order of scientific thought is quite incongruent either with the way in which reality exists or with the way in which it comes before us. Scientific thought goes by selection and emphasis exclusively. We break the solid plenitude of fact into separate essences, conceive generally what only exists particularly, and by our classifications leave nothing in its natural neighborhood, but separate the contiguous, and join what the poles divorce. The reality *exists* as a *plenum*. All its parts are contemporaneous, each is as real as any other, and each as essential for making the whole just what it is and nothing else. But we can neither experience nor think this *plenum*. What we experience, what *comes before us,* is a chaos of fragmentary impressions interrupting each other;[2] what we

[1] From *The Principles of Psychology,* vol. ii, pp. 633-640.

[2] "The order of nature, as perceived at a first glance, presents at every instant a chaos followed by another chaos. We must decompose each chaos into single facts. We must learn to see in the chaotic antecedent a multitude of distinct antecedents, in the chaotic consequent a multitude of distinct consequents. This, supposing it done,

think is an abstract system of hypothetical data and laws.[1]

This sort of scientific algebra, little as it immediately resembles the reality given to us, turns out (strangely enough) applicable to it. That is, it yields expressions which, at given places and times, can be translated into real values, or interpreted as definite portions of the chaos that falls upon our sense. It becomes thus a practical guide to our expectations as well as a theoretic delight. But I do not see how any one with a sense for the facts can possibly call our systems immediate results of "experience" in the ordinary sense. Every

will not of itself tell us on which of the antecedents each consequent is invariably attendant. To determine that point, we must endeavor to effect a separation of the facts from one another, not in our minds only, but in nature. The mental analysis, however, must take place first. And every one knows that in the mode of performing it, one intellect differs immensely from another." (J. S. Mill, *Logic,* bk. iii, chap. vii, § 1.)

[1] I quote from an address entitled "Reflex Action and Theism," published in the *Unitarian Review* for November, 1881, and translated in the *Critique Philosophique* for January and February, 1882. "The conceiving or theorizing faculty works exclusively for the sake of ends that do not exist at all in the world of the impressions received by way of our senses, but are set by our emotional and practical subjectivity. It is a transformer of the world of our impressions into a totally different world, the world of our conception; and the transformation is effected in the interests of our volitional nature, and for no other purpose whatsoever. Destroy the volitional nature, the definite subjective purposes, preferences, fondness for certain effects, forms, orders, and not the slightest motive would remain for the brute order of our experience to be remodeled at all. But, as we have the elaborate volitional constitution we do have, the remodeling must be effected, there is no escape." . . . *See page 19 for conclusion of note.*—ED.

scientific conception is in the first instance a "spontaneous variation" in some one's brain.[1] For one that proves useful and applicable there are a thousand that perish through their worthlessness. Their genesis is strictly akin to that of the flashes of poetry and sallies of wit to which the instable brain-paths equally give rise. But whereas the poetry and wit (like the science of the ancients) are their "own excuse for being," and have to run the gauntlet of no farther test, the "scientific" conceptions must prove their worth by being "verified." This test, however, is the cause of their *preservation,* not that of their production; and one might as well account for the origin of Artemus Ward's jokes by the "cohesion" of subjects with predicates in proportion to the "persistence of the outer relations" to which they "correspond" as to treat the genesis of scientific conceptions in the same ponderously unreal way. The most persistent outer relations which science believes in are never matters of experience at all, but have to be disengaged from under experience by a process of elimination, that is, by ignoring conditions which are always present. The *elementary* laws of

[1] In an article entitled "Great Men, Great Thoughts, and the Environment," published in the *Atlantic Monthly* for October, 1880, the reader will find some ampler illustrations of these remarks. I have there tried to show that both mental and social evolution are to be conceived after the Darwinian fashion, and that the function of the environment properly so called is much more that of *selecting* forms, produced by invisible forces, than *producing* of such forms,— producing being the only function thought of by the pre-Darwinian evolutionists, and the only one on which stress is laid by such contemporary ones as Mr. Spencer and Mr. Allen.

mechanics, physics, and chemistry are all of this sort. The principle of uniformity in nature is of this sort; it has to be *sought* under and in spite of the most rebellious appearances; and our conviction of its truth is far more like a religious faith than like assent to a demonstration. The only cohesions which experience in the literal sense of the word produces in our mind are, as we contended some time back the proximate laws of nature, and habitudes of concrete things, that heat melts ice, that salt preserves meat, that fish die out of water, and the like. Such "empirical truths" as these we admitted to form an enormous part of human wisdom. The "scientific" truths have to harmonize with these truths, or be given up as useless; but they arise in the mind in no such passive associative way as that in which the simpler truths arise. Even those experiences which are used to prove a scientific truth are for the most part artificial experiences of the laboratory gained after the truth itself has been conjectured. Instead of experiences engendering the "inner relations," the inner relations are what engender the experiences here.

What happens in the brain after experience has done its utmost is what happens in every material mass which has been fashioned by an outward force,—in every pudding or mortar, for example, which I may make with my hands. The fashioning from without brings the elements into collocations which set new internal forces free to exert their effects in turn. And the random irradiations and resettlements of our ideas, which *supervene upon experience*, and constitute our free mental play, are due entirely to those secondary internal processes, which vary enormously from brain to brain, even though the brains be exposed to exactly the same "outer relations."   The higher thought-processes owe their being to causes which correspond far more to the sourings and fermentations of dough, the setting of mortar, or the subsidence of sediments in mixtures, than to the manipulations by which these physical aggregates came to be compounded.   Our study of similar association and reasoning taught us that the whole superiority of man depended on the facility with which in his brain the paths worn by the most frequent outer cohesions could be ruptured.   The causes of the instability, the reasons why now this point and now that become in him the seat of rupture, we saw to be entirely obscure.   (Vol. I. p. 580; Vol. II. p. 364.)   The only clear thing about the peculiarity seems to be its interstitial character, and the certainty that no mere appeal to man's "experience" suffices to explain it.

When we pass from scientific to æsthetic and ethical systems, every one readily admits that, although the elements are matters of experience, the peculiar forms of relation into which they are woven are incongruent with the order of passively received experience.   The world of æsthetics and ethics is an ideal world, a Utopia, a world which the outer relations persist in contradicting, but which we as stubbornly persist in striving to make actual. Why do we thus invincibly crave to alter the given order of nature? Simply because other relations among things are far more interesting to us and more charming than the mere rates of frequency of their time- and space-conjunctions. These other relations are all secondary and brain-born, "spontaneous variations" most of them, of our sensibility, whereby certain elements of experience, and certain arrangements in time and space, have acquired an agreeableness which otherwise would not have been felt. It is true that habitual arrangements may also become agreeable. But this agreeableness of the merely habitual is felt to be a mere ape and counterfeit of real inward fitness; and one sign of intelligence is never to mistake the one for the other.

There are then ideal and inward relations amongst the objects of our thought which can in no intelligible sense whatever be interpreted as reproductions of the order of outer experience. In the æsthetic and ethical realms they conflict with its order—the early Christian with his kingdom of heaven, and the contemporary anarchist with his abstract dream of justice, will tell you that the existing order must perish, root and branch, ere the true order can come. Now the peculiarity of those relations among the objects of our thought which are dubbed "scientific" is this, that although they no more are inward *reproductions* of the outer order than the ethical and æsthetic relations are, yet they do not conflict with that order, but, once having sprung up by the play of the inward forces, are found—some of them at least, namely the only ones which have survived long enough to be matters of record—to be *congruent* with the time- and space-relations which our impressions affect.

In other words, though nature's materials lend themselves slowly and discouragingly to our translation of them into ethical forms, but more readily into æsthetic forms; to translation into scientific forms they lend themselves with relative ease and completeness. The translation, it is true, will probably never be ended. The perceptive order does not give way, nor the right conceptive substitute for it arise, at our bare word of command.[1] It is often a deadly fight; and many a man of science can say, like Johannes Müller, after an investigation, *"Es klebt Blut an der Arbeit."* But victory after victory makes us sure that the essential doom of our enemy is defeat.[2]

[1] Cf. Hodgson: *Philosophy of Reflection,* book ii, chap. v.

[2] The aspiration to be "scientific" is such an idol of the tribe to the present generation, is so sucked in with his mother's milk by every one of us, that we find it hard to conceive of a creature who should not feel it, and harder still to treat it freely as the altogether peculiar and one-sided subjective interest which it is. But as a matter of fact, few even of the cultivated members of the race have shared it; it was invented but a generation or two ago. In the middle ages it meant only impious magic; and the way in which it even now strikes Orientals is charmingly shown in the letter of a Turkish cadi to an English traveler asking him for statistical information, which Sir A. Layard prints at the end of his *Nineveh and Babylon.* The document is too full of edification not to be given in full. It runs thus:

"My Illustrious Friend, and Joy of my Liver!

"The thing you ask of me is both difficult and useless. Although I have passed all my days in this place, I have neither counted the houses nor inquired into the number of the inhabitants; and as to what one person loads on his mules and the other stows away in the bottom of his ship, that is no business of mine. But, above all, as to the previous history of this city, God only knows the amount of dirt and confusion that the infidels may have eaten before the coming of the sword of Islam. It were unprofitable for us to inquire into it.

"O my soul! O my lamb! seek not after the things which concern thee not. Thou camest unto us and we welcomed thee: go in peace.

"Of a truth thou hast spoken many words; and there is no harm done, for the speaker is one and the listener is another. After the fashion of thy people thou hast wandered from one place to another, until thou art happy and content in none. We (praise be to God) were born here, and never desire to quit it. Is it possible, then, that the idea of a general intercourse between mankind should make any impression on our understandings? God forbid!

"Listen, O my son! There is no wisdom equal unto the belief in God! He created the world, and shall we liken ourselves unto Him in seeking to penetrate into the mysteries of His creation? Shall we say, Behold this star spinneth round that star, and this other star with a tail goeth and cometh in so many years! Let it go! He from whose hand it came will guide and direct it.

"But thou wilt say unto me, Stand aside, O man, for I am more learned than thou art, and have seen more things. If thou thinkest that thou art in this respect better than I am, thou art welcome. I praise God that I seek not that which I require not. Thou art learned in the things I care not for; and as for that which thou hast seen, I spit upon it. Will much knowledge create thee a double belly, or wilt thou seek Paradise with thine eyes?

"O my friend! if thou wilt be happy, say, There is no God but God! Do no evil, and thus wilt thou fear neither man nor death; for surely thine hour will come!

"The meek in spirit (El Fakir),

"IMAUM ALI ZADI."

CHAPTER VI

THE REALITIES OF RELIGION

What the Mystic Experience Signifies [1]

. . . Mr. Chesterton, I think, says somewhere, that the Greeks and Romans, in all that concerned their moral life, were an extraordinarily solemn set of folks. The Athenians thought that the very gods must admire the rectitude of Phocion and Aristides; and those gentlemen themselves were apparently of much the same opinion. Cato's veracity was so impeccable that the extremest incredulity a Roman could express of anything was to say, "I would not believe it even if Cato had told me." Good was good, and bad was bad, for these people. Hypocrisy, which church-Christianity brought in, hardly existed; the naturalistic system held firm; its values showed no hollowness and brooked no irony. The individual, if virtuous enough, could meet all possible requirements. The pagan pride had never crumbled. Luther was the first moralist who broke with any effectiveness through the crust of all this naturalistic self-sufficiency, thinking (and possibly he was right) that Saint Paul had done it already. Religious experience of the Lutheran type brings all our

[1] From *A Pluralistic Universe*, Lecture viii, pp. 303-316.

naturalistic standards to bankruptcy. You are strong only by being weak, it shows. You cannot live on pride or self-sufficingness. There is a light in which all naturally founded and currently accepted distinctions, excellences, and safeguards of our characters appear as utter childishness. Sincerely to give up one's conceit or hope of being good in one's own right is the only door to the universe's deeper reaches. . . .

Here is a world in which all is well, in *spite* of certain forms of death, indeed *because* of certain forms of death—death of hope, death of strength, death of responsibility, of fear and worry, competency and desert, death of everything that paganism, naturalism, and legalism pin their faith on and tie their trust to.

Reason, operating on our other experiences, even our psychological experiences, would never have inferred these specifically religious experiences in advance of their actual coming. She could not suspect their existence, for they are discontinuous with the "natural" experiences they succeed upon and invert their values. But as they actually come and are given, creation widens to the view of their recipients. They suggest that our natural experience, our strictly moralistic and prudential experience, may be only a fragment of real human experience. They soften nature's outlines and open out the strangest possibilities and perspectives.

This is why it seems to me that the logical understanding, working in abstraction from such specifically religious experiences, will always omit something, and fail to reach completely adequate conclusions. Death and failure, it will always say, *are* death and failure simply, and can nevermore be one with life; so religious experience, peculiarly so called, needs, in my opinion, to be carefully considered and interpreted by every one who aspires to reason out a more complete philosophy. . . .

To quote words which I have used elsewhere, the believer finds that the tenderer parts of his personal life are continuous with a *more* of the same quality which is operative in the universe outside of him and which he can keep in working touch with, and in a fashion get on board of and save himself, when all his lower being has gone to pieces in the wreck. In a word, the believer is continuous, to his own consciousness, at any rate, with a wider self from which saving experiences flow in. Those who have such experiences distinctly enough and often enough to live in the light of them remain quite unmoved by criticism, from whatever quarter it may come, be it academic or scientific, or be it merely the voice of logical common sense. They have had their vision and they *know*—that is enough—that we inhabit an invisible spiritual environment from which help comes, our soul being mysteriously one with a larger soul whose instruments we are.

One may therefore plead, I think, that Fechner's ideas are not without direct empirical verification. There is at any rate one side of life which would be easily explicable if those ideas were true, but of which there appears no clear explanation so long as we assume either with naturalism that human consciousness is the highest consciousness there is, or with dualistic theism that there is a higher mind in cosmos, but that it is discontinuous with our own. . . .

In spite of rationalism's disdain for the particular, the personal, and the unwholesome, the drift of all the evidence we have seems to me to sweep us very strongly towards the belief in some form of superhuman life with which we may, unknown to ourselves, be co-conscious. We may be in the universe as dogs and cats are in our libraries, seeing the books and hearing the conversation, but having no inkling of the meaning of it all. The intellectualist objections to this fall away when the authority of intellectualist logic is undermined by criticism, and then the positive empirical evidence remains. The analogies with ordinary psychology and with the facts of pathology, with those of psychical research, so called, and with those of religious experience, establish, when taken together, a decidedly *formidable* probability in favor of a general view of the world almost identical with Fechner's. The outlines of the superhuman consciousness thus made probable must remain, however, very vague, and the number of functionally distinct "selves" it comports and carries has to be left entirely problematic. It may be polytheistically or it may be monotheistically conceived of. Fechner, with his distinct earth-soul functioning as our guardian angel, seems to me clearly polytheistic;

but the word "polytheism" usually gives offense, so perhaps it is better not to use it. . . .

The line of least resistance, then, as it seems to me, both in theology and in philosophy, is to accept, along with the superhuman consciousness, the notion that it is not all-embracing, the notion, in other words, that there is a God, but that He is finite, either in power or in knowledge, or in both at once. These, I need hardly tell you, are the terms in which common men have usually carried on their active commerce with God; and the monistic perfections that make the notion of Him so paradoxical practically and morally are the colder addition of remote professorial minds operating *in distans* upon conceptual substitutes for Him alone. . . .

It is true that superstitions and wild-growing over-beliefs of all sorts will undoubtedly begin to abound if the notion of higher consciousness enveloping ours, of fechnerian earth-souls and the like, grows orthodox and fashionable; still more will they superabound if science ever puts her approving stamp on the phenomena of which Frederic Myers so earnestly advocated the scientific recognition, the phenomena of psychic research so called—and I myself firmly believe that most of these phenomena are rooted in reality. But ought one seriously to allow such a timid consideration as that to deter one from following the evident path of greatest religious promise? Since when, in this mixed world, was any good thing given us in purest outline and isolation? One of the chief characteristics of life is life's redundancy. The sole condition of our having anything, no matter what, is that we should have so much of it, that we are fortunate if we do not grow sick of the sight and sound of it altogether. Everything is smothered in the litter that is fated to accompany it. Without too much you cannot have enough, of any-thing. Lots of inferior books, lots of bad statues, lots of dull speeches, of tenth-rate men and women, as a condition of the few precious specimens in either kind being realized! The gold-dust comes to birth with the quartz-sand all around it, and this is as much a condi-tion of religion as of any other excellent possession. There must be extrication; there must be competition for survival; but the clay matrix and the noble gem must first come into being unsifted. Once extricated, the gem can be examined separately, conceptualized, defined, and insulated.

What Religion Is [1]

CHOCORUA, *Aug.* 17, 1897.

DEAR GODKIN,—Thanks for your kind note *in re* "Will to Believe." I suppose you expect as little a reply to it as I expected one from you to the book; but since you ask what I *du* mean by Religion, and add that until I define that word my essay cannot be effec-tive, I can't forbear sending you a word to clear up that point. I mean by religion for a man *anything* that

[1] From a letter to E. L. Godkin, in *The Letters of William James,* vol. ii, pp. 64-65.

for *him* is a live hypothesis in that line, although it may be a dead one for any one else. And what I try to show is that whether the man believes, disbelieves, or doubts his hypothesis, the moment he does either, on principle and methodically, he runs a risk of one sort or the other from his own point of view. There is no escaping the risk; why not then admit that one's human function is to run it? By settling down on that basis, and respecting each other's choice of risk to run, it seems to me that we should be in a clearer-headed condition than we now are in, postulating as most all of us do a rational certitude which doesn't exist and disowning the semi-voluntary mental action by which we continue in our own severally characteristic attitudes of belief. Since our willing natures are active here, why not face squarely the fact without humbug and get the benefits of the admission?

Religious Belief and National Idiosyncrasy [1]

CAMBRIDGE, *Apr.* 8, 1871.

. . . So the gallant Gauls are shooting each other again! I wish we knew what it all meant. From the apparent generality of the movement in Paris, it seems as if it must be something more dignified than it at first appeared. But can anything great be expected now from a nation between the two factions of which there is such hopeless enmity and mistrust as between the

[1] From a letter to Henry P. Bowditch, in *The Letters of William James,* vol. ii, pp. 161-162.

religious and the revolutionary parties in France? No mediation is possible between them. In England, America and Germany, a regular advance is possible, because each man confides in his brothers. However great the superficial differences of opinion, there is at bottom a trust in the power of the deep forces of human nature to work out their salvation, and the minority is contented to bide its time. But in France, nothing of the sort; no one feels secure against what he considers evil, by any guaranty but force; and if his opponents get uppermost, he thinks all is forever lost. How much Catholic education is to answer for this and how much national idiosyncrasy, it is hard to say. But I am inclined to think the latter is a large factor. The want of true sympathy in the French character, their love of external mechanical order, their satisfaction in police-regulation, their everlasting cry of "traitor," all point to it. But, on the other hand, protestantism would seem to have a good deal to do with the fundamental cohesiveness of society in the countries of Germanic blood. For what may be called the revolutionary party there has *developed* through insensible grades of rationalism out of the old orthodox conceptions, religious and social. The process has been a continuous modification of positive belief, and the extremes, even if they had no respect for each other and no desire for mutual accommodation (which I think at bottom they have), would yet be kept from cutting each other's throats by the intermediate links. But in

France Belief and Denial are separated by a chasm. The step once made, "écrasez l'infâme" is the only watchword on each side. How any order is possible except by a Cæsar to hold the balance, it is hard to see.

Science and the Struggle Among Religious Beliefs [1]

. . . I quite agree that what mankind most lacks is criticism and caution, not faith. Its cardinal weakness is to let belief follow recklessly upon lively conception, especially when the conception has instinctive liking at its back. I admit, then, that were I addressing the Salvation Army or a miscellaneous popular crowd it would be a misuse of opportunity to preach the liberty of believing as I have in these pages preached it. What such audiences most need is that their faith should be broken up and ventilated, that the northwest wind of science should get into them and blow their sickliness and barbarism away. But academic audiences, fed already on science, have a very different need. Paralysis of their native capacity for faith and timorous *abulia* in the religious field are their special forms of mental weakness, brought about by the notion, carefully instilled, that there is something called scientific evidence by waiting upon which they shall escape all danger of shipwreck in regard to truth. But there is really no scientific or other method by which men can steer safely between the opposite dangers of believing too little or of believing too much. To face such dan-

[1] From *The Will to Believe*, Preface, pp. x-xiii.

gers is apparently our duty, and to hit the right chan-
nel between them is the measure of our wisdom as men.
It does not follow, because recklessness may be a
vice in soldiers, that courage ought never to be preached
to them. What *should* be preached is courage weighted
with responsibility,—such courage as the Nelsons and
Washingtons never failed to show after they had taken
everything into account that might tell against their
success, and made every provision to minimize disaster
in case they met defeat. I do not think that any one
can accuse me of preaching reckless faith. I have
preached the right of the individual to indulge his personal faith at his personal risk. I have discussed the
kinds of risk; I have contended that none of us escape
all of them; and I have only pleaded that it is better
to face them open-eyed than to act as if we did not
know them to be there.

After all, though, you will say, Why such an ado
about a matter concerning which, however we may
theoretically differ, we all practically agree? In this
age of toleration, no scientist will ever try actively to
interfere with our religious faith, provided we enjoy
it quietly with our friends and do not make a public
nuisance of it in the market-place. But it is just
on this matter of the market-place that I think the
utility of such essays as mine may turn. If religious
hypotheses about the universe be in order at all, then
the active faiths of individuals in them, freely express-
ing themselves in life, are the experimental tests by

which they are verified, and the only means by which
their truth or falsehood can be wrought out. The truest
scientific hypothesis is that which, as we say, "works"
best; and it can be no otherwise with religious
hypotheses. Religious history proves that one
hypothesis after another has worked ill, has crumbled
at contact with a widening knowledge of the world,
and has lapsed from the minds of men. Some articles
of faith, however, have maintained themselves through
every vicissitude, and possess even more vitality today
than ever before: it is for the "science of religions"
to tell us just which hypotheses these are. Meanwhile
the freest competition of the various faiths with one
another, and their openest application to life by their
several champions, are the most favorable conditions
under which the survival of the fittest can proceed.
They ought therefore not to lie hid each under his
bushel, indulged-in quietly with friends. They ought
to live in publicity, vying with each other; and it
seems to me that (the régime of tolerance once granted,
and a fair field shown) the scientist has nothing to
fear for his own interests from the liveliest possible
state of fermentation in the religious world of his time.
Those faiths will best stand the test which adopt also
his hypotheses, and make them integral elements of
their own. He should welcome therefore every species
of religious agitation and discussion, so long as he is
willing to allow that some religious hypothesis *may* be
true. Of course there are plenty of scientists who

would deny that dogmatically, maintaining that science has already ruled all possible religious hypotheses out of court. Such scientists ought, I agree, to aim at imposing privacy on religious faiths, the public manifestation of which could only be a nuisance in their eyes. With all such scientists, as well as with their allies outside of science, my quarrel openly lies; and I hope that my book may do something to persuade the reader of their crudity, and range him on my side. Religious fermentation is always a symptom of the intellectual vigor of a society; and it is only when they forget that they are hypotheses and put on rationalistic and authoritative pretensions, that our faiths do harm. The most interesting and valuable things about a man are his ideals and over-beliefs. The same is true of nations and historic epochs; and the excesses of which the particular individuals and epochs are guilty are compensated in the total, and become profitable to mankind in the long run. . . .

The Common Content of All Religions [1]

First, is there, under all the discrepancies of the creeds, a common nucleus to which they bear their testimony unanimously?

And second, ought we to consider the testimony true?

I will take up the first question first, and answer it immediately in the affirmative. The warring gods and

[1] From *The Varieties of Religious Experience*, pp. 507-519.

formulas of the various religions do indeed cancel each other, but there is a certain uniform deliverance in which religions all appear to meet. It consists of two parts:—

1. An uneasiness; and
2. Its solution.

1. The uneasiness, reduced to its simplest terms, is a sense that there is *something wrong about us* as we naturally stand.

2. The solution is a sense that *we are saved from the wrongness* by making proper connection with the higher powers.

In those more developed minds which alone we are studying, the wrongness takes a moral character, and the salvation takes a mystical tinge. I think we shall keep well within the limits of what is common to all such minds if we formulate the essence of their religious experience in terms like these:—

The individual, so far as he suffers from his wrongness and criticizes it, is to that extent consciously beyond it, and in at least possible touch with something higher, if anything higher exist. Along with the wrong part there is thus a better part of him, even though it may be but a most helpless germ. With which part he should identify his real being is by no means obvious at this stage; but when stage 2 (the stage of solution or salvation) arrives,[1] the man identifies his real being

---

[1] Remember that for some men it arrives suddenly, for others gradually, whilst others again practically enjoy it all their life.

with the germinal higher part of himself; and does so in the following way: *He becomes conscious that this higher part is conterminous and continuous with a* MORE *of the same quality, which is operative in the universe outside of him, and which he can keep in working touch with, and in a fashion get on board of and save himself when all his lower being has gone to pieces in the wreck.*

It seems to me that all the phenomena are accurately describable in these very simple general terms. They allow for the divided self and the struggle; they involve the change of personal center and the surrender of the lower self; they express the appearance of exteriority of the helping power and yet account for our sense of union with it; and they fully justify our feelings of security and joy. There is probably no autobiographic document, among all those which I have quoted, to which the description will not well apply. One need only add such specific details as will adapt it to various theologies and various personal temperaments, and one will then have the various experiences reconstructed in their individual forms.

So far, however, as this analysis goes, the experiences are only psychological phenomena. They possess, it is true, enormous biological worth. Spiritual strength really increases in the subject when he has them, a new life opens for him, and they seem to him a place of conflux where the forces of two universes meet; and yet this may be nothing but his subjective way of feeling things, a mood of his own fancy, in spite of the effects produced.   I now turn to my second question: What is the objective "truth" of their content?

The part of the content concerning which the question of truth most pertinently arises is that "MORE of the same quality" with which our own higher self appears in the experience to come into harmonious working relation.   Is such a "more" merely our own notion, or does it really exist?   If so, in what shape does it exist?   Does it act, as well as exist?   And in what form should we conceive of that "union" with it of which religious geniuses are so convinced?

It is in answering these questions that the various theologies perform their theoretic work, and that their divergencies most come to light.   They all agree that the "more" really exists; though some of them hold it to exist in the shape of a personal god or gods, while others are satisfied to conceive it as a stream of ideal tendency embedded in the eternal structure of the world.   They all agree, moreover, that it acts as well as exists, and that something really is effected for the better when you throw your life into its hands.   It is when they treat of the experience of "union" with it that their speculative differences appear most clearly. Over this point pantheism and theism, nature and second birth, works and grace and karma, immortality and reincarnation, rationalism and mysticism, carry on inveterate disputes. . . .

The "more," as we called it, and the meaning of our "union" with it, form the nucleus of our inquiry. Into what definite description can these words be translated, and for what definite facts do they stand? . . .

The *subconscious self* is nowadays a well-accredited psychological entity; and I believe that in it we have exactly the mediating term required. Apart from all religious considerations, there is actually and literally more life in our total soul than we are at any time aware of. . . .

Much of the content of this larger background against which our conscious being stands out in relief is insignificant. Imperfect memories, silly jingles, inhibitive timidities, "dissolutive" phenomena of various sorts, as Myers calls them, enter into it for a large part. But in it many of the performances of genius seem also to have their origin; and in our study of conversion, of mystical experiences, and of prayer, we have seen how striking a part invasions from this region play in the religious life.

Let me then propose, as an hypothesis, that whatever it may be on its *farther* side, the "more" with which in religious experience we feel ourselves connected is on its *hither* side the subconscious continuation of our conscious life. Starting thus with a recognized psychological fact as our basis, we seem to preserve a contact with "science" which the ordinary theologian lacks. At the same time the theologian's contention that the religious man is moved by an external power is vindicated, for it is one of the peculiarities of invasions from the subconscious region to take on objective appearances, and to suggest to the Subject an external control. In the religious life the control is felt as "higher"; but since on our hypothesis it is primarily the higher faculties of our own hidden mind which are controlling, the sense of union with the power beyond us is a sense of something, not merely apparently, but literally true.

This doorway into the subject seems to me the best one for a science of religions, for it mediates between a number of different points of view. Yet it is only a doorway, and difficulties present themselves as soon as we step through it, and ask how far our transmarginal consciousness carries us if we follow it on its remoter side. Here the over-beliefs begin: here mysticism and the conversion-rapture and Vedantism and transcendental idealism bring in their monistic interpretations and tell us that the finite self rejoins the absolute self, for it was always one with God and identical with the soul of the world. Here the prophets of all the different religions come with their visions, voices, raptures, and other openings, supposed by each to authenticate his own peculiar faith. . . .

Disregarding the over-beliefs, and confining ourselves to what is common and generic, we have in *the fact that the conscious person is continuous with a wider self through which saving experiences come,* a positive content of religious experience which, it seems to me, *is literally and objectively true as far as it goes.*

If I now proceed to state my own hypothesis about the farther limits of this extension of our personality, I shall be offering my own over-belief—though I know it will appear a sorry under-belief to some of you—for which I can only bespeak the same indulgence which in a converse case I should accord to yours.

The further limits of our being plunge, it seems to me, into an altogether other dimension of existence from the sensible and merely "understandable" world. Name it the mystical region, or the supernatural region, whichever you choose. So far as our ideal impulses originate in this region (and most of them do originate in it, for we find them possessing us in a way for which we cannot articulately account), we belong to it in a more intimate sense than that in which we belong to the visible world, for we belong in the most intimate sense wherever our ideals belong. Yet the unseen region in question is not merely ideal, for it produces effects in this world. When we commune with it, work is actually done upon our finite personality, for we are turned into new men, and consequences in the way of conduct follow in the natural world upon our regenerative change. But that which produces effects within another reality must be termed a reality itself, so I feel as if we had no philosophic excuse for calling the unseen or mystical world unreal. . . .

What the more characteristically divine facts are, apart from the actual inflow of energy in the faith-state and the prayer-state, I know not.   But the over-belief on which I am ready to make my personal venture is that they exist.   The whole drift of my education goes to persuade me that the world of our present consciousness is only one out of many worlds of consciousness that exist, and that those other worlds must contain experiences which have a meaning for our life also; and that although in the main their experiences and those of this world keep discrete, yet the two become continuous at certain points, and higher energies filter in.

Religious Experience Points to Polytheism [1]

. . . If asked just where the differences in fact which are due to God's existence come in, I should have to say that in general I have no hypothesis to offer beyond what the phenomenon of "prayerful communion," especially when certain kinds of incursion from the subconscious region take part in it, immediately suggests.   The appearance is that in this phenomenon something ideal, which in one sense is part of ourselves and in another sense is not ourselves, actually exerts an influence, raises our center of personal energy, and produces regenerative effects unattainable in other ways.   If, then, there be a wider world of being than that of our every-day consciousness, if in it there be forces whose effects on us are intermittent, if one facilitating condition of the effects be the open-

[1] From *The Varieties of Religious Experience*, pp. 523-526.

ness of the "subliminal" door, we have the elements of a theory to which the phenomena of religious life lend plausibility. I am so impressed by the importance of these phenomena that I adopt the hypothesis which they so naturally suggest. At these places at least, I say, it would seem as though transmundane energies, God, if you will, produced immediate effects within the natural world to which the rest of our experience belongs.

. . . Meanwhile the practical needs and experiences of religion seem to me sufficiently met by the belief that beyond each man and in a fashion continuous with him there exists a larger power which is friendly to him and to his ideals. All that the facts require is that the power should be both other and larger than our conscious selves. Anything larger will do, if only it be large enough to trust for the next step. It need not be infinite, it need not be solitary. It might conceivably even be only a larger and more godlike self, of which the present self would then be but the mutilated expression, and the universe might conceivably be a collection of such selves, of different degrees of inclusiveness, with no absolute unity realized in it at all. Thus would a sort of polytheism return upon us—a polytheism which I do not on this occasion defend, for my only aim at present is to keep the testimony of religious experience clearly within its proper bounds.

CHAPTER VII

THE INDIVIDUAL AND SOCIETY

Why Communities Change [1]

Our problem is, What are the causes that make communities change from generation to generation,—that make the England of Queen Anne so different from the England of Queen Elizabeth, the Harvard College of today so different from that of thirty years ago?

I shall reply to this problem, The difference is due to the accumulated influence of individuals, of their examples, their initiatives, and their decisions. The Spencerian school replies, The changes are irrespective of persons, and independent of individual control. They are due to the environment, to the circumstances, the physical geography, the ancestral conditions, the increasing experience of outer relations; to everything, in fact, except the Grants and the Bismarcks, the Joneses and the Smiths. . . .

The causes of production of great men lie in a sphere wholly inaccessible to the social philosopher. He must simply accept geniuses as data, just as Darwin accepts his spontaneous variations. For him, as for Darwin, the only problem is, these data being given,

[1] From "Great Men and Their Environment," in *The Will to Believe*, p. 218.

234

How does the environment affect them, and how do they affect the environment? Now, I affirm that the relation of the visible environment to the great man is in the main exactly what it is to the "variation" in the Darwinian philosophy. It chiefly adopts or rejects, preserves or destroys, in short *selects* him.[1] And whenever it adopts and preserves the great man, it becomes modified by his influence in an entirely original and peculiar way. He acts as a ferment, and changes its constitution, just as the advent of a new zoölogical species changes the faunal and floral equilibrium of the region in which it appears. We all recollect Mr. Darwin's famous statement of the influence of cats on the growth of clover in their neighborhood. We all have read of the effects of the European rabbit in New Zealand, and we have many of us taken part in the controversy about the English sparrow here,—whether he kills most canker-worms, or drives away most native birds. Just so the great man, whether he be an importation from without like Clive in India or Agassiz here, or whether he spring from the soil like Mahomet or Franklin, brings about a rearrangement, on a large or a small scale, of the pre-existing social relations.

The mutations of societies, then, from generation

[1] It is true that it remodels him, also, to some degree, by its educative influence, and that this constitutes a considerable difference between the social case and the zoölogical case. I neglect this aspect of the relation here, for the other is the more important. At the end of the article I will return to it incidentally.

to generation, are in the main due directly or indirectly to the acts or the example of individuals whose genius was so adapted to the receptivities of the moment, or whose accidental position of authority was so critical that they became ferments, initiators of movement, setters of precedent or fashion, centers of corruption, or destroyers of other persons, whose gifts, had they had free play, would have led society in another direction.

We see this power of individual initiative exemplified on a small scale all about us, and on a large scale in the case of the leaders of history. It is only following the common-sense method of a Lyell, a Darwin, and a Whitney to interpret the unknown by the known, and reckon up cumulatively the only causes of social change we can directly observe. Societies of men are just like individuals in that both at any given moment offer ambiguous potentialities of development. Whether a young man enters business or the ministry may depend on a decision which has to be made before a certain day. He takes the place offered in the counting-house, and is *committed*.

Little by little, the habits, the knowledges, of the other career, which once lay so near, cease to be reckoned even among his possibilities. At first, he may sometimes doubt whether the self he murdered in that decisive hour might not have been the better of the two; but with the years such questions themselves expire, and the old alternative *ego*, once so vivid, fades into something less substantial than a dream. It is no otherwise with nations. They may be committed by kings and ministers to peace or war, by generals to victory or defeat, by prophets to this religion or to that, by various geniuses to fame in art, science, or industry. A war is a true point of bifurcation of future possibilities. Whether it fail or succeed, its declaration must be the starting-point of new policies. Just so does a revolution, or any great civic precedent, become a deflecting influence, whose operations widen with the course of time. Communities obey their ideals; and an accidental success fixes an ideal as an accidental failure blights it.

Would England have today the "imperial" ideal which she now has, if a certain boy named Bob Clive had shot himself, as he tried to do, at Madras? Would she be the drifting raft she is now in European affairs [1] if a Frederick the Great had inherited her throne instead of a Victoria, and if Messrs. Bentham, Mill, Cobden, and Bright had all been born in Prussia? England has, no doubt, today precisely the same intrinsic value relatively to the other nations that she ever had. There is no such fine accumulation of human material upon the globe. But in England the material has lost effective form, while in Germany it has found it. Leaders give the form. Would England be crying forward and backward at once, as she does now, "letting I will not wait upon I would,"

[1] The reader will remember when this was written.

wishing to conquer but not to fight, if her ideal had in all these years been fixed by a succession of states-men of supremely commanding personality, working in one direction? Certainly not. She would have espoused, for better or worse, either one course or another. Had Bismarck died in his cradle, the Ger-mans would still be satisfied with appearing to them-selves as a race of spectacled *Gelehrten* and political herbivora, and to the French as *ces bons,* or *ces naifs, Allemands.* Bismarck's will showed them, to their own great astonishment, that they could play a far livelier game. The lesson will not be forgotten. Germany may have many vicissitudes, but they—

> "will never do away, I ween,
> The marks of that which once hath been"—

of Bismarck's initiative, namely, from 1860 to 1873.

The fermentative influence of geniuses must be admitted as, at any rate, one factor in the changes that constitute social evolution. The community *may* evolve in many ways. The accidental presence of this or that ferment decides in which way it *shall* evolve. Why, the very birds of the forest, the par-rot, the mino, have the power of human speech, but never develop it of themselves; some one must be there to teach them. So with us individuals. Rem-brandt must teach us to enjoy the struggle of light with darkness, Wagner to enjoy peculiar musical effects; Dickens gives a twist to our sentimentality,

Artemus Ward to our humor; Emerson kindles a
new moral light within us. But it is like Columbus's
egg. "All can raise the flowers now, for all have
got the seed." But if this is true of the individuals in
the community, how can it be false of the community
as a whole? If shown a certain way, a community
may take it; if not, it will never find it. And the
ways are to a large extent indeterminate in advance.
A nation may obey either of many alternative impulses given by different men of genius, and still live
and be prosperous, just as a man may enter either of
many businesses. Only, the prosperities may differ in
their type.

But the indeterminism is not absolute. Not every
"man" fits every "hour." Some incompatibilities there
are. A given genius may come either too early or
too late. Peter the Hermit would now be sent to a
lunatic asylum. John Mill in the tenth century
would have lived and died unknown. Cromwell and
Napoleon need their revolutions, Grant his civil war.
An Ajax gets no fame in the day of telescopic-sighted
rifles; and, to express differently an instance which
Spencer uses, what could a Watt have effected in a
tribe which no precursive genius had taught to smelt
iron or to turn a lathe?

Now, the important thing to notice is that what
makes a certain genius now incompatible with his
surroundings is usually the fact that some previous
genius of a different strain has warped the community

away from the sphere of his possible effectiveness.
After Voltaire, no Peter the Hermit; after Charles
IX. and Louis XIV., no general Protestantization of
France; after a Manchester school, a Beaconfield's
success is transient; after a Philip II., a Castelar
makes little headway; and so on. Each bifurcation
cuts off certain sides of the field altogether, and limits
the future possible angles of deflection. A community is a living thing, and in words which I can do no
better than quote from Professor Clifford,[1] "it is the
peculiarity of living things not merely that they
change under the influence of surrounding circumstances, but that any change which takes place in
them is not lost but retained, and as it were built into
the organism to serve as a foundation for future
actions. If you cause any distortion in the growth
of a tree and make it crooked, whatever you may do
afterwards to make the tree straight the mark of your
distortion is there; it is absolutely indelible; it has
become a part of the tree's nature. . . . Suppose, however, that you take a lump of gold, melt it, and let it
cool. . . . No one can tell by examining a piece of
gold how often it has been melted and cooled in geo-
logic ages, or even in the last year by the hand of
man. Any one who cuts down an oak can tell by the
rings in its trunk how many times winter has frozen it
into widowhood, and how many times summer has
warmed it into life. A living being must always con-

[1] *Lectures and Essays.* i. 82.

tain within itself the history, not merely of its own existence, but of all its ancestors."

Every painter can tell us how each added line deflects his picture in a certain sense. Whatever lines follow must be built on those first laid down. Every author who starts to rewrite a piece of work knows how impossible it becomes to use any of the first-written pages again. The new beginning has already excluded the possibility of those earlier phrases and transitions, while it has at the same time created the possibility of an indefinite set of new ones, no one of which, however, is completely determined in advance. Just so the social surroundings of the past and present hour exclude the possibility of accepting certain contributions from individuals; but they do not positively define what contributions shall be accepted, for in themselves they are powerless to fix what the nature of the individual offering shall be.[1]

Thus social evolution is a resultant of the interaction of two wholly distinct factors,—the individual, deriving his peculiar gifts from the play of physiological and infra-social forces, but bearing all the power of initiative and origination in his hands; and, second, the social environment, with its power of adopting or

[1] Mr. Grant Allen himself . . . admits that a set of people who, if they had been exposed ages ago to the geographical agencies of Timbuctoo, would have developed into negroes might now, after a protracted exposure to the conditions of Hamburg, never become negroes if transplanted to Timbuctoo.

rejecting both him and his gifts. Both factors are essential to change. The community stagnates without the impulse of the individual. The impulse dies away without the sympathy of the community.

. . . The evolutionary view of history, when it denies the vital importance of individual initiative, is, then, an utterly vague and unscientific conception, a lapse from modern scientific determinism into the most ancient oriental fatalism. The lesson of the analysis that we have made (even on the completely deterministic hypothesis with which we started) forms an appeal of the most stimulating sort to the energy of the individual. Even the dogged resistance of the reactionary conservative to changes which he cannot hope entirely to defeat is justified and shown to be effective. He retards the movement; deflects it a little by the concessions he extracts; gives it a resultant momentum, compounded of his inertia and his adversaries' speed; and keeps up, in short, a constant lateral pressure, which, to be sure, never heads it round about, but brings it up at last at a goal far to the right or left of that to which it would have drifted had he allowed it to drift alone.

The Importance of Individuals [1]

An unlearned carpenter of my acquaintance once said in my hearing: "There is very little difference between one man and another; but what little there is,

[1] From *The Will to Believe,* pp. 256-262.

is very important." This distinction seems to me to go to the root of the matter. It is not only the size of the difference which concerns the philosopher, but also its place and its kind. An inch is a small thing, but we know the proverb about an inch on a man's nose. . . .

Now, there is a striking law over which few people seem to have pondered. It is this: That among all the differences which exist, the only ones that interest us strongly are those *we do not take for granted*. We are not a bit elated that our friend should have two hands and the power of speech, and should practice the matter-of-course human virtues; and quite as little are we vexed that our dog goes on all fours and fails to understand our conversation. Expecting no more from the latter companion, and no less from the former, we get what we expect and are satisfied. We never think of communing with the dog by discourse of philosophy, or with the friend by head-scratching or the throwing of crusts to be snapped at. But if either dog or friend fall above or below the expected standard, they arouse the most lively emotion. On our brother's vices or genius we never weary of descanting; to his bipedism or his hairless skin we do not consecrate a thought. *What* he says may transport us; that he is able to speak at all leaves us stone cold. The reason of all this is that his virtues and vices and utterances might, compatibly with the current range of variation in our tribe, be just the opposites of what they are, while his zoölogically human attributes cannot possibly go astray. There is thus a zone of insecurity in human affairs in which all the dramatic interest lies; the rest belongs to the dead machinery of the stage. This is the formative zone, the part not yet ingrained into the race's average, not yet a typical, hereditary, and constant factor of the social community in which it occurs. It is like the soft layer beneath the bark of the tree in which all the year's growth is going on. Life has abandoned the mighty trunk inside, which stands inert and belongs almost to the inorganic world. . . .

The zone of the individual differences, and of the social "twists" which by common confession they initiate, is the zone of formative processes, the dynamic belt of quivering uncertainty, the line where past and future meet. It is the theater of all we do not take for granted, the stage of the living drama of life; and however narrow its scope, it is roomy enough to lodge the whole range of human passions. The sphere of the race's average, on the contrary, no matter how large it may be, is a dead and stagnant thing, an achieved possession, from which all insecurity has vanished. Like the trunk of a tree, it has been built up by successive concretions of successive active zones. The moving present in which we live with its problems and passions, its individual rivalries, victories, and defeats, will soon pass over to the majority and leave its small deposit on this static mass, to make room for fresh actors and a newer play.

And though it may be true, as Mr. Spencer predicts, that each later zone shall fatally be narrower than its forerunners; and that when the ultimate lady-like tea-table elysium of the Data of Ethics shall prevail, such questions as the breaking of eggs at the large or the small end will span the whole scope of possible human warfare,—still even in this shrunken and enfeebled generation, *spatio aetatis defessa vetusto,* what eagerness there will be! Battles and defeats will occur, the victors will be glorified and the vanquished dishonored just as in the brave days of yore, the human heart still withdrawing itself from the much it has in safe possession, and concentrating all its passion upon those evanescent possibilities of fact which still quiver in fate's scale.

And is not its instinct right? Do not we here grasp the race-differences *in the making,* and catch the only glimpse it is allotted to us to attain of the working units themselves, of whose differentiating action the race-gaps form but the stagnant sum? What strange inversion of scientific procedure does Mr. Allen practice when he teaches us to neglect elements and attend only to aggregate resultants? On the contrary, simply because the active ring, whatever its bulk, *is elementary,* I hold that the study of its conditions (be these never so "proximate") is the highest of topics for the social philosopher. If individual variations determine its ups and downs and hair-breadth escapes and twists and turns, as Mr.

Allen and Mr. Fiske both admit, Heaven forbid us from tabooing the study of these in favor of the average! On the contrary, let us emphasize these, and the importance of these; and in picking out from history our heroes, and communing with their kindred spirits,—in imagining as strongly as possible what differences their individualities brought about in this world, while its surface was still plastic in their hands, and what whilom feasibilities they made impossible,—each one of us may best fortify and inspire what creative energy may lie in his own soul.[1]

This is the lasting justification of hero-worship, and the pooh-poohing of it by "sociologists" is the everlasting excuse for popular indifference to their general laws and averages. The difference between an America rescued by a Washington or a "Jenkins" may, as Mr. Allen says, be "little," but it is, in the words of my carpenter friend, "important." Some organizing genius must in the nature of things have emerged from the French Revolution; but what Frenchman will affirm it to have been an accident of no consequence that he should have had the supernumerary idiosyncrasies of a Bonaparte? What animal, domestic or wild, will call it a matter of no moment that scarce a word of sympathy with brutes

---

[1] M. G. Tarde's book (itself a work of genius), *Les Lois de l'Imitation, Étude Sociologique* (2me Édition, Paris, Alcan, 1895), is the best possible commentary on this text,—"invention" on the one hand, and "imitation" on the other, being for this author the two sole factors of social change.

should have survived from the teachings of Jesus of Nazareth?

The preferences of sentient creatures are what *create* the importance of topics. They are the absolute and ultimate law-giver here. And I for my part cannot but consider the talk of the contemporary sociological school about averages and general laws and predetermined tendencies, with its obligatory undervaluing of the importance of individual differences, as the most pernicious and immoral of fatalisms. Suppose there is a social equilibrium fated to be, whose it is to be,—that of your preference, or mine? There lies the question of questions, and it is one which no study of averages can decide.

The Wealth of a Nation [1]

The world . . . is only beginning to see that the wealth of a nation consists more than in anything else in the number of superior men that it harbors. In the practical realm it has always recognized this, and known that no price is too high to pay for a great statesman or great captain of industry. But it is equally so in the religious and moral sphere, in the poetic and artistic sphere and in the philosophic and scientific sphere. Geniuses are ferments; and when they come together as they have done in certain lands at certain times, the whole population seems to share in the higher energy which they awaken. The effects are

[1] From "Stanford's Ideal Destiny," in *Memories and Studies,* pp. 363-366.

incalculable and often not easy to trace in detail, but they are pervasive and momentous. Who can measure the effects on the national German soul of the splendid series of German poets and German men of learning, most of them academic personages?

From the bare economic point of view the importance of geniuses is only beginning to be appreciated. How can we measure the cash-value to France of a Pasteur, to England of a Kelvin, to Germany of an Ostwald, to us here of a Burbank? One main care of every country in the future ought to be to find out who its first-rate thinkers are and to help them. Cost here becomes something entirely irrelevant, the returns are sure to be so incommensurable.

. . . Geniuses are sensitive plants, in some respects like *prima donnas*. They have to be treated tenderly. They don't need to live in superfluity; but they need freedom from harassing care; they need books and instruments; they are always overworking, so they need generous vacations; and above all things they need occasionally to travel far and wide in the interests of their souls' development. Where quality is the thing sought after, the thing of supreme quality is cheap, whatever be the price one has to pay for it.

The Social Sources of Individuality [1]

We long for sympathy, for a purely *personal* communication, first with the soul of the world, and then

[1] From a letter to Thomas W. Ward, in *The Letters of William James*, vol. i, pp. 131-132.

with the soul of our fellows. And happy are they who think, or know, that they have got them! But to those who must confess with bitter anguish that they are perfectly isolated from the soul of the world, and that the closest human love incloses a potential germ of estrangement or hatred, that all *personal* relation is finite, conditional, mixed (*vide* in Dana's "Household Book of Poetry," stanzas by C. P. Cranch, "Thought is deeper than speech," etc., etc.), it may not prove such an unfruitful substitute. At least, when you have added to the property of the race, even if no one knows your name, yet it is certain that, without what you have done, some individuals must needs be acting now in a somewhat different manner. You have modified their life; you are in *real* relation with them; you have in so far forth entered into their being. And is that such an unworthy stake to set up for our good, after all? Who are these men anyhow? Our predecessors, even apart from the physical link of generation, have made us what we are. Every thought you now have and every act and intention owes its complexion to the acts of your dead and living brothers. *Everything* we know and are is through men. We have no revelation but through man. Every sentiment that warms your gizzard, every brave act that ever made your pulse bound and your nostril open to a confident breath was a man's act. However mean a man may be, man is *the best we know;* and your loathing as you turn from what you probably call the vulgarity of human life—your homesick yearning for a *Better,* somewhere—is furnished by your manhood; your ideal is made up of traits suggested by past men's words and actions. Your manhood shuts you in forever, bounds all your thoughts like an overarching sky—and all the Good and True and High and Dear that you know by virtue of your sharing in it. They are the Natural Product of our Race. So that it seems to me that a sympathy with men as such, and a desire to contribute to the weal of a species, which, whatever may be said of it, contains All that we acknowledge as good, may very well form an external interest sufficient to keep one's moral pot boiling in a very lively manner to a good old age. The idea, in short, of becoming an accomplice in a sort of "Mankind its own God or Providence" scheme is a *practical* one.

I don't mean, by any means, to affirm that we must come to that, I only say it is *a* mode of envisaging life; which is capable of affording moral support—and may at any rate help to bridge over the despair of skeptical intervals. I confess that, in the lonesome gloom which beset me for a couple of months last summer, the only feeling that kept me from giving up was that by waiting and living, by hook or crook, long enough, I might make my nick, however small a one, in the raw stuff the race has got to shape, and so assert my reality. The stoic feeling of being a sentinel obeying orders without knowing the general's plans is a noble one. And so is the divine enthusiasm of moral culture (Channing, etc.), and I think that, successively, they may all help to ballast the same man.

An Example of Effective Individualism [1]

. . . If one asks, now, what the *value* of Thomas Davidson was, what was the general significance of his life, apart from his particular books and articles, I have to say that it lay in the example he set to us all of how, even in the midst of this intensely worldly social system of ours, in which each human interest is organized so collectively and so commercially, a single man may still be a knight-errant of the intellectual life, and preserve full freedom in the midst of sociability. Extreme as was his need of friends, and faithful as he was to them, he yet lived mainly in reliance on his private inspiration. Asking no man's permission, bowing the knee to no tribal idol, renouncing the conventional channels of recognition, he showed us how a life of purely intellectual ends could be beautifully wholesome outwardly, and overflow with inner contentment. Fortunately this type of man is recurrent, and from generation to generation literary history preserves examples. But it is infrequent enough for few of us to have known more than one example—I count myself happy in knowing two and a half! The memory of Davidson will always strengthen my faith in personal freedom and its spontaneities, and make me less unqualifiedly respectful than ever of "Civilization,"

[1] From "Thomas Davidson," in *Memories and Studies*, pp. 101-103.

with its herding and branding, licensing and degree-giving, authorizing and appointing, and in general regulating and administering by system the lives of human beings. Surely the individual, the person in the singular number, is the more fundamental phenomenon, and the social institution, of whatever grade, is but secondary and ministerial. Many as are the interests which social systems satisfy, always unsatisfied interests remain over, and among them are interests to which system, as such, does violence whenever it lays its hand upon us. The best Commonwealth will always be the one that most cherishes the men who represent the residual interests, the one that leaves the largest scope to their peculiarities.

The Uniqueness of Nationality [1]

I

BAD-NAUHEIM, *Sept.* 17, 1899.

. . . God bless the American climate, with its transparent, passionate, impulsive variety and headlong fling. There are deeper, slower tones of earnestness and moral gravity here, no doubt, but ours is more like youth and youth's infinite and touching promise. God bless America in general! *Conspuez* McKinley and the Republican party and the Philippine war, and the Methodists, and the voices, etc., as much as you please, but bless the innocence. Talk of corruption! We don't know what the word corruption means at home, with

[1] From a letter to Miss Frances R. Morse, in *The Letters of William James.* vol. ii. pp. 102-103.

our improvised and shifting agencies of crude pecuniary bribery, compared with the solidly intrenched and permanently organized corruptive geniuses of monarchy, nobility, church, army, that penetrate the very bosom of the higher kind as well as the lower kind of people in all the European states (except Switzerland) and sophisticate their motives away from the impulse to straightforward handling of any simple case. *Temoin* the Dreyfus case! But no matter! Of all the forms of mental crudity, that of growing earnest over international comparisons is probably the most childish. Every nation has its ideals which are a dead secret to other nations, and it has to develop in its own way, in touch with them. It can only be judged by itself. If each of us does as well as he can in his own sphere at home, he will do all he *can* do; that is why I hate to remain so long abroad. . . .

II [1]

. . . Seriously speaking, though, I believe that international comparisons are a great waste of time—at any rate, international judgments and passings of sentence are. Every nation has ideals and difficulties and sentiments which are an impenetrable secret to one not of the blood. Let them alone, let each one work out its own salvation on its own lines. They talk of the decadence of France. The hatreds, and the *coups de gueule* of the newspapers there are awful. But I doubt if the

[1] From a letter to Mrs. Henry Whitman, in *The Letters of William James*, vol. ii, pp. 105-106.

better ideals were ever so aggressively strong; and I fancy it is the fruit of the much decried republican régime that they have become so. My brother represents English popular opinion as less cock-a-whoop for war than newspaper accounts would lead one to imagine; but I don't know that he is in a good position for judging. I hope if they do go to war that the Boers will give them fits, and I heartily emit an analogous prayer on behalf of the Philippinos.

War and the Crowd Mind [1]

. . . How much has happened since I last heard from you! To say nothing of the Zola trial, we now have the Cuban War! A curious episode of history, showing how a nation's ideals can be changed in the twinkling of an eye, by a succession of outward events partly accidental. It is quite possible that, without the explosion of the *Maine,* we should still be at peace, though, since the *basis* of the whole American attitude is the persuasion on the part of the people that the cruelty and misrule of Spain in Cuba call for her expulsion (so that in that sense our war is just what a war of "the powers" against Turkey for the Armenian atrocities would have been), it is hardly possible that peace could have been maintained indefinitely longer, unless Spain had gone out—a consummation hardly to be expected by peaceful means. The actual declaration of war by

[1] From a letter to François Pillon, in *The Letters of William James,* vol. ii, pp. 73-74.

Congress, however, was a case of *psychologie des foules*, a genuine hysteric stampede at the last moment, which shows how unfortunate that provision of our written constitution is which takes the power of declaring war from the Executive and places it in Congress. Our Executive has behaved very well   The European nations of the Continent cannot believe that our pretense of humanity, and our disclaiming of all ideas of conquest, is sincere.   It has been *absolutely* sincere! The self-conscious feeling of our people has been entirely based in a sense of philanthropic duty, without which not a step would have been taken.   And when, in its ultimatum to Spain, Congress denied any project of conquest in Cuba, it generally meant every word it said.   But here comes in the psychologic factor: once the excitement of action gets loose, the taxes levied, the victories achieved, etc., the old human instincts will get into play with all their old strength, and the ambition and sense of mastery which our nation has will set up new demands.   We shall never take Cuba; I imagine that to be very certain—unless indeed after years of unsuccessful police duty there, for that is what we have made ourselves responsible for.   But Porto Rico, and even the Philippines, are not so sure.   We had supposed ourselves (with all our crudity and barbarity in certain ways) a better nation morally than the rest, safe at home, and without the old savage ambition, destined to exert great international influence by throwing in our "moral weight," etc.   Dreams!

Human Nature is everywhere the same; and at the least temptation all the old military passions rise, and sweep everything before them. It will be interesting to see how it will end.

War and Human Nature [1]

. . . Man, biologically considered, and whatever else he may be into the bargain, is the most formidable of all beasts of prey, and, indeed, the only one that preys systematically on his own species. We are once for all adapted to the military status. A millennium of peace would not breed the fighting disposition out of our bone and marrow, and a function so ingrained and vital will never consent to die without resistance and will always find impassioned apologists and idealizers.

Not only men born to be soldiers, but non-combatants by trade and nature, historians in their studies, and clergymen in their pulpits, have been war's idealizers. They have talked of war as of God's court of justice. And, indeed, if we think how many things besides the frontiers of states the wars of history have decided, we must feel some respectful awe, in spite of all the horrors. Our actual civilization, good and bad alike, has had past wars for its determining condition. Great mindedness among the tribes of men has always meant the will to prevail, and all the more so if prevailing included slaughtering and being slaugh-

[1] From "The Remarks at the Peace Banquet," in *Memories and Studies,* pp. 301-306.

tered.   Rome, Paris, England, Brandenburg, Pied-
mont,—possibly soon Japan,—along with their arms
have their traits of character and habits of thought
prevail among their conquered neighbors.   The blessings we actually enjoy, such as they are, have grown up
in the shadow of the wars of antiquity.   The various
ideals were backed by fighting wills, and when neither
would give way, the God of battles had to be the
arbiter.   A shallow view this, truly; for who can say
what might have prevailed if man had ever been a
reasoning and not a fighting animal?   Like dead men,
dead causes tell no tales, and the ideals that went under
in the past, along with all the tribes that represented
them, find today no recorder, no explainer, no defender.

But apart from theoretic defenders, and apart from
every soldierly individual straining at the leash and
clamoring for opportunity, war has an omnipotent support in the form of our imagination.   Man lives *by*
habits indeed, but what he lives *for* is thrills and excitements.   The only relief from habit's tediousness is
periodical excitement.   From time immemorial wars
have been, especially for non-combatants, the supremely
thrilling excitement.   Heavy and dragging at its end,
at its outset every war means an explosion of imaginative energy.   The dams of routine burst, and boundless prospects open.   The remotest spectators share the
fascination of that awful struggle now in process on the
confines of the world.[1]   There is not a man in this

[1] The Russo-Japanese War.—*Ed*

room, I suppose, who doesn't buy both an evening and a morning paper, and first of all pounce on the war column.

A deadly listlessness would come over most men's imagination of the future if they could seriously be brought to believe that never again *in sœcula sœculorum* would a war trouble human history. In such a stagnant summer afternoon of a world, where would be the zest or interest?

This is the constitution of human nature which we have to work against. The plain truth is that people *want* war. They want it anyhow; for itself, and apart from each and every possible consequence. It is the final bouquet of life's fireworks. The born soldiers want it hot and actual. The non-combatants want it in the background, and always as an open possibility, to feed imagination on and keep excitement going. Its clerical and historical defenders fool themselves when they talk as they do about it. What moves them is not the blessings it has won for us, but a vague religious exaltation. War is human nature at its uttermost. We are here to do our uttermost. It is a sacrament. Society would rot without the mystical blood-payment.

We do ill, I think, therefore, to talk much of universal peace or of a general disarmament. We must go in for preventive medicine, not for radical cure. We must cheat our foe, circumvent him in detail, not try to change his nature. In one respect war is like love, though in no other. Both leave us intervals of rest; and in the intervals life goes on perfectly well without them, though the imagination still dallies with their possibility. Equally insane when once aroused and under headway, whether they shall be aroused or not depends on accidental circumstances. How are old maids and old bachelors made? Not by deliberate vows of celibacy, but by sliding on from year to year with no sufficient matrimonial provocation. So of the nations with their wars. Let the general possibility of war be left open, in Heaven's name, for the imagination to dally with. Let the soldiers dream of killing, as the old maids dream of marrying.

But organize in every conceivable way the practical machinery for making each successive chance of war abortive. Put peace men in power; educate the editors and statesmen to responsibility. How beautifully did their trained responsibility in England make the Venezuela incident abortive! Seize every pretext, however small, for arbitration methods, and multiply the precedents; foster rival excitements, and invent new outlets for heroic energy; and from one generation to another the chances are that irritation will grow less acute and states of strain less dangerous among the nations. Armies and navies will continue, of course, and fire the minds of populations with their potentialities of greatness. But their officers will find that somehow or other, with no deliberate intention on any one's part, each successive "incident" has managed to evaporate and to lead nowhere, and that the thought of what might have been remains their only consolation.

The last weak runnings of the war spirit will be "punitive expeditions." A country that turns its arms only against uncivilized foes is, I think, wrongly taunted as degenerate. Of course it has ceased to be heroic in the old grand style. But I verily believe that this is because it now sees something better. It has a conscience. It will still perpetrate peccadillos. But it is afraid, afraid in the good sense, to engage in absolute crimes against civilization.

The Psychological Basis of Peace [1]

. . . I devoutly believe in the reign of peace and in the gradual advent of some sort of a socialistic equilibrium. The fatalistic view of the war-function is to me nonsense, for I know that war-making is due to definite motives and subject to prudential checks and reasonable criticisms, just like any other form of enterprise. And when whole nations are the armies, and the science of destruction vies in intellectual refinement with the sciences of production, I see that war becomes absurd and impossible from its own monstrosity. Extravagant ambitions will have to be replaced by reasonable claims, and nations must make common cause against them. I see no reason why all this should not apply to yellow as well as to white countries, and I

[1] From "The Moral Equivalent for War," in *Memories and Studies*, pp. 286-292.

look forward to a future when acts of war shall be formally outlawed as between civilized peoples.

All these beliefs of mine put me squarely into the anti-militarist party.   But I do not believe that peace either ought to be or will be permanent on this globe, unless the states pacifically organized preserve some of the old elements of army-discipline.   A permanently successful peace-economy cannot be a simple pleasure-economy.   In the more or less socialistic future towards which mankind seems drifting we must still subject ourselves collectively to those severities which answer to our real position upon this only partly hospitable globe.   We must make new energies and hardihoods continue the manliness to which the military mind so faithfully clings.   Martial virtues must be the enduring cement; intrepidity, contempt of softness, surrender of private interest, obedience to command, must still remain the rock upon which states are built—unless, indeed, we wish for dangerous reactions against commonwealths fit only for contempt, and liable to invite attack whenever a center of crystallization for military-minded enterprise gets formed anywhere in their neighborhood.

The war-party is assuredly right in affirming and reaffirming that the martial virtues, although originally gained by the race through war, are absolute and permanent human goods.   Patriotic pride and ambition in their military form are, after all, only specifications of a more general competitive passion.   They are its first form, but that is no reason for supposing them to be its last form. Men now are proud of belonging to a conquering nation, and without a murmur they lay down their persons and their wealth, if by so doing they may fend off subjection. But who can be sure that *other aspects of one's country* may not, with time and education and suggestion enough, come to be regarded with similarly effective feelings of pride and shame? Why should men not some day feel that it is worth a blood-tax to belong to a collectivity superior in *any* ideal respect? Why should they not blush with indignant shame if the community that owns them is vile in any way whatsoever? Individuals, daily more numerous, now feel this civic passion. It is only a question of blowing on the spark till the whole population gets incandescent, and on the ruins of the old morals of military honor, a stable system of morals of civic honor builds itself up. What the whole community comes to believe in grasps the individual as in a vise. The war-function has grasped us so far; but constructive interests may some day seem no less imperative, and impose on the individual a hardly lighter burden.

Let me illustrate my idea more concretely. There is nothing to make one indignant in the mere fact that life is hard, that men should toil and suffer pain. The planetary conditions once for all are such, and we can stand it. But that so many men, by mere accidents of birth and opportunity, should have a life of

nothing else but toil and pain and hardness and in-
feriority imposed upon them, should have *no* vacation,
while others natively no more deserving never get any
taste of this campaigning life at all,—*this* is capable of
arousing indignation in reflective minds. It may end
by seeming shameful to all of us that some of us have
nothing but campaigning, and others nothing but un-
manly ease. If now—and this is my idea—there
were, instead of military conscription a conscription of
the whole youthful population to form for a certain
number of years a part of the army enlisted against
Nature, the injustice would tend to be evened out, and
numerous other goods to the commonwealth would
follow. The military ideals of hardihood and discipline would be wrought into the growing fiber of the
people; no one would remain blind as the luxurious
classes now are blind, to man's relations to the globe he
lives on, and to the permanently sour and hard foundations of his higher life. To coal and iron mines, to
freight trains, to fishing fleets in December, to dish-
washing, clothes-washing, and window-washing, to road-
building and tunnel-making, to foundries and stoke-
holes, and to the frames of skyscrapers, would our
gilded youths be drafted off, according to their choice,
to get the childishness knocked out of them, and to
come back into society with healthier sympathies and
soberer ideas. They would have paid their blood-tax,
done their own part in the immemorial human warfare
against nature; they would tread the earth more

proudly, the women would value them more highly, they would be better fathers and teachers of the following generation.

Such a conscription, with the state of public opinion that would have required it, and the many moral fruits it would bear, would preserve in the midst of a pacific civilization the manly virtues which the military party is so afraid of seeing disappear in peace. We should get toughness without callousness, authority with as little criminal cruelty as possible, and painful work done cheerily because the duty is temporary, and threatens not, as now, to degrade the whole remainder of one's life. I spoke of the "moral equivalent" of war. So far, war has been the only force that can discipline a whole community, and until an equivalent discipline is organized, I believe that war must have its way. But I have no serious doubt that the ordinary prides and shames of social man, once developed to a certain intensity, are capable of organizing such a moral equivalent as I have sketched, or some other just as effective for preserving manliness of type. It is but a question of time, of skillful propagandism, and of opinion-making men seizing historic opportunities.

The Place of Labor Troubles in Social Evolution [1]

Don't be alarmed about the labor troubles here.[2]   I

[1] From a letter to Henry James, in *The Letters of William James*, vol. i, p. 252.

[2] The "troubles" referred to were the Pullman strike in Chicago and its consequences.

am quite sure they are a most healthy phase of evolution, a little costly, but normal, and sure to do lots of good to all hands in the end.

The Function of Education in a Democracy [1]

. . . "The people in their wisdom"—this is the kind of wisdom most needed by the people. Democracy is on its trial, and no one knows how it will stand the ordeal. Abounding about us are pessimistic prophets. Fickleness and violence used to be, but are no longer, the vices which they charge to democracy. What its critics now affirm is that its preferences are inveterately for the inferior. So it was in the beginning, they say, and so it will be world without end. Vulgarity enthroned and institutionalized, elbowing everything superior from the highway, this, they tell us, is our irremediable destiny; and the picture papers of the European Continent are already drawing Uncle Sam with the hog instead of the eagle for his heraldic emblem. The privileged aristocracies of the foretime, with all their iniquities, did at least preserve some taste for higher human quality, and honor certain forms of refinement by their enduring traditions. But when democracy is sovereign, its doubters say, nobility will form a sort of invisible church, and sincerity and refinement, stripped of honor, precedence, and favor, will have to vegetate on sufferance in private

[1] From "The Social Value of the College-Bred," in *Memories and Studies*, pp. 316-324.

corners. They will have no general influence. They will be harmless eccentricities.

Now, who can be absolutely certain that this may not be the career of democracy? Nothing future is quite secure; states enough have inwardly rotted; and democracy as a whole may undergo self-poisoning. But, on the other hand, democracy is a kind of religion, and we are bound not to admit its failure. Faiths and utopias are the noblest exercise of human reason, and no one with a spark of reason in him will sit down fatalistically before the croaker's picture. The best of us are filled with the contrary vision of a democracy stumbling through every error till its institutions glow with justice and its customs shine with beauty. Our better men *shall* show the way and we *shall* follow them; so we are brought round again to the mission of the higher education in helping us to know the better kind of man whenever we see him.

The notion that a people can run itself and its affairs anonymously is now well known to be the silliest of absurdities. Mankind does nothing save through initiatives on the part of inventors, great or small, and imitation by the rest of us—these are the sole factors active in human progress. Individuals of genius show the way, and set the patterns, which common people then adopt and follow. *The rivalry of the patterns is the history of the world*. Our democratic problem thus is statable in ultra-simple terms: Who are the kind of men from whom our majorities

shall take their cue?   Whom shall they treat as right-
ful leaders?   We and our leaders are the x and the y
of the equation here; all other historic circumstances,
be they economical, political, or intellectual, are only
the background of occasion on which the living drama
works itself out between us.

In this very simple way does the value of our
educated class define itself: we more than others should
be able to divine the worthier and better leaders.   The
terms here are monstrously simplified, of course, but
such a bird's-eye view lets us immediately take our
bearings.   In our democracy, where everything else
is so shifting, we alumni and alumnæ of the colleges are
the only permanent presence that corresponds to the
aristocracy in older countries.   We have continuous
traditions, as they have; our motto, too, is *noblesse
oblige;* and, unlike them, we stand for ideal interests
solely, for we have no corporate selfishness and wield
no powers of corruption.   We ought to have our own
class-consciousness.   *"Les   Intellectuels!"*   What
prouder club-name could there be than this one, used
ironically by the party of "redblood," the party
of every stupid prejudice and passion, during the anti-
Dreyfus craze, to satirize the men in France who still
retained some critical sense and judgment!   Critical
sense, it has to be confessed, is not an exciting term,
hardly a banner to carry in processions.   Affections for
old habit, currents of self-interest, and gales of passion
are the forces that keep the human ship moving; and

the pressure of the judicious pilot's hand upon the tiller is a relatively insignificant energy. But the affections, passions, and interests are shifting, successive, and distraught; they blow in alternation while the pilot's hand is steadfast. He knows the compass, and, with all the leeways he is obliged to tack toward, he always makes some headway. A small force, if it never lets up, will accumulate effects more considerable than those of much greater forces if these work inconsistently. The ceaseless whisper of the more permanent ideals, the steady tug of truth and justice, give them but time, *must* warp the world in their direction. . . .

. . . It would be a pity if any future historian were to have to write words like these: "By the middle of the twentieth century the higher institutions of learning had lost all influence over public opinion in the United States. But the mission of raising the tone of democracy, which they had proved themselves so lamentably unfitted to exert, was assumed with rare enthusiasm and prosecuted with extraordinary skill and success by a new educational power; and for the clarification of their human sympathies and elevation of their human preferences, the people at large acquired the habit of resorting exclusively to the guidance of certain private literary adventures, commonly designated in the market by the affectionate name of ten-cent magazines. . . ."

CHAPTER VIII

EDUCATION

Education and Behavior [1]

In our foregoing talk we were led to frame a very simple conception of what an education means. In the last analysis it consists in the organizing of *resources* in the human being, of powers of conduct which shall fit him to his social and physical world. An "uneducated" person is one who is nonplussed by all but the most habitual situations. On the contrary, one who is educated is able practically to extricate himself, by means of the examples with which his memory is stored and of the abstract conceptions which he has acquired, from circumstances in which he never was placed before. Education, in short, cannot be better described than by calling it *the organization of acquired habits of conduct and tendencies to behavior*.

To illustrate. You and I are each and all of us educated, in our several ways; and we show our education at this present moment by different conduct. It would be quite impossible for me, with my mind technically and professionally organized as it is, and with the optical stimulus which your presence affords, to

[1] From *Talks to Teachers on Psychology,* pp. 29-36.

remain sitting here entirely silent and inactive. Something tells me that I am expected to speak, and must speak; something forces me to keep on speaking. My organs of articulation are continuously innervated by outgoing currents, which the currents passing inward at my eyes and through my educated brain have set in motion; and the particular movements which they make have their form and order determined altogether by the training of all my past years of lecturing and reading. Your conduct, on the other hand, might seem at first sight purely receptive and inactive,—leaving out those among you who happen to be taking notes. But the very listening which you are carrying on is itself a determinate kind of conduct. All the muscular tensions of your body are distributed in a peculiar way as you listen. Your head, your eyes, are fixed characteristically. And, when the lecture is over, it will inevitably eventuate in some stroke of behavior, as I said on the previous occasion: you may be guided differently in some special emergency in the schoolroom by words which I now let fall.—So it is with the impressions you will make there on your pupil. You should get into the habit of regarding them all as leading to the acquisition by him of capacities for behavior, —emotional, social, bodily, vocal, technical, or what not. And, this being the case, you ought to feel willing, in a general way, and without hair-splitting or farther ado, to take up for the purposes of these lectures with the biological conception of the mind, as of something given us for practical use. That conception will certainly cover the greater part of your own educational work.

If we reflect upon the various ideals of education that are prevalent in the different countries, we see that what they all aim at is to organize capacities for conduct. This is most immediately obvious in Germany, where the explicitly avowed aim of the higher education is to turn the student into an instrument for advancing scientific discovery. The German universities are proud of the number of young specialists whom they turn out every year,—not necessarily men of any original force of intellect, but men so trained to research that when their professor gives them an historical or philological thesis to prepare, or a bit of laboratory work to do, with a general indication as to the best method, they can go off by themselves and use apparatus and consult sources in such a way as to grind out in the requisite number of months some little pepper-corn of new truth worthy of being added to the store of extant human information on that subject. Little else is recognized in Germany as a man's title to academic advancement than his ability thus to show himself an efficient instrument of research.

In England, it might seem at first sight as if the higher education of the universities aimed at the production of certain static types of character rather than at the development of what one may call this dynamic scientific efficiency. Professor Jowett, when asked

what Oxford could do for its students, is said to have
replied, "Oxford can teach an English gentleman how
to *be* an English gentleman." But, if you ask what it
means to "be" an English gentleman, the only reply is
in terms of conduct and behavior. An English gentleman is a bundle of specifically qualified reactions, a
creature who for all the emergencies of life has his line
of behavior distinctly marked out for him in advance.
Here, as elsewhere, England expects every man to do
his duty.

If all this be true, then immediately one general
aphorism emerges which ought by logical right to
dominate the entire conduct of the teacher in the class-
room.

*No reception without reaction, no impression without
correlative expression,*—this is the great maxim which
the teacher ought never to forget.

An impression which simply flows in at the pupil's
eyes or ears, and in no way modifies his active life, is
an impression gone to waste. It is physiologically incomplete. It leaves no fruits behind it in the way of
capacity acquired. Even as mere impression, it fails
to produce its proper effect upon the memory; for, to
remain fully among the acquisitions of this latter faculty, it must be wrought into the whole cycle of our
operations. Its *motor consequences* are what clinch it.
Some effect due to it in the way of an activity must
return to the mind in the form of the *sensation of having
acted*, and connect itself with the impression. The most

durable impressions are those on account of which we speak or act, or else are inwardly convulsed.

The older pedagogic method of learning things by rote, and reciting them parrot-like in the schoolroom, rested on the truth that a thing merely read or heard, and never verbally reproduced, contracts the weakest possible adhesion in the mind. Verbal recitation or reproduction is thus a highly important kind of reactive behavior on our impressions; and it is to be feared that, in the reaction against the old parrot-recitations as the beginning and end of instruction, the extreme value of verbal recitation as an element of complete training may nowadays be too much forgotten.

When we turn to modern pedagogics, we see how enormously the field of reactive conduct has been extended by the introduction of all those methods of concrete object teaching which are the glory of our contemporary schools. Verbal reactions, useful as they are, are insufficient. The pupil's words may be right, but the conceptions corresponding to them are often direfully wrong. In a modern school, therefore, they form only a small part of what the pupil is required to do. He must keep notebooks, make drawings, plans, and maps, take measurements, enter the laboratory and perform experiments, consult authorities, and write essays. He must do in his fashion what is often laughed at by outsiders when it appears in prospectuses under the title of "original work," but what is really the only possible training for the doing of original work there-

after. The most colossal improvement which recent
years have seen in secondary education lies in the introduction of the manual training schools; not because
they will give us a people more handy and practical for
domestic life and better skilled in trades, but because
they will give us citizens with an entirely different intellectual fiber. Laboratory work and shop work engender a habit of observation, a knowledge of the difference between accuracy and vagueness, and an insight into nature's complexity and into the inadequacy
of all abstract verbal accounts of real phenomena,
which once wrought into the mind, remain there as life-
long possessions. They confer precision; because, if
you are *doing* a thing, you must do it definitely right
or definitely wrong. They give honesty; for, when you
express yourself by making things, and not by using
words, it becomes impossible to dissimulate your vagueness or ignorance by ambiguity. They beget a habit
of self-reliance; they keep the interest and attention
always cheerfully engaged, and reduce the teacher's dis-
ciplinary functions to a minimum.

The Laws of Habit [1]

It is very important that teachers should realize the
importance of habit, and psychology helps us greatly
at this point. We speak, it is true, of good habits and
of bad habits; but, when people use the word "habit,"
in the majority of instances it is a bad habit which

[1] From *Talks to Teachers on Psychology,* pp. 64-78.

they have in mind. They talk of the smoking-habit and the swearing-habit and the drinking-habit, but not of the abstention-habit or the moderation-habit or the courage-habit. But the fact is that our virtues are habits as much as our vices. All our life, so far as it has definite form, is but a mass of habits—practical, emotional, and intellectual—systematically organized for our weal or woe, and bearing us irresistibly toward our destiny, whatever the latter may be.

Since pupils can understand this at a comparatively early age, and since to understand it contributes in no small measure to their feeling of responsibility, it would be well if the teacher were able himself to talk to them of the philosophy of habit in some such abstract terms as I am now about to talk of it to you.

I believe that we are subject to the law of habit in consequence of the fact that we have bodies. The plasticity of the living matter of our nervous system, in short, is the reason why we do a thing with difficulty the first time, but soon do it more and more easily, and finally, with sufficient practice, do it semi-mechanically, or with hardly any consciousness at all. Our nervous systems have (in Dr. Carpenter's words) *grown* to the way in which they have been exercised, just as a sheet of paper or a coat, once creased or folded, tends to fall forever afterward into the same identical folds.

Habit is thus a second nature, or rather, as the Duke of Wellington said, it is "ten times nature"—at any rate as regards its importance in adult life; for the acquired habits of our training have by that time inhibited or strangled most of the natural impulsive tendencies which were originally there. Ninety-nine hundredths or, possibly, nine hundred and ninety-nine thousandths of our activity is purely automatic and habitual, from our rising in the morning to our lying down each night. Our dressing and undressing, our eating and drinking, our greetings and partings, our hat-raisings and giving way for ladies to precede, nay, even most of the forms of our common speech, are things of a type so fixed by repetition as almost to be classed as reflex actions. To each sort of impression we have an automatic, ready-made response. My very words to you now are an example of what I mean; for having already lectured upon habit and printed a chapter about it in a book, and read the latter when in print, I find my tongue inevitably falling into its old phrases and repeating almost literally what I said before.

So far as we are thus mere bundles of habit, we are stereotyped creatures, imitators and copiers of our past selves. And since this, under any circumstances, is what we always tend to become, it follows first of all that the teacher's prime concern should be to ingrain into the pupil that assortment of habits that shall be most useful to him throughout life. Education is for behavior, and habits are the stuff of which behavior consists.

To quote my earlier book directly, the great thing in all education is to *make our nervous system our ally instead of our enemy.* It is to fund and capitalize our acquisitions, and live at ease upon the interest of the fund. *For this we must make automatic and habitual, as early as possible, as many useful actions as we can,* and as carefully guard against the growing into ways that are likely to be disadvantageous. The more of the details of our daily life we can hand over to the effortless custody of automatism, the more our higher powers of mind will be set free for their own proper work. There is no more miserable human being than one in whom nothing is habitual but indecision, and for whom the lighting of every cigar, the drinking of every cup, the time of rising and going to bed every day, and the beginning of every bit of work are subjects of express volitional deliberation. Full half the time of such a man goes to the deciding or regretting of matters which ought to be so ingrained in him as practically not to exist for his consciousness at all. If there be such daily duties not yet ingrained in any one of my hearers, let him begin this very hour to set the matter right.

In Professor Bain's chapter on "The Moral Habits" there are some admirable practical remarks laid down. Two great maxims emerge from the treatment. The first is that in the acquisition of a new habit, or the leaving off of an old one, we must take care to *launch ourselves with as strong and decided an initiative as possible.* Accumulate all the possible circumstances which shall reinforce the right motives; put yourself assiduously in conditions that encourage the new way; make engagements incompatible with the old; take a public pledge, if the case allows; in short, envelope your resolution with every aid you know. This will give your new beginning such a momentum that the temptation to break down will not occur as soon as it otherwise might; and every day during which a break-down is postponed adds to the chances of its not oc-curring at all.

I remember long ago reading in an Austrian paper the advertisement of a certain Rudolph Somebody, who promised fifty gulden reward to any one who after that date should find him at the wine-shop of Ambrosius So-and-so. "This I do," the advertisement continued, "in consequence of a promise which I have made my wife." With such a wife, and such an understanding of the way in which to start new habits, it would be safe to stake one's money on Rudolph's ultimate success.

The second maxim is, *Never suffer an exception to occur till the new habit is securely rooted in your life.* Each lapse is like the letting fall of a ball of string which one is carefully winding up: a single slip undoes more than a great many turns will wind again. Con-tinuity of training is the great means of making the nervous system act infallibly right. As Professor Bain says:

"The peculiarity of the moral habits, contradistin-guishing them from the intellectual acquisitions, is the presence of two hostile powers, one to be gradually raised into the ascendant over the other. It is necessary above all things, in such a situation, never to lose a battle. Every gain on the wrong side undoes the effect of many conquests on the right. The essential precaution, therefore, is so to regulate the two opposing powers that the one may have a series of uninterrupted successes, until repetition has fortified it to such a degree as to enable it to cope with the opposition, under any circumstances. This is the theoretically best career of mental progress."

A third maxim may be added to the preceding pair: *Seize the very first possible opportunity to act on every resolution you make, and on every emotional prompting you may experience in the direction of the habits you aspire to gain.* It is not in the moment of their forming, but in the moment of their producing motor effects, that resolves and aspirations communicate the new "set" to the brain.

No matter how full a reservoir of maxims one may possess, and no matter how good one's sentiments may be, if one have not taken advantage of every concrete opportunity to act, one's character may remain entirely unaffected for the better. With good intentions, hell proverbially is paved. This is an obvious consequence of the principles I have laid down. A "character," as J. S. Mill says, "is a completely fashioned will"; and a will, in the sense in which he means it, is an aggregate of tendencies to act in a firm and prompt and definite way upon all the principal emergencies of life. A tendency to act only becomes effectively ingrained in us in proportion to the uninterrupted frequency with which the actions actually occur, and the brain "grows" to their use. When a resolve or a fine glow of feeling is allowed to evaporate without bearing practical fruit, it is worse than a chance lost: it works so as positively to hinder future resolutions and emotions from taking the normal path of discharge. There is no more contemptible type of human character than that of the nerveless sentimentalist and dreamer, who spends his life in a weltering sea of sensibility, but never does a concrete manly deed.

This leads to a fourth maxim. *Don't preach too much to your pupils or abound in good talk in the abstract.* Lie in wait rather for the practical opportunities, be prompt to seize those as they pass, and thus at one operation get your pupils both to think, to feel, and to do. The strokes of *behavior* are what give the new set to the character, and work the good habits into its organic tissue. Preaching and talking too soon become an ineffectual bore.

There is a passage in Darwin's short autobiography which has been often quoted, and which, for the sake of its bearing on our subject of habit, I must now quote again. Darwin says: "Up to the age of thirty or beyond it, poetry of many kinds gave me great pleasure; and even as a schoolboy I took intense delight in

Shakespeare, especially in the historical plays. I have also said that pictures formerly gave me considerable, and music very great delight. But now for many years I cannot endure to read a line of poetry. I have tried lately to read Shakespeare, and found it so intolerably dull that it nauseated me. I have also almost lost my taste for pictures or music. . . . My mind seems to have become a kind of machine for grinding general laws out of large collections of facts; but why this should have caused the atrophy of that part of the brain alone, on which the higher tastes depend, I cannot conceive. . . . If I had to live my life again, I would have made a rule to read some poetry and listen to some music at least once every week; for perhaps the parts of my brain now atrophied would thus have been kept alive through use. The loss of these tastes is a loss of happiness, and may possibly be injurious to the intellect, and more probably to the moral character, by enfeebling the emotional part of our nature."

We all intend when young to be all that may become a man, before the destroyer cuts us down. We wish and expect to enjoy poetry always, to grow more and more intelligent about pictures and music, to keep in touch with spiritual and religious ideas, and even not to let the greater philosophic thoughts of our time develop quite beyond our view. We mean all this in youth, I say; and yet in how many middle-aged men and women is such an honest and sanguine expectation fulfilled? Surely, in comparatively few; and the laws of habit show us why. Some interest in each of these things arises in everybody at the proper age; but, if not persistently fed with the appropriate matter, instead of growing into a powerful and necessary habit, it atrophies and dies, choked by the rival interests to which the daily food is given. We make ourselves into Darwins in this negative respect by persistently ignoring the essential practical conditions of our case. We say abstractly: "I mean to enjoy poetry, and to absorb a lot of it, of course. I fully intend to keep up my love of music, to read the books that shall give new turns to the thought of my time, to keep my higher spiritual side alive," etc. But we do not attack these things concretely, and we do not begin *today*. We forget that every good that is worth possessing must be paid for in strokes of daily effort. We postpone and postpone, until those smiling possibilities are dead. Whereas ten minutes a day of poetry, of spiritual reading or meditation, and an hour or two a week at music, pictures, or philosophy, provided we began *now* and suffered no remission, would infallibly give us in due time the fullness of all we desire. By neglecting the necessary concrete labor, by sparing ourselves the little daily tax, we are positively digging the graves of our higher possibilities. This is a point concerning which you teachers might well give a little timely information to your older and more aspiring pupils.

According as a function receives daily exercise or not, the man becomes a different kind of being in later life. We have lately had a number of accomplished Hindoo visitors at Cambridge, who talked freely of life and philosophy. More than one of them has confided to me that the sight of our faces, all contracted as they are with the habitual American over-intensity and anxiety of expression, and our ungraceful and distorted attitudes when sitting, made on him a very painful impression. "I do not see," said one, "how it is possible for you to live as you do, without a single minute in your day deliberately given to tranquillity and meditation. It is an invariable part of our Hindoo life to retire for at least half an hour daily into silence, to relax our muscles, govern our breathing, and meditate on eternal things. Every Hindoo child is trained to this from a very early age." The good fruits of such a discipline were obvious in the physical repose and lack of tension, and the wonderful smoothness and calmness of facial expression, and imperturbability of manner of these Orientals. I felt that my countrymen were depriving themselves of an essential grace of character. How many American children ever hear it said by parent or teacher, that they should moderate their piercing voices, that they should relax their unused muscles, and as far as possible, when sitting, sit quite still? Not one in a thousand, not one in five thousand! Yet, from its reflex influence on the inner mental states, this ceaseless over-tension, over-motion, and over-expression are working on us grievous national harm.

I beg you teachers to think a little seriously of this

matter.   Perhaps you can help our rising generation of Americans toward the beginning of a better set of personal ideals.

To go back now to our general maxims, I may at last, as a fifth and final practical maxim about habits, offer something like this: *Keep the faculty of effort alive in you by a little gratuitous exercise every day.* That is, be systematically heroic in little unnecessary points, do every day or two something for no other reason than its difficulty, so that, when the hour of dire need draws nigh, it may find you not unnerved and untrained to stand the test.   Asceticism of this sort is like the insurance which a man pays on his house and goods.   The tax does him no good at the time, and possibly may never bring him a return.   But, if the fire *does* come, his having paid it will be his salvation from ruin.   So with the man who has daily inured himself to habits of concentrated attention, energetic volition, and self-denial in unnecessary things.   He will stand like a tower when everything rocks around him, and his softer fellow-mortals are winnowed like chaff in the blast.

I have been accused, when talking of the subject of habit, of making old habits appear so strong that the acquiring of new ones, and particularly anything like a sudden reform or conversion, would be made impossible by my doctrine.   Of course, this would suffice to condemn the latter; for sudden conversions, however infrequent they may be, unquestionably do occur. But there is no incompatibility between the general laws I have laid down and the most startling sudden alterations in the way of character. New habits *can* be launched, I have expressly said, on condition of there being new stimuli and new excitements. Now life abounds in these, and sometimes they are such critical and revolutionary experiences that they change a man's whole scale of values and system of ideas. In such cases, the old order of his habits will be ruptured; and, if the new motives are lasting, new habits will be formed, and build up in him a new or regenerate "nature."

All this kind of fact I fully allow. But the general laws of habit are no wise altered thereby, and the physiological study of mental conditions still remains on the whole the most powerful ally of hortatory ethics. The hell to be endured hereafter, of which theology tells, is no worse than the hell we make for ourselves in this world by habitually fashioning our characters in the wrong way. Could the young but realize how soon they will become mere walking bundles of habits, they would give more heed to their conduct while in the plastic state. We are spinning our own fates, good or evil, and never to be undone. Every smallest stroke of virtue or of vice leaves its never-so-little scar. The drunken Rip Van Winkle, in Jefferson's play, excuses himself for every fresh dereliction by saying, "I won't count this time!" Well, he may not count it, and a kind Heaven may not count it, but it is being counted none the less. Down among his nerve-cells and fibers the molecules are counting it, registering and storing it up to be used against him when the next temptation comes. Nothing we ever do is, in strict scientific literalness, wiped out.

Of course, this has its good side as well as its bad one. As we become permanent drunkards by so many separate drinks, so we become saints in the moral, and authorities and experts in the practical and scientific spheres, by so many separate acts and hours of work. Let no youth have any anxiety about the upshot of his education, whatever the line of it may be. If he keep faithfully busy each hour of the working day, he may safely leave the final result to itself. He can with perfect certainty count on waking up some fine morning to find himself one of the competent ones of his generation, in whatever pursuit he may have singled out. Silently, between all the details of his business, the *power of judging* in all that class of matter will have built itself up within him as a possession that will never pass away. Young people should know this truth in advance. The ignorance of it has probably engendered more discouragement and faint-heartedness in youths embarking on arduous careers than all other causes put together.

The Ideal College Education [1]

Of what use is a college training? We who have had it seldom hear the question raised; we might be a little nonplussed to answer it offhand. A certain amount of meditation has brought me to this as the pithiest reply which I myself can give: The best claim that a college education can possibly make on your respect, the best thing it can aspire to accomplish for you, is this: that it should *help you to know a good man when you see him.* This is as true of women's as of men's colleges; but that it is neither a joke nor a one-sided abstraction I shall now endeavor to show.

What talk do we commonly hear about the contrast between college education and the education which business or technical or professional schools confer? The college education is called higher because it is supposed to be so general and so disinterested. At the "schools" you get a relatively narrow practical skill, you are told, whereas the "colleges" give you the more liberal culture, the broader outlook, the historical perspective, the philosophic atmosphere, or something which phrases of that sort try to express. You are made into an efficient instrument for doing a definite thing, you hear, at the schools; but, apart from that, you may remain a crude and smoky kind of petroleum, incapable of spreading light. The universities and colleges, on the other hand, although they may leave you

[1] From "The Social Value of the College-Bred," in *Memories and Studies,* pp. 309-314.

less efficient for this or that practical task, suffuse your whole mentality with something more important than skill. They redeem you, make you well-bred; they make "good company" of you mentally. If they find you with a naturally boorish or caddish mind, they cannot leave you so, as a technical school may leave you. This, at least, is pretended; this is what we hear among college-trained people when they compare their education with every other sort. Now, exactly how much does this signify?

It is certain, to begin with, that the narrowest trade or professional training does something more for a man than to make a skillful practical tool of him—it makes him also a judge of other men's skill. Whether his trade be pleading at the bar or surgery or plastering or plumbing, it develops a critical sense in him for that sort of occupation. He understands the difference between second-rate and first-rate work in his whole branch of industry; he gets to know a good job in his own line as soon as he sees it; and getting to know this in his own line, he gets a faint sense of what good work may mean anyhow, that may, if circumstances favor, spread into his judgments elsewhere. Sound work, clean work, finished work: feeble work, slack work, sham work—these words express an identical contrast in many different departments of activity. In so far forth, then, even the humblest manual trade may beget in one a certain small degree of power to judge of good work generally.

Now, what is supposed to be the line of us who have the higher college training? Is there any broader line— since our education claims primarily not to be "narrow"—in which we also are made good judges between what is first-rate and what is second-rate only? What is especially taught in the colleges has long been known by the name of the "humanities," and these are often identified with Greek and Latin. But it is only as literatures, not as languages, that Greek and Latin have any general humanity-value; so that in a broad sense the humanities mean literature primarily, and in a still broader sense the study of masterpieces in almost any field of human endeavor. Literature keeps the primacy; for it not only *consists* of masterpieces, but is largely *about* masterpieces, being little more than an appreciative chronicle of human master-strokes, so far as it takes the form of criticism and history. You can give humanistic value to almost anything by teaching it historically. Geology, economics, mechanics, are humanities when taught with reference to the successive achievements of the geniuses to which these sciences owe their being. Not taught thus literature remains grammar, art a catalogue, history a list of dates, and natural science a sheet of formulas and weights and measures.

The sifting of human creations!—nothing less than this is what we ought to mean by the humanities. Essentially this means biography; what our colleges should teach is, therefore, biographical history, that not of politics merely, but of anything and everything so far as human efforts and conquests are factors that have played their part. Studying in this way, we learn what types of activity have stood the test of time; we acquire standards of the excellent and durable. All our arts and sciences and institutions are but so many quests of perfection on the part of men; and when we see how diverse the types of excellence may be, how various the tests, how flexible the adaptations, we gain a richer sense of what the terms "better" and "worse" may signify in general. Our critical sensibilities grow both more acute and less fanatical. We sympathize with men's mistakes even in the act of penetrating them; we feel the pathos of lost causes and misguided epochs even while we applaud what overcame them.

Such words are vague and such ideas are inadequate, but their meaning is unmistakable. What the colleges —teaching humanities by examples which may be special, but which must be typical and pregnant—should at least try to give us, is a general sense of what, under various disguises, *superiority* has always signified and may still signify. The feeling for a good human job anywhere, the admiration of the really admirable, the disesteem of what is cheap and trashy and impermanent,—this is what we call the critical sense, the sense for ideal values. It is the better part of what men know as wisdom. . . .

CHAPTER IX

THE AMERICAN SCENE

The Land [1]

THE SALTERS' HILL-TOP
[near CHOCORUA], *Sept. 22,* 1893.

. . . I am up here for a few days with Billy, to close our house for the winter, and get a sniff of the place. The Salters have a noble hill with such an outlook! and a very decent little house and barn. But oh! the difference from Switzerland, the thin grass and ragged waysides, the poverty-stricken land, and sad American sunlight over all—sad because so empty. There is a strange thinness and femininity hovering over all America, so different from the stoutness and masculinity of land and air and everything in Switzerland and England, that the coming back makes one feel strangely sad and hardens one in the resolution never to go away again unless one can go to end one's days. Such a divided soul is very bad. To you, who now have real practical relations and a place in the old world, I should think there was no necessity of ever coming back again. But Europe has been made what it is by men staying in their homes and fighting

[1] From a letter to Henry James, in *The Letters of William James*, vol. i, pp. 346-347.

291

stubbornly generation after generation for all the beauty, comfort and order that they have got—we must abide and do the same. As England struck me newly and differently last time, so America now—force and directness in the people, but a terrible grimness, more ugliness than I ever realized in things, and a greater weakness in nature's beauty, such as it is. One must pitch one's whole sensibility first in a different key—then gradually the quantum of personal happiness of which one is susceptible fills the cup—but the moment of change of key is lonesome. . . .

Colorado [1]

I, you see, am farther away from home than I have ever been before on this side of the Atlantic, namely, in the state of Colorado, and just now in the heart of the Rocky Mountains. I have been giving a course of six lectures on psychology "for teachers" at a socalled "summer-school" in Colorado Springs. I had to remain for three nights and three days in the train to get there, and it has made me understand the vastness of my dear native land better than I ever did before. . . . The trouble with all this new civilization is that it is based, not on saving, but on borrowing; and when hard times come, as they did come three years ago, every one goes bankrupt. But the vision of the future, the dreams of the possible, keep every one

[1] From a letter to Theodore Flournoy, 1895, in *The Letters of William James,* vol. ii, p. 24.

enthusiastic, and so the work goes on. Such conditions have never existed before on so enormous a scale.

California [1]

. . . You've seen this wonderful spot, so I needn't describe it. It is really a miracle; and so simple the life and so benign the elements, that for a young ambitious professor who wishes to leave his mark on Pacific civilization while it is most plastic, or for *any one* who wants to teach and work under the most perfect conditions for eight or nine months, and *who is able to get to the East, or Europe, for the remaining three,* I can't imagine anything finer. It is Utopian. Perfection of weather. Cold nights, though above freezing. Fire pleasant until 10 o'clock A. M., then unpleasant. In short, the "simple life" with all the essential higher elements thrown in as communal possessions. The drawback is, of course, the great surrounding human vacuum—the historic silence fairly rings in your ears when you listen—and the social insipidity. . . .

New York City [2]

The first impression of New York, if you stay there not more than 36 hours, which has been my limit

[1] From a letter to Henry James, 1906, in *The Letters of William James,* vol. ii, p. 241.

[2] From a letter to Henry James, 1907, in *The Letters of William James,* vol. ii, p. 264.

for twenty years past, is one of repulsion at the clangor, disorder, and permanent earthquake conditions. But this time, installed as I was at the Harvard Club (44th St.) in the center of the cyclone, I caught the pulse of the machine, took up the rhythm, and vibrated *mit*, and found it simply magnificent. I'm surprised at you, Henry, not having been more enthusiastic, but perhaps that superbly powerful and beautiful subway was not opened when you were there. It is an *entirely* new New York, in soul as well as in body, from the old one, which looks like a village in retrospect. The courage, the heaven-scaling audacity of it all, and the *lightness* withal, as if there was nothing that was not easy, and the great pulses and bounds of progress, so many in directions all simultaneous that the coördination is indefinitely future, give a kind of *drumming background* of life that I never felt before. I'm sure that once *in* that movement, and at home, all other places would seem insipid.

American Energy and Tension [1]

I

I am beginning to get impatient with the Brazilian sleepiness and ignorance. These Indians are particularly exasperating by their laziness and stolidity. It would be amusing if it were not so infuriating to see how impossible it is to make one hurry, no matter how

[1] From a letter to his father, 1868, in *The Letters of William James*, vol. i, p. 64.

imminent the emergency. How queer and how exhilarating all those home letters were, with their accounts of what every one was doing, doing, doing. To me, just awakening from my life of forced idleness and from an atmosphere of Brazilian inanity, it seemed as if a little window had been opened and a life-giving blast of one of our October nor'westers had blown into my lungs for half an hour. I had no idea before of the real greatness of American energy. They wood up the steamer here for instance at the rate (accurately counted) of eight to twelve logs a minute. It takes them two and one-half hours to put in as much wood as would go in at home in less than fifteen minutes.

II

The apophthegm,[1] "a fat man consequently a good man," has much of truth in it. The Germans come out strong on their abdomens—even when these are not vast in capacity, one feels that they are of mighty powerful construction, and play a much weightier part in the economy of the man than with us—affording a massive, immovable background to the consciousness, over which, as on the surface of a deep and tranquil sea, the motley images contributed by the other senses to life's drama glide and play without raising more than a pleasant ripple—while with *us*, who have no such voluminous background, they forever touch bottom,

[1] From a letter to O. W. Holmes (now Justice Holmes of the Supreme Court), 1867, in *The Letters of William James*, vol. i, p. 100

or come out on the other side, or kick up such a tempest and fury that we enjoy no repose. . . .

III

[1] Many years ago a Scottish medical man, Dr. Clouston, a mad-doctor as they call him there, or what we should call an asylum physician (the most eminent one in Scotland), visited this country, and said something that has remained in my memory ever since. "You Americans," he said, "wear too much expression on your faces. You are living like an army with all its reserves engaged in action. The duller countenances of the British population betoken a better scheme of life. They suggest stores of reserved nervous force to fall back upon, if any occasion should arise that requires it. This inexcitability, this presence at all times of power not used, I regard," continued Dr. Clouston, "as the great safeguard of our British people. The other thing in you gives me a sense of insecurity, and you ought somehow to tone yourselves down. You really do carry too much expression, you take too intensely the trivial moments of life."

Now Dr. Clouston is a trained reader of the secrets of the soul as expressed upon the countenance, and the observation of his which I quote seems to me to mean a great deal. And all Americans who stay in Europe long enough to get accustomed to the spirit that reigns and expresses itself there, so unexcitable as compared

[1] From "The Gospel of Relaxation," in *Talks to Teachers on Psychology,* etc., pp. 207-217.

with ours, make a similar observation when they return
to their native shores. They find a wild-eyed look upon
their compatriots' faces, either of too desperate eagerness and anxiety or of too intense responsiveness and
good-will. It is hard to say whether the men or the
women show it most. It is true that we do not all
feel about it as Dr. Clouston felt. Many of us, far
from deploring it, admire it. We say: "What intelligence it shows! How different from the stolid cheeks,
the codfish eyes, the slow, inanimate demeanor we
have been seeing in the British Isles!" Intensity, ra-
pidity, vivacity of appearance, are indeed with us something of a nationally accepted ideal; and the medical
notion of "irritable weakness" is not the first thing
suggested by them to our mind, as it was to Dr. Clouston's. In a weekly paper not very long ago I remember reading a story in which, after describing the beauty
and interest of the heroine's personality, the author
summed up her charms by saying that to all who
looked upon her an impression as of "bottled lightning"
was irresistibly conveyed.

Bottled lightning, in truth, is one of our American
ideals, even of a young girl's character! Now it is
most ungracious, and it may seem to some persons
unpatriotic, to criticize in public the physical peculiarities of one's own people, of one's own family, so to
speak. Besides, it may be said, and said with justice,
that there are plenty of bottled-lightning temperaments
in other countries, and plenty of phlegmatic tempera-

ments here; and that, when all is said and done, the more or less of tension about which I am making such a fuss is a very small item in the sum total of a nation's life, and not worth solemn treatment at a time when agreeable rather than disagreeable things should be talked about. Well, in one sense the more or less of tension in our faces and in our unused muscles *is* a small thing: not much mechanical work is done by these contractions. But it is not always the material size of a thing that measures its importance: often it is its place and function. One of the most philosophical remarks I ever heard made was by an unlettered workman who was doing some repairs at my house many years ago. "There is very little difference between one man and another," he said, "when you go to the bottom of it. But what little there is, is very important." And the remark certainly applies to this case. The general over-contraction may be small when estimated in foot-pounds, but its importance is immense on account of its *effects on the over-contracted person's spiritual life*. This follows as a necessary consequence from the theory of our emotions to which I made reference at the beginning of this article. For by the sensations that so incessantly pour in from the over-tense excited body the over-tense and excited habit of mind is kept up; and the sultry, threatening, exhausting, thunderous inner atmosphere never quite clears away. If you never wholly give yourself up to the chair you sit in, but always keep your leg- and body-muscles half contracted for a rise; if you breathe eighteen or nineteen instead of sixteen times a minute, and never quite breathe out at that—what mental mood *can* you be in but one of inner panting and expectancy, and how can the future and its worries possibly forsake your mind? On the other hand, how can they gain admission to your mind if your brow be unruffled, your respiration calm and complete, and your muscles all relaxed?

Now what is the cause of this absence of repose, this bottled-lightning quality in us Americans? The explanation of it that is usually given is that it comes from the extreme dryness of our climate and the acrobatic performances of our thermometer, coupled with the extraordinary progressiveness of our life, the hard work, the railroad speed, the rapid success, and all the other things we know so well by heart. Well, our climate is certainly exciting, but hardly more so than that of many parts of Europe, where nevertheless no bottled-lightning girls are found. And the work done and the pace of life are as extreme in every great capital of Europe as they are here. To me both of these pretended causes are utterly insufficient to explain the facts.

To explain them, we must go not to physical geography, but to psychology and sociology. The latest chapter both in sociology and in psychology to be developed in a manner that approaches adequacy is the chapter on the imitative impulse. First Bagehot, then Tarde, then Royce and Baldwin here, have shown that invention and imitation, taken together, form, one may say, the entire warp and woof of human life, in so far as it is social. The American over-tension and jerkiness and breathlessness and intensity and agony of expression are primarily social, and only secondarily physiological, phenomena. They are *bad habits,* nothing more or less, bred of custom and example, born of the imitation of bad models and the cultivation of false personal ideals. How are idioms acquired, how do local peculiarities of phrase and accent come about? Through an accidental example set by some one, which struck the ears of others, and was quoted and copied till at last every one in the locality chimed in. Just so it is with national tricks of vocalization or intonation, with national manners, fashions of movement and gesture, and habitual expressions of face. We, here in America, through following a succession of pattern-setters whom it is now impossible to trace, and through influencing each other in a bad direction, have at last settled down collectively into what, for better or worse, is our own characteristic national type—a type with the production of which, so far as these habits go, the climate and conditions have had practically nothing at all to do.

This type, which we have thus reached by our imitativeness, we now have fixed upon us, for better or worse. Now no type can be *wholly* disadvantageous; but, so far as our type follows the bottled-lightning

fashion, it cannot be wholly good. Dr. Clouston was
certainly right in thinking that eagerness, breathlessness, and anxiety are not signs of strength: they are
signs of weakness and of bad coördination. The even
forehead, the slab-like cheek, the codfish eye, may be
less interesting for the moment; but they are more
promising signs than intense expression is of what we
may expect of their possessor in the long run. Your
dull, unhurried worker gets over a great deal of ground,
because he never goes backward or breaks down. Your
intense, convulsive worker breaks down and has bad
moods so often that you never know where he may
be when you most need his help—he may be having
one of his "bad days." We say that so many of our
fellow-countrymen collapse, and have to be sent abroad
to rest their nerves, because they work so hard. I
suspect that this is an immense mistake. I suspect
that neither the nature nor the amount of our work
is accountable for the frequency and severity of our
breakdowns, but that their cause lies rather in those
absurd feelings of hurry and having no time, in that
breathlessness and tension, that anxiety of feature and
that solicitude for results, that lack of inner harmony
and ease, in short, by which with us the work is so
apt to be accompanied, and from which a European
who should do the same work would nine times out
of ten be free. These perfectly wanton and unnecessary
tricks of inner attitude and outer manner in us, caught
from the social atmosphere, kept up by tradition, and

idealized by many as the admirable way of life, are the last straws that break the American camel's back, the final overflowers of our measure of wear and tear and fatigue.

The voice, for example, in a surprisingly large number of us has a tired and plaintive sound. Some of us are really tired (for I do not mean absolutely to deny that our climate has a tiring quality); but far more of us are not tired at all, or would not be tired at all unless we had got into a wretched trick of feeling tired, by following the prevalent habits of vocalization and expression. And if talking high and tired, and living excitedly and hurriedly, would only enable us to *do* more by the way, even while breaking us down in the end, it would be different. There would be some compensation, some excuse, for going on so. But the exact reverse is the case. It is your relaxed and easy worker, who is in no hurry, and quite thoughtless most of the while of consequences, who is your efficient worker; and tension and anxiety, and present and future, all mixed up together in our mind at once, are the surest drags upon steady progress and hindrances to our success. My colleague, Professor Münsterberg, an excellent observer, who came here recently, has written some notes on America to German papers. He says in substance that the appearance of unusual energy in America is superficial and illusory, being really due to nothing but the habits of jerkiness and bad coördination for which we have to thank the defective training of our people. I think myself that it is high time for old legends and traditional opinions to be changed: and that, if any one should begin to write about Yankee inefficiency and feebleness, and inability to do anything with time except to waste it, he would have a very pretty paradoxical little thesis to sustain, with a great many facts to quote, and a great deal of experience to appeal to in its proof.

Well, my friends, if our dear American character is weakened by all this over-tension—and I think, whatever reserves you may make, that you will agree as to the main facts—where does the remedy lie? It lies, of course, where lay the origins of the disease. If a vicious fashion and taste are to blame for the thing, the fashion and taste must be changed. And, though it is no small thing to inoculate seventy millions of people with new standards, yet, if there is to be any relief, that will have to be done. We must change ourselves from a race that admires jerk and snap for their own sakes, and looks down upon low voices and quiet ways as dull, to one that, on the contrary, has calm for its ideal, and for their own sakes loves harmony, dignity, and ease.

American Vices [1]

I

I have been growing lately to feel that a great mistake of my past life—which has been prejudicial to

[1] From a letter to Thomas W. Ward, 1868, in *The Letters of William James,* vol. i, p. 133.

my education, and by telling me which, and by making me understand it some years ago, some one might have conferred a great benefit on me—is an impatience of *results*. Inexperience of life is the cause of it, and I imagine it is generally an American characteristic. I think you suffer from it. Results should not be too voluntarily aimed at or too busily thought of. They are *sure* to float up of their own accord, from a long enough daily work at a given matter; and I think the work as a mere occupation ought to be the primary interest with us.

II

[1] The old notion that book learning can be a panacea for the vices of society lies pretty well shattered to-day. . . . vice will never cease. Every level of culture breeds its own peculiar brand of it as surely as one soil breeds sugar-cane, and another soil breeds cranberries. If we were asked that disagreeable question, "What are the bosom-vices of the level of culture which our land and day have reached?" we should be forced, I think, to give the still more disagreeable answer that they are swindling and adroitness, and the indulgence of swindling and adroitness, and cant, and sympathy with cant—natural fruits of that extraordinary idealization of "success" in the mere outward sense of "getting there," and getting there on as big a scale as we can,

[1] From "The True Harvard," in *Memories and Studies*, pp. 50-51.

which characterizes our present generation. What was Reason given to man for, some satirist has said, except to enable him to invent reasons for what he wants to do?

III

[1] *Rem acu tetegisti!* Exactly that callousness to abstract justice is *the* sinister feature and, to me as well as to you, the incomprehensible feature, of our U. S. civilization. How you hit upon it so neatly and singled it out so truly (and talked of it so tactfully!) God only knows: He evidently created you to do such things! I never heard of the MacQueen case before, but I've known of plenty of others. When the ordinary American hears of them, instead of the idealist within him beginning to "see red" with the higher indignation, instead of the spirit of English history growing alive in his breast, he begins to pooh-pooh and minimize and tone down the thing, and breed excuses from his general fund of optimism and respect for expediency. "It's probably right enough"; "Scoundrelly, as you say," but understandable, "from the point of view of parties interested"—but understandable in onlooking citizens only as a symptom of the moral flabbiness born of the exclusive worship of the bitch-goddess SUCCESS. That —with the squalid cash interpretation put on the word success—is our national disease.

[1] From a letter to H. G. Wells, 1906, in *The Letters of William James,* vol. ii, p. 260.

Our Optimism [1]

The horrors of *not* living in America, as you so well put it, are not shared by those who do live here. All that the telegraph imparts are the shocks; the "happy homes," good husbands and fathers, fine weather, honest business men, neat new houses, punctual meetings of engagements, etc., of which the country mainly consists, are never cabled over. Of course, the Saint Louis disaster is dreadful, but it will very likely end by "improving" the city. The really bad thing here is the silly wave that has gone over the public mind— protection humbug, silver, jingoism, etc. It is a case of "mob-psychology." Any country is liable to it if circumstances conspire, and our circumstances have conspired. It is very hard to get them out of the rut. It *may* take another financial crash to get them out— which, of course, will be an expensive method. It is no more foolish and considerably less damnable than the Russophobia of England, which would seem to have been responsible for the Armenian massacres. That to me is the biggest indictment "of our boasted civilization"!!

[1] From a letter to Henry James, written in 1896, in answer to one in which the novelist had said: "Life *is* heroic, however we 'fix' it! Even as I write these words the St. Louis horror bursts in upon me in the evening paper. Inconceivable—I can't try, and I *won't*. Strange how practically all one's sense of news from the U. S. here is Horrors and Catastrophes. It's a terrible country *not* to live in." Cf. *The Letters of William James*, vol. i.

Churchmen and Reformers [1]

. . . Jones spoilt my incipient nap this afternoon and I adjourned to his room to meet Smith and Brown [2] again, with another American wild-cat reformer. Jones is too many for me—I'm glad I'm to get far off. Religion is well, moral regeneration is well, so is improvement of society, so are the courage, disinterestedness, ideality of all sorts, these men show in their lives; but I verily believe that the condition of being a man of the world, a gentleman, etc., carries something with it, an atmosphere, an outlook, a play, that all these things together fail to carry, and that is worth them all. I got so suffocated with their everlasting spiritual gossip! The falsest views and tastes somehow in a man of fashion are truer than the truest in a plebeian cad. And when I told the new man there that a "materialist" would have no difficulty in keeping his place in Harvard College provided he was well-bred, I said what was really the highest test of the College excellence. I suppose he thought it sounded cynical. *Their* sphere is with the masses struggling into light, not with us at Harvard; though I'm glad I can meet them cordially for a while now and then. Thou see'est I have some "spleen" on me today. . . .

---

[1] From a letter to Mrs. James, 1882, in *The Letters of William James,* vol. i, pp. 214-215.

[2] The true names of three compatriots, who may be living, are

American Superiority [1]

The total lesson of what I have done in the past month is to make me quieter with my home-lot and readier to believe that it is one of the chosen places of the Earth. Certainly the instruction and facilities at our university are on the whole superior to anything I have seen; the rawnesses we mention with such affliction at home belong rather to the century than to us (witness the houses here); we are not a whit more isolated than they are here. In all Belgium there seem to be but two genuine philosophers; in Berlin they have little to do with each other, and I really believe that in my way I have a wider view of the field than any one I've seen (I count out, of course, my ignorance of ancient authors). We are a sound country and my opinion of our essential worth has risen and not fallen. We only lack abdominal depth of temperament and the power to sit for an hour over a single pot of beer without being able to tell at the end of it what we've been thinking about. Also to reform our altogether abominable, infamous and infra-human voices and way of talking. (What *further* fatal defects hang together with that I don't know—it seems as if it must carry something very bad with it.)

[1] From a letter to Mrs. James, 1882, in *The Letters of William James,* vol. i, p. 216.

Our Timid Idealism [1]

The whole thing *might* be Utopian; it *is* only half-Utopian. A characteristic American affair! But the half-success is great enough to make one see the great advantages that come to this country from encouraging public-spirited millionaires to indulge their freaks, however eccentric.

Professorial English [2]

I am pleased, but also amused, by what you say of Woodbridge's Journal: "la palme est maintenant à l'Amérique." It is true that a lot of youngsters in that Journal are doing some real thinking, but of all the *bad writing* that the world has seen, I think that our American writing is getting to be the worst. X——'s ideas have unchained formlessness of expression that beats the bad writing of the Hegelian epoch in Germany. I can hardly believe you sincere when you praise that journal as you do. . . .

On the Fear of Catholicism [3]

I doubt whether the earth supports a more genuine enemy of all that the Catholic Church *inwardly* stands

[1] From a letter to Theodore Flournoy, describing Stanford University, where James was lecturing in 1906, in *The Letters of William James*, vol. ii, p. 244.

[2] From the same letter.

[3] From a letter to Mrs. Henry Whitman, in *The Letters of William James*, vol. i, pp. 296-297.

for than I do—*écrasez l'infâme* is the only way I can feel about it. But the concrete Catholics, including the common priests in this country, are an entirely different matter. Their wish to educate their own, and to do what proselytizing they can, is natural enough; so is their wish to get state money. "Destroying American institutions" is a widely different matter; and instead of this vague phrase, I should like to hear one specification laid down of an "institution" which they are now threatening. The only way to resist them is absolute firmness and impartiality, and continuing in the line which you point out, bless your 'art! Down with demagogism! . . .

Against the Mania for Bigness [1]

As for me, my bed is made: I am against bigness and greatness in all their forms, and with the invisible molecular moral forces that work from individual to individual, stealing in through the crannies of the world like so many soft rootlets, or like the capillary oozing of water, and yet rending the hardest monuments of man's pride, if you give them time. The bigger the unit you deal with, the hollower, the more brutal, the more mendacious is the life displayed. So I am against all big organizations as such, national ones first and foremost; against all big successes and big results; and

[1] From a letter to Mrs. Henry Whitman, in the course of comment on G. E. Woodberry's *The Heart of Man,* especially the paper on "Democracy," in *The Letters of William James,* vol. ii, p. 90.

in favor of the eternal forces of truth which always work in the individual and immediately unsuccessful way, under-dogs always, till history comes, after they are long dead, and puts them on the top.

American Journalism [1]

. . . Sooth to say the "———" and the "———," the reception of whose "weeklies" has become one of the solaces of my life, do make a first-rate showing for her (America's) civilization. One can't just say what "tone" consists in, but these papers hold their own excellently in comparison with the English papers. There is far less alertness of mind in the general make-up of the latter; and the "respectability" of the English editorial columns, though it shows a correcter literary drill, is apt to be due to a remorseless longitude of commonplace conventionality that makes them deadly dull. (The "Spectator" appears to be the only paper with a nervous system, in England—that of a *carnassier* at present!) The English people seem to have positively a passionate hunger for this mass of prosy stupidity, never less than a column and a quarter long. The Continental papers of course are "nowhere." As for our yellow papers—every country has its criminal classes, and with us and in France, they have simply got into journalism as part of their professional evolution, and they must be got out. Mr. Bosanquet

[1] From a letter to Miss Frances R. Morse, 1900, in *The Letters of William James,* vol. ii, pp. 126-127.

somewhere says that so far from the "dark ages" being over, we are just at the beginning of a new dark-age period. He means that ignorance and unculture, which then were merely brutal, are now articulate and possessed of a literary voice, and the fight is transferred from fields and castles and town walls to "organs of publicity"; but it is the same fight, of reason and goodness against stupidity and passions; and it must be fought through to the same kind of success. But it means the reëducating of perhaps twenty more generations; and by that time some altogether new kind of institutional opportunity for the Devil will have been evolved.

The American Religion [1]

Our great western republic had from its origin been a singular anomaly. A land of freedom, boastfully so-called, with human slavery enthroned at the heart of it, and at last dictating terms of unconditional surrender to every other organ of its life, what was it but a thing of falsehood and horrible self-contradiction? For three-quarters of a century it had nevertheless endured, kept together by policy, compromise, and concession. But at the last that republic was torn in two; and truth was to be possible under the flag. Truth, thank God, truth! even though for the moment it must be truth written in hell-fire.

And this, fellow-citizens, is why, after the great gen-

[1] From "Robert Gould Shaw." in *Memories and Studies*, pp. 42-43.

erals have had their monuments, and long after the abstract soldier's-monuments have been reared on every village green, we have chosen to take Robert Shaw and his regiment as the subjects of the first soldier's-monument to be raised to a particular set of comparatively undistinguished men. The very lack of external complication in the history of these soldiers is what makes them represent with such typical purity the profounder meaning of the Union cause.

Our nation had been founded in what we may call our American religion, baptized and reared in the faith that a man requires no master to take care of him, and that common people can work out their salvation well enough together if left free to try. But the founders had not dared to touch the great intractable exception; and slavery had wrought until at last the only alternative for the nation was to fight or die. What Shaw and his comrades stand for and show us is that in such an emergency Americans of all complexions and conditions can go forth like brothers, and meet death cheerfully if need be, in order that this religion of our native land shall not become a failure on earth.

The Moral Legacy of the Civil War [1]

The deadliest enemies of nations are not their foreign foes; they always dwell within their borders. And from these internal enemies civilization is always in need of being saved. The nation blest above all nations

[1] From "Robert Gould Shaw," in *Memories and Studies*, pp. 58-59.

is she in whom the civic genius of the people does the saving day by day, by acts without external picturesqueness; by speaking, writing, voting reasonably; by smiting corruption swiftly; by good temper between parties; by the people knowing true men when they see them, and preferring them as leaders to rabid partisans or empty quacks. Such nations have no need of wars to save them. Their accounts with righteousness are always even; and God's judgments do not have to overtake them fitfully in bloody spasms and convulsions of the race.

The lesson that our war ought most of all to teach us is the lesson that evils must be checked in time, before they grow so great. The Almighty cannot love such long-postponed accounts, or such tremendous settlements. And surely He hates all settlements that do such quantities of incidental devils' work. Our present situation, with its rancors and delusions, what is it but the direct outcome of the added powers of government, the corruptions and inflations of the war? Every war leaves such miserable legacies, fatal seeds of future war and revolution, unless the civic virtues of the people save the State in time.

What Will Save Democracy on Trial [1]

Democracy is still upon its trial. The civic genius of our people is its only bulwark, and neither laws nor monuments, neither battleships nor public libraries,

[1] From "Robert Gould Shaw," in *Memories and Studies*, pp. 60-61.

nor great newspapers nor booming stocks; neither mechanical invention nor political adroitness, nor churches nor universities nor civil service examinations can save us from degeneration if the inner mystery be lost. That mystery, at once the secret and the glory of our English-speaking race, consists in nothing but two common habits, two inveterate habits carried into public life—habits so homely that they lend themselves to no rhetorical expression, yet habits more precious, perhaps, than any that the human race has gained. They can never be too often pointed out or praised. One of them is the habit of trained and disciplined good temper towards the opposite party when it fairly wins its innings. It was by breaking away from this habit that the Slave States nearly wrecked our Nation. The other is that of fierce and merciless resentment toward every man or set of men who break the public peace. By holding to this habit the free States saved her life.

CHAPTER X

DEATH AND THE VALUE OF LIFE

At the Parting of the Generations [1]

BOLTON ST., LONDON, *Dec.* 14, 1882.

DARLING OLD FATHER—Two letters, one from my Alice last night, and one from Aunt Kate to Harry just now, have somewhat dispelled the mystery in which the telegrams left your condition; and although their news is several days earlier than the telegrams, I am free to suppose that the latter report only an aggravation of the symptoms the letters describe. It is far more agreeable to think of this than of some dreadful unknown and sudden malady.

We have been so long accustomed to the hypothesis of your being taken away from us, especially during the past ten months, that the thought that this may be your last illness conveys no very sudden shock. You are old enough, you've given your message to the world in many ways and will not be forgotten; you are here left alone, and on the other side, let us hope and pray, dear, dear old Mother is waiting for you to join her. If you go, it will not be an inharmonious thing. Only,

[1] From a letter to his father, in *The Letters of William James*, vol. i, pp. 218-220.

if you are still in possession of your normal consciousness, I should like to see you once again before we part.
I stayed here only in obedience to the last telegram, and
am waiting now for Harry—who knows the exact state
of my mind, and who will know yours—to telegraph
again what I shall do. Meanwhile, my blessed old
Father, I scribble this line (which may reach you
though I should come too late), just to tell you how full
of the tenderest memories and feelings about you my
heart has for the last few days been filled. In that mysterious gulf of the past into which the present soon
will fall and go back and back, yours is still for me the
central figure. All my intellectual life I derive from
you; and though we have often seemed at odds in the
expression thereof, I'm sure there's a harmony somewhere, and that our strivings will combine. What my
debt to you is goes beyond all my power of estimating
—so early, so penetrating and so constant has been the
influence. You need be in no anxiety about your literary
remains. I will see them well taken care of, and that
your words shall not suffer for being concealed. At
Paris I heard that Milsand, whose name you may remember in the "Revue des Deux Mondes" and elsewhere, was an admirer of the "Secret of Swedenborg,"
and Hodgson told me your last book had deeply impressed him. So will it be; especially, I think, if a
collection of *extracts* from your various writings were
published, after the manner of the extracts from Carlyle, Ruskin, & Co. I have long thought such a volume

would be the best monument to you.—As for us; we shall live on each in his way—feeling somewhat unprotected, old as we are, for the absence of the parental bosoms as a refuge, but holding fast together in that common sacred memory. We will stand by each other and by Alice, try to transmit the torch in our offspring as you did in us, and when the time comes for being gathered in, I pray we may, if not all, some at least, be as ripe as you. As for myself, I know what trouble I've given you at various times through my peculiarities; and as my own boys grow up, I shall learn more and more of the kind of trial you had to overcome in superintending the development of a creature different from yourself, for whom you felt responsible. I say this merely to show how my *sympathy* with you is likely to grow much livelier, rather than to fade—and not for the sake of regrets.—As for the other side, and Mother, and our all possibly meeting, I *can't* say anything. More than ever at this moment do I feel that if that *were* true, all would be solved and justified. And it comes strangely over me in bidding you good-bye how a life is but a day and expresses mainly but a single note. It is so much like the act of bidding an ordinary good-night. Good-night, my sacred old Father! If I don't see you again—Farewell! a blessed farewell! Your

WILLIAM.

Release from Living [1]

CHOCORUA, N. H., *July* 6, 1891.

DEAREST ALICE— . . . Of course [this medical verdict on your case may mean] as all men know, a finite length of days; and then, good-bye to neurasthenia and neuralgia and headache, and weariness and palpitation and disgust all at one stroke—I should think you would be reconciled to the prospect with all its pluses and minuses! I know you've never cared for life, and to me, now at the age of nearly fifty, life and death seem singularly close together in all of us—and life a mere farce of frustration in all, so far as the realization of the innermost ideals go to which we are made respectively capable of feeling an affinity and responding. Your frustrations are only rather more flagrant than the rule; and you've been saved many forms of self-dissatisfaction and misery which appertain to such a multiplication of responsible relations to different people as I, for instance, have got into. Your fortitude, good spirits and unsentimentality have been simply unexampled in the midst of your physical woes; and when you're relieved from your post, just *that* bright note will remain behind together with the inscrutable and mysterious character of the doom of nervous weakness which has chained you down for all these years. As for that, there's more in it than has ever been told to so-called science. These inhibitions, these split-up selves,

[1] From a letter to his sister, in *The Letters of William James*, vol. i, pp. 309-311.

all these new facts that are gradually coming to light about our organization, these enlargements of the self in trance, etc., are bringing me to turn for light in the direction of all sorts of despised spiritualistic and unscientific ideas. Father would find in me today a much more receptive listener—all *that* philosophy has got to be brought in. And what a queer contradiction comes to the ordinary scientific argument against immortality (based on body being mind's condition and mind going *out* when body is gone), when one must believe (as now, in these neurotic cases) that some infernality in the body *prevents* really existing parts of the mind from coming to their effective rights at all, suppresses them, and blots them out from participation in this world's experiences, although they are *there* all the time. When that which is *you* passes out of the body, I am sure that there will be an explosion of liberated force and life till then eclipsed and kept down. I can hardly imagine *your* transition without a great oscillation of both "worlds" as they regain their new equilibrium after the change! Every one will feel the shock, but you yourself will be more surprised than anybody else.

It may seem odd for me to talk to you in this cool way about your end; but, my dear little sister, if one has things present to one's mind, and I know they are present enough to *your* mind, why not speak them out? I am sure you appreciate that best. How many times I have thought, in the past year, when my days were so full of strong and varied impression and activities, of the long unchanging hours in bed which those days stood for with you, and wondered how you bore the slow-paced monotony at all, as you did! You can't tell how I've pitied you. But you *shall* come to your rights erelong. Meanwhile take things gently. Look for the little good in each day as if life were to last a hundred years. Above all things, save yourself from bodily pain, if it can be done. You've had too much of that. Take all the morphia (or other forms of opium if that disagrees) you want, and don't be afraid of becoming an opium-drunkard. What was opium created for except for such times as this? Beg the good Katharine (to whom *our* debt can never be extinguished) to write me a line every week, just to keep the currents flowing, and so farewell until I write again.

Your ever loving,

W. J.

Suffering and the Zest for Life [1]

. . . It is, indeed, a remarkable fact that suffering and hardships do not, as a rule, abate the love of life; they seem, on the contrary, usually to give it a keener zest. The sovereign source of melancholy is repletion. Need and struggle are what excite and inspire us; our hour of triumph is what brings the void. Not the Jews of the captivity, but those of the days of Solomon's glory are those from whom the pessimistic utterances in

[1] From "Is Life Worth Living?" in *The Will to Believe*, pp. 47-50.

our Bible come. Germany, when she lay trampled beneath the hoofs of Bonaparte's troopers, produced perhaps the most optimistic and idealistic literature that
the world has seen; and not till the French "milliards"
were distributed after 1871 did pessimism overrun the
country in the shape in which we see it there today.
The history of our own race is one long commentary
on the cheerfulness that comes with fighting ills.

Life is worth living, no matter what it bring, if only
such combats may be carried to successful terminations
and one's heel set on the tyrant's throat. To the suicide, then, in his supposed world of multifarious and
immoral nature, you can appeal—and appeal in the
name of the very evils that make his heart sick there—
to wait and see *his* part of the battle out. And the
consent to live on, which you ask of him under these
circumstances, is not the sophistical "resignation"
which devotees of cowering religions preach: it is not
resignation in the sense of licking a despotic Deity's
hand. It is, on the contrary, a resignation based on
manliness and pride.

What Survives the Dead [1]

The pathos of death is this, that when the days of
one's life are ended, those days that were so crowded

---

[1] From "The Address at the Emerson Centenary in Concord," in
Memories and Studies, p. 19. An address delivered at the Centenary
of the Birth of Ralph Waldo Emerson in Concord, May 25, 1903
and printed in the published proceedings of that meeting.

with business and felt so heavy in their passing, what remains of one in memory should usually be so slight a thing. The phantom of an attitude, the echo of a certain mode of thought, a few pages of print, some invention, or some victory we gained in a brief critical hour, are all that can survive the best of us. It is as if the whole of a man's significance had now shrunk into the phantom of an attitude, into a mere musical note or phrase suggestive of his singularity—happy are those whose singularity gives a note so clear as to be victorious over the inevitable pity of such a diminution and abridgment.

Cosmic Processes and Human Values

BAD-NAUHEIM, *June* 17, 1910.

DEAR HENRY ADAMS,[1]—I have been so "slim" since seeing you, and the baths here have so weakened my brain, that I have been unable to do any reading except trash, and have only just got round to finishing your "letter," which I had but half-read when I was with you at Paris. To tell the truth, it doesn't impress me at all, save by its wit and erudition; and I ask you whether an old man soon about to meet his Maker can hope to save himself from the consequences of his life by pointing to the wit and learning he has shown in treating a tragic subject. No, sir, you can't do it,

[1] To Henry Adams, on his "Letter to American Teachers," originally printed for private circulation, but recently published, with a preface by Mr. Brooks Adams, under the title: "The Degradation of Democratic Dogma"; in *The Letters of William James*, vol. ii, pp. 344-347

can't impress God in that way. So far as our scientific
conceptions go, it may be admitted that your Creator
(and mine) started the universe with a certain amount
of "energy" latent in it, and decreed that everything
that should happen thereafter should be a result of
parts of that energy falling to lower levels; raising
other parts higher, to be sure, in so doing, but never
in equivalent amount, owing to the constant radiation
of unrecoverable warmth incidental to the process.
It is customary for gentlemen to pretend to believe
one another, and until some one hits upon a newer
revolutionary concept (which may be tomorrow) all
physicists must play the game by holding religiously
to the above doctrine. It involves of course the ultimate cessation of all perceptible happening, and the
end of human history. With this general conception
as *surrounding* everything you say in your "letter,"
no one can find any fault—in the present stage of
scientific conventions and fashions. But I protest
against your interpretation of some of the specifications
of the great statistical drift downwards of the original
high-level energy. If, instead of criticizing what you
seem to me to say, I express my own interpretation
dogmatically, and leave you to make the comparison,
it will doubtless conduce to brevity and economize
recrimination.

To begin with, the *amount* of cosmic energy it costs
to buy a certain distribution of fact which humanly
we regard as precious, seems to me to be an altogether

secondary matter as regards the question of history and progress. Certain arrangements of matter *on the same energy-level* are, from the point of view of man's appreciation, superior, while others are inferior. Physically a dinosaur's brain may show as much intensity of energy-exchange as a man's, but it can do infinitely fewer things, because as a force of detent it can only unlock the dinosaur's muscles, while the man's brain, by unlocking far feebler muscles, indirectly can by their means issue proclamations, write books, describe Chartres Cathedral, etc., and guide the energies of the shrinking sun into channels which never would have been entered otherwise—in short, *make* history. Therefore the man's brain and muscles are, from the point of view of the historian, the more important place of energy-exchange, small as this may be when measured in absolute physical units.

The "second law" is wholly irrelevant to "history"—save that it sets a terminus—for history is the course of things before that terminus, and all that the second law says is that, whatever the history, it must invest itself between that initial maximum and that terminal minimum of difference in energy-level. As the great irrigation-reservoir empties itself, the whole question for us is that of the distribution of its effects, of *which* rills to guide it into; and the size of the rills has nothing to do with their significance. Human cerebration is the most important rill we know of, and both the "capacity" and the "intensity" factor thereof may be treated as infinitesimal. Yet the filling of such rills would be cheaply bought by the waste of whole sums spent in getting a little of the down-flowing torrent to enter them. Just so of human institutions—their value has in strict theory nothing whatever to do with their energy-budget—being wholly a question of the form the energy flows through. Though the *ultimate* state of the universe may be its vital and psychical extinction, there is nothing in physics to interfere with the hypothesis that the penultimate state might be the millennium—in other words a state in which a minimum of difference of energy-level might have its exchanges so skillfully *canalisés* that a maximum of happy and virtuous consciousness would be the only result. In short, the last expiring pulsation of the universe's life might be, "I am so happy and perfect that I can stand it no longer." You don't believe this and I don't say I do. But I can find nothing in "Energetik" to conflict with its possibility. You seem to me not to discriminate, but to treat quantity and distribution of energy as if they formed one question.

There! that's pretty good for a brain after 18 Nauheim baths—so I won't write another line, nor ask you to reply to me. In case you can't help doing so, however, I will gratify you now by saying that I probably won't jaw back. It was pleasant at Paris to hear your identically unchanged and "undegraded" voice after so many years of loss of solar energy. Yours ever truly,   WM. JAMES.

[Post-card]

NAUHEIM, *June* 19, 1910.

P. S. Another illustration of my meaning: The clock of the universe is running down, and by so doing makes the hands move. The energy absorbed by the hands and the *mechanical* work they do is the same day after day, no matter how far the weights have descended from the position they were originally wound up to. The *history* which the hands perpetrate has nothing to do with the *quantity* of this work, but follows the *significance* of the figures which they cover on the dial. If they move from O to XII, there is "progress," if from XII to O, there is "decay," etc., etc.

W. J.

To Henry Adams.

[Post-card]

CONSTANCE, *June* 26 [1910].

Yours of the 20th, just arriving, pleases me by its docility of spirit and passive subjection to philosophic opinion. Never, never pretend to an opinion of your own! that way lies every annoyance and madness! You tempt me to offer you another illustration—that of the *hydraulic ram* (thrown back to me in an exam. as a "hydraulic goat" by an insufficiently intelligent student). Let this arrangement of metal, placed in the course of a brook, symbolize the machine of human life. It works, clap, clap, clap, day and night, so long as the brook runs *at all,* and no matter how full the brook (which symbolizes the descending cosmic energy) may be, it works always to the same effect, of raising so many kilogrammeters of water. What the *value* of this work as history may be, depends on the uses to which the water is put in the house which the ram serves.

W. J.

Why Free Will

[1] . . . The distinctions between *vis impressa* and *vis insita,* and compulsion and "reaction" *mean* nothing in a monistic world; and any world is a monism in which the parts to come are, as they are in your world, absolutely involved and presupposed in the parts that are already given. Were such a monism a palpable optimism, no man would be so foolish as to care whether it was predetermined or not, or to ask whether he was or was not what you call a "real agent." He would acquiesce in the flow and drift of things, of which he found himself a part, and rejoice that it was such a whole. The question of free will owes its entire being to a difficulty you disdain to notice, namely that we *cannot* rejoice in such a whole, for it is *not* a palpable optimism, and yet, if it be predetermined, we *must treat* it as a whole. Indeterminism is the only way to *break* the world into good parts and into bad,

[1] From a letter to Shadworth Hodgson, in *The Letters of William James,* vol. i, pp. 245-247.

and to stand by the former as against the latter.

I can understand the determinism of the mere mechanical intellect which will not hear of a moral dimension to existence. I can understand that of mystical monism shutting its eyes on the concretes of life, for the sake of its abstract rapture. I can understand that of mental defeat and despair saying, "it's all a muddle, and here I go, along with it." I can *not* understand a determinism like yours, which rejoices in clearness and distinctions, and which is at the same time alive to moral ones—unless it be that the latter are purely speculative for it, and have little to do with its real feeling of the way life *is* made up.

For life *is* evil. Two souls are in my breast; I see the better, and in the very act of seeing it I do the worse. To say that the molecules of the nebula implied this and *shall have implied it* to all eternity, so often as it recurs, is to condemn me to that "dilemma" of pessimism or subjectivism of which I once wrote, and which seems to have so little urgency to you, and to which all talk about abstractions erected into entities; and compulsion *vs.* "freedom" are simply irrelevant. What living man cares for such niceties, when the real problem stares him in the face of how practically to meet a world foredone, with no possibilities left in it?

What a mockery then seems your distinction between determination and compulsion, between passivity and an "activity" every minutest feature of which is

preappointed, both as to its *whatness* and as to its *thatness,* by what went before! What an insignificant difference then the difference between "impediments from
within" and "impediments from without"!—between
being fated to do the thing *willingly* or not! The point
is not as to how it is done, but as to its being done
at all. It seems a wrong complement to the rest of
life, which rest of life (according to your precious
"free-will determinism," as to any other fatalism),
whilst shrieking aloud at its *whatness,* nevertheless
exacts rigorously its *thatness* then and there. Is that
a reasonable world from the moral point of view? And
is it made more reasonable by the fact that when I
brought about the *thatness* of the evil *whatness* decreed
to come by the *thatness* of all else beside, I did so con-
sentingly and aware of no "impediments outside of my
own nature"? With what can I *side* in such a world
as this? this monstrous indifferentism which brings forth
everything *eodem jure?* Our nature demands something
objective to take sides with. If the world is a Unit
of this sort there *are* no sides—there's the moral rub!
And you don't see it!

Ah, Hodgson! Hodgson *mio!* from whom I hoped so
much! Most spirited, most clean, most thoroughbred
of philosophers! *Perchè di tanto inganni i figli tuoi?* [1]
If you want to reconcile us rationally to Determinism,
write a Theodicy, reconcile us to *Evil,* but don't talk

---

[1] "Why so heartlessly deceive your sons?"
    LEOPARDI, *To Sylvia.*

of the distinction between impediments from within and without when the within and the without of which you speak are both within that *Whole* which is the only real agent in your philosophy. There is no such superstition as the idolatry of the *Whole*.

[1] What I care for is that my moral reactions should find a real outward application. All those who, like you, hold that the world is a system of "uniform law" which repels all variation as so much "chaos," oblige, it seems to me, the world to be judged integrally. Now the only *integral* emotional reaction which can be called forth by such a world as this of our experience, is that of dramatic or melodramatic interest—romanticism—which *is* the emotional reaction upon it of all intellects who are neither religious nor moral. The moment you seek to go deeper, you must break the world into parts, the parts that seem good and those that seem bad. Whatever Indian mystics may say about overcoming the bonds of good and evil, for *us* there is no higher synthesis in which their contradiction merges, no *one* way of judging that world which holds them both. Either close your eyes and adopt an optimism or a pessimism equally daft; or exclude moral categories altogether from a place in the world's definition, which leaves the world *unheimlich*, reptilian, and foreign to man; or else, sticking to it that the

[1] From a letter to Shadworth Hodgson, in *The Letters of William James*, vol. i, pp. 256-257.

moral judgment *is* applicable, give up the hope of applying it to the *whole*, and admit that, whilst some parts are good, others are bad, and being bad, *ought* not to have been, "argal," possibly *might* not have been. In short, be an indeterminist on moral grounds with which the differences between compulsory or sponta neous uniformity and perceptive and conceptive order have absolutely nothing to do.

Effort and Worth [1]

. . . If the "searching of our heart and reins" be the purpose of this human drama, then what is sought seems to be what effort we can make. He who can make none is but a shadow; he who can make much is a hero. The huge world that girdles us about puts all sorts of questions to us, and tests us in all sorts of ways. Some of the tests we meet by actions that are easy, and some of the questions we answer in articulately formulated words. But the deepest question that is ever asked admits of no reply but the dumb turning of the will and tightening of our heartstrings as we say, "*Yes, I will even have it so!*" When a dreadful object is presented, or when life as a whole turns up its dark abysses to our view, then the worthless ones among us lose their hold on the situation altogether, and either escape from its difficulties by averting their attention, or if they cannot do that, collapse into yielding masses of plaintiveness and fear.

[1] From "The Question of Free Will," in *The Principles of Psychology*, vol. ii, chap. xxvi, on Will, pp. 578-579.

The effort required for facing and consenting to such objects is beyond their power to make. But the heroic mind does differently. To it, too, the objects are sinister and dreadful, unwelcome, incompatible with wished-for things. But it can face them if necessary, without for that losing its hold upon the rest of life. The world thus finds in the heroic man its worthy match and mate; and the effort which he is able to put forth to hold himself erect and keep his heart unshaken is the direct measure of his worth and function in the game of human life. He can *stand* this Universe. He can meet it and keep up his faith in it in presence of those same features which lay his weaker brethren low. He can still find a zest in it, not by "ostrich-like forgetfulness," but by pure inward willingness to face the world with those deterrent objects there. And hereby he becomes one of the masters and the lords of life. He must be counted with henceforth; he forms a part of human destiny. Neither in the theoretic nor in the practical sphere do we care for, or go for help to, those who have no head for risks, or sense for living on the perilous edge. Our religious life lies more, our practical life lies less, than it used to, on the perilous edge. But just as our courage is so often a reflex of another's courage, so our faith is apt to be, as Max Müller somewhere says, a faith in someone else's faith. We draw new life from the heroic example. The prophet has drunk more deeply than any one of the cup of bitterness, but his counte-

nance is so unshaken and he speaks such mighty words
of cheer that his will becomes our will, and our life is
kindled at his own.

Thus not only our morality but our religion, so far as
the latter is deliberate, depend on the effort which
we can make. *"Will you or won't you have it so?"*
is the most probing question we are ever asked; we
are asked it every hour of the day, and about the
largest as well as the smallest, the most theoretical as
well as the most practical, things. We answer by *con-
sents or non-consents* and not by words. What wonder
that these dumb responses should seem our deepest
organs of communication with the nature of things!
What wonder if the effort demanded by them be the
measure of our worth as men! What wonder if the
amount which we accord of it be the one strictly un-
derived and original contribution which we make to the
world!

Facts and Values [1]

Some years ago, while journeying in the mountains
of North Carolina, I passed by a large number of
"coves," as they call them there, or heads of small
valleys between the hills, which had been newly cleared
and planted. The impression on my mind was one of
unmitigated squalor. The settler had in every case cut
down the more manageable trees, and left their charred
stumps standing. The larger trees he had girdled and

[1] From "On a Certain Blindness in Human Beings," in *Talks to
Teachers,* etc., pp. 231-234; 264-265.

killed, in order that their foliage should not cast a shade. He had then built a log cabin, plastering its chinks with clay, and had set up a tall zigzag rail fence around the scene of his havoc, to keep the pigs and cattle out. Finally, he had irregularly planted the intervals between the stumps and trees with Indian corn, which grew among the chips; and there he dwelt with his wife and babes—an axe, a gun, a few utensils, and some pigs and chickens feeding in the woods, being the sum total of his possessions.

The forest had been destroyed; and what had "improved" it out of existence was hideous, a sort of ulcer, without a single element of artificial grace to make up for the loss of Nature's beauty. Ugly, indeed, seemed the life of the squatter, scudding, as the sailors say, under bare poles, beginning again away back where our first ancestors started, and by hardly a single item the better off for all the achievements of the intervening generations.

Talk about going back to nature! I said to myself, oppressed by the dreariness, as I drove by. Talk of a country life for one's old age and for one's children! Never thus, with nothing but the bare ground and one's bare hands to fight the battle! Never, without the best spoils of culture woven in! The beauties and commodities gained by the centuries are sacred. They are our heritage and birthright. No modern person ought to be willing to live a day in such a state of rudimentariness and denudation.

Then I said to the mountaineer who was driving me, "What sort of people are they who have to make these new clearings?" "All of us," he replied. "Why, we ain't happy here, unless we are getting one of these coves under cultivation." I instantly felt that I had been losing the whole inward significance of the situation. Because to me the clearings spoke of naught but denudation, I thought that to those whose sturdy arms and obedient axes had made them they could tell no other story. But, when *they* looked on the hideous stumps, what they thought of was personal victory. The chips, the girdled trees, and the vile split rails spoke of honest sweat, persistent toil and final reward. The cabin was a warrant of safety for self and wife and babes. In short, the clearing, which to me was a mere ugly picture on the retina, was to them a symbol redolent with moral memories and sang a very pæan of duty, struggle, and success.

I had been as blind to the peculiar ideality of their conditions as they certainly would also have been to the ideality of mine, had they had a peep at my strange indoor academic ways of life at Cambridge.

Wherever a process of life communicates an eagerness to him who lives it, there the life becomes genuinely significant. Sometimes the eagerness is more knit up with the motor activities, sometimes with the perceptions, sometimes with the imagination, sometimes with reflective thought. But, wherever it is found, there is the zest, the tingle, the excitement of reality; and there *is* "importance" in the only real and positive sense in which importance ever anywhere can be. . . .

And now what is the result of all these considerations and quotations? It is negative in one sense, but positive in another. It absolutely forbids us to be forward in pronouncing on the meaninglessness of forms of existence other than our own; and it commands us to tolerate, respect, and indulge those whom we see harmlessly interested and happy in their own ways, however unintelligible these may be to us. Hands off: neither the whole of truth nor the whole of good is revealed to any single observer, although each observer gains a partial superiority of insight from the peculiar position in which he stands. Even prisons and sick-rooms have their special revelations. It is enough to ask of each of us that he should be faithful to his own opportunities and make the most of his own blessings, without presuming to regulate the rest of the vast field.

The Sacredness of Individuality

[1] I wish I were able to make the second [Essay in this volume], "On a Certain Blindness in Human Beings," more impressive. It is more than the mere piece of sentimentalism which it may seem to some readers. It connects itself with a definite view of the world and of our moral relations to the same. . . . I mean the pluralistic or individual-

[1] From the Preface to *Talks to Teachers on Psychology*, pp. v-vi.

istic philosophy. According to that philosophy, the truth is too great for any one actual mind, even though that mind be dubbed "the Absolute," to know the whole of it. The facts and worths of life need many cognizers to take them in. There is no point of view absolutely public and universal. Private and uncommunicable perceptions always remain over, and the worst of it is that those who look for them from the outside never know *where*.

The practical consequence of such a philosophy is the well-known democratic respect for the sacredness of individuality—is, at any rate, the outward tolerance of whatever is not itself intolerant. These phrases are so familiar that they sound now rather dead in our ears. Once they had a passionate inner meaning. Such a passionate inner meaning they may easily acquire again if the pretension of our nation to inflict its own inner ideals and institutions *vi et armis* upon Orientals should meet with a resistance as obdurate as so far it has been gallant and spirited. Religiously and philosophically, our ancient national doctrine of live and let live may prove to have a far deeper meaning than our people now seem to imagine it to possess.

What Makes a Life Significant [1]

In my previous talk, "On a Certain Blindness," I tried to make you feel how soaked and shot-through life is with values and meanings which we fail to realize be-

[1] From *Talks to Teachers on Psychology*, etc., pp. 265-301.

cause of our external and insensible point of view. The meanings are there for the others, but they are not there for us. There lies more than a mere interest of curious speculation in understanding this. It has the most tremendous practical importance. I wish that I could convince you of it as I feel it myself. It is the basis of all our tolerance, social, religious, and political. The forgetting of it lies at the root of every stupid and sanguinary mistake that rulers over subject-peoples make. The first thing to learn in intercourse with others is non-interference with their own peculiar ways of being happy, provided those ways do not assume to interfere by violence with ours. No one has insight into all the ideals. No one should presume to judge them off-hand. The pretension to dogmatize about them in each other is the root of most human injustices and cruelties, and the trait in human character most likely to make the angels weep.

Every Jack sees in his own particular Jill charms and perfections to the enchantment of which we stolid onlookers arc stone-cold. And which has the superior view of the absolute truth, he or we? Which has the more vital insight into the nature of Jill's existence, as a fact? Is he in excess, being in this matter a maniac? or are we in defect, being victims of a pathological anæsthesia as regards Jill's magical importance? Surely the latter; surely to Jack are the profounder truths revealed; surely poor Jill's palpitating little life-throbs *are* among the wonders of creation, *are* worthy of this sympathetic interest; and it is to our shame that the rest of us cannot feel like Jack. For Jack realizes Jill concretely, and we do not. He struggles toward a union with her inner life, divining her feelings, anticipating her desires, understanding her limits as manfully as he can, and yet inadequately, too; for he is also afflicted with some blindness, even here. Whilst we, dead clods that we are, do not even seek after these things, but are contented that that portion of eternal fact named Jill should be for us as if it were not. Jill, who knows her inner life, knows that Jack's way of taking it— so importantly—is the true and serious way; and she responds to the truth in him by taking him truly and seriously, too. May the ancient blindness never wrap its clouds about either of them again! Where would any of *us* be, were there no one willing to know us as we really are or ready to repay us for *our* insight by making recognizant return? We ought, all of us, to realize each other in this intense, pathetic, and important way.

If you say that this is absurd, and that we cannot be in love with every one at once, I merely point out to you that, as a matter of fact, certain persons do exist with an enormous capacity for friendship and for taking delight in other people's lives; and that such persons know more of truth than if their hearts were not so big. The vice of ordinary Jack and Jill affection is not its intensity, but its exclusions and its jealousies. Leave those out, and you see that the ideal I am holding un before you, however impracticable today, yet contains nothing intrinsically absurd.

We have unquestionably a great cloud-bank of ancestral blindness weighing down upon us, only transiently riven here and there by fitful revelations of the truth. It is vain to hope for this state of things to alter much. Our inner secrets must remain for the most part impenetrable by others, for beings as essentially practical as we are are necessarily short of sight. But, if we cannot gain much positive insight into one another, cannot we at least use our sense of our own blindness to make us more cautious in going over the dark places? Cannot we escape some of those hideous ancestral intolerances and cruelties, and positive reversals of the truth?

For the remainder of this hour I invite you to seek with me some principle to make our tolerance less chaotic. And, as I began my previous lecture by a personal reminiscence, I am going to ask your indulgence for a similar bit of egotism now.

A few summers ago I spent a happy week at the famous Assembly Grounds on the borders of Chautauqua Lake. The moment one treads that sacred enclosure, one feels one's self in an atmosphere of success. Sobriety and industry, intelligence and goodness, orderliness and ideality, prosperity and cheerfulness, pervade the air. It is a serious and studious picnic on a gigantic scale. Here you have a town of many thousands of inhabitants, beautifully laid out in the forest and drained, and equipped with means for satisfying all the necessary lower and most of the superfluous higher wants of man. You have a first-class college in full blast. You have magnificent music—a chorus of seven hundred voices, with possibly the most perfect open-air auditorium in the world. You have every sort of athletic exercise from sailing, rowing, swimming, bicycling, to the ball-field and the more artificial doings which the gymnasium affords. You have kindergartens and model secondary schools. You have general religious services and special club-houses for the several sects. You have perpetually running soda-water fountains, and daily popular lectures by distinguished men. You have the best of company, and yet no effort. You have no zymotic diseases, no poverty, no drunkenness, no crime, no police. You have culture, you have kindness, you have cheapness, you have equality, you have the best fruits of what mankind has fought and bled and striven for under the name of civilization for centuries. You have, in short, a foretaste of what human society might be, were it all in the light, with no suffering and no dark corners.

I went in curiosity for a day. I stayed for a week, held spell-bound by the charm and ease of everything, by the middle-class paradise, without a sin, without a victim, without a blot, without a tear.

And yet what was my own astonishment, on emerging into the dark and wicked world again, to catch myself quite unexpectedly and involuntarily saying:

"Ouf! what a relief! Now for something primordial and savage, even though it were as bad as an Armenian massacre, to set the balance straight again. This order is too tame, this culture too second-rate, this goodness too uninspiring. This human drama without a villain or a pang; this community so refined that ice-cream soda-water is the utmost offering it can make to the brute animal in man; this city simmering in the tepid lakeside sun; this atrocious harmlessness of all things —I cannot abide with them. Let me take my chances again in the big outside worldly wilderness with all its sins and sufferings. There are the heights and depths, the precipices and the steep ideals, the gleams of the awful and the infinite; and there is more hope and help a thousand times than in this dead level and quintes-sence of every mediocrity."

Such was the sudden right-about-face performed for me by my lawless fancy! There had been spread before me the realization—on a small, sample scale of course —of all the ideals for which our civilization has been striving: security, intelligence, humanity, and order; and here was the instinctive hostile reaction, not of the natural man, but of a so-called cultivated man upon such a Utopia. There seemed thus to be a self-contra-diction and paradox somewhere, which I, as a professor drawing a full salary, was in duty bound to unravel and explain, if I could.

So I meditated. And, first of all, I asked myself what the thing was that was so lacking in this Sabbatical city, and the lack of which kept one forever falling short of the higher sort of contentment. And I soon recognized that it was the element that gives to the wicked outer world all its moral style, expressiveness and picturesqueness—the element of precipitousness, so to call it, of strength and strenuousness, intensity and danger. What excites and interests the looker-on at life, what the romances and the statues celebrate and the grim civic monuments remind us of, is the everlasting battle of the powers of light with those of darkness; with heroism, reduced to its bare chance, yet ever and anon snatching victory from the jaws of death. But in this unspeakable Chautauqua there was no potentiality of death in sight anywhere, and no point of the compass visible from which danger might possibly appear. The ideal was so completely victorious already that no sign of any previous battle remained, the place just resting on its oars. But what our human emotions seem to require is the sight of the struggle going on. The moment the fruits are being merely eaten, things become ignoble. Sweat and effort, human nature strained to its uttermost and on the rack, yet getting through alive, and then turning its back on its success to pursue another more rare and arduous still—this is the sort of thing the presence of which inspires us, and the reality of which it seems to be the function of all the higher forms of literature and fine art to bring home to us and suggest. At Chautauqua there were no racks, even in the place's historical museum; and no sweat, except possibly the gentle moisture on the brow of some lecturer, or on the sides of some player in the ball-field.

Such absence of human nature *in extremis* anywhere seemed, then, a sufficient explanation for Chautauqua's flatness and lack of zest.

But was not this a paradox well calculated to fill one with dismay? It looks indeed, thought I, as if the romantic idealists with their pessimism about our civilization were, after all, quite right. An irremediable flatness is coming over the world. Bourgeoisie and mediocrity, church sociables and teachers' conventions, are taking the place of the old heights and depths and romantic chiaroscuro. And, to get human life in its wild intensity, we must in future turn more and more away from the actual, and forget it, if we can, in the romancer's or the poet's pages. The whole world, delightful and sinful as it may still appear for a moment to one just escaped from the Chautauquan enclosure, is nevertheless obeying more and more just those ideals that are sure to make of it in the end a mere Chautauqua Assembly on an enormous scale. *Was im Gesang soll leben muss im Leben untergehn.* Even now, in our own country, correctness, fairness, and compromise for every small advantage are crowding out all other qualities. The higher heroisms and the old rare flavors are passing out of life.[1]

[1] This address was composed before the Cuban and Philippine wars. Such outbursts of the passion of mastery are, however, only episodes in a social process which in the long run seems everywhere tending toward the Chautauquan ideals.

With these thoughts in my mind, I was speeding with the train toward Buffalo, when, near that city, the sight of a workman doing something on the dizzy edge of a sky-scaling iron construction brought me to my senses very suddenly. And now I perceived, by a flash of insight, that I had been steeping myself in pure ancestral blindness, and looking at life with the eyes of a remote spectator. Wishing for heroism and the spectacle of human nature on the rack, I had never noticed the great fields of heroism lying round about me, I had failed to see it present and alive. I could only think of it as dead and embalmed, labeled and costumed, as it is in the pages of romance. And yet there it was before me in the daily lives of the laboring classes. Not in clanging fights and desperate marches only is heroism to be looked for, but on every railway bridge and fire-proof building that is going up today. On freight-trains, on the decks of vessels, in cattle-yards and mines, on lumber-rafts, among the firemen and the policemen, the demand for courage is incessant; and the supply never fails. There, every day of the year somewhere, is human nature *in extremis* for you. And wherever a scythe, an axe, a pick, or a shovel is wielded, you have it sweating and aching and with its powers of patient endurance racked to the utmost under the length of hours of the strain.

As I awoke to all this unidealized heroic life around me, the scales seemed to fall from my eyes; and a wave of sympathy greater than anything I had ever before felt with the common life of common men began to fill my soul. It began to seem as if virtue with horny hands and dirty skin were the only virtue genuine and vital enough to take account of. Every other virtue poses; none is absolutely unconscious and simple, and unexpectant of decoration or recognition, like this. These are our soldiers, thought I, these our sustainers, these the very parents of our life.

Many years ago, when in Vienna, I had had a similar feeling of awe and reverence in looking at the peasant-women, in from the country on their business at the market for the day. Old hags many of them were, dried and brown and wrinkled, kerchiefed and short-petticoated, with thick wool stockings on their bony shanks, stumping through the glittering thoroughfares, looking neither to the right nor the left, bent on duty, envying nothing, humble-hearted, remote—and yet at bottom, when you came to think of it, bearing the whole fabric of the splendors and corruptions of that city on their laborious backs. For where would any of it have been without their unremitting, unrewarded labor in the fields? And so with us: not to our generals and poets, I thought, but to the Italian and Hungarian laborers in the Subway, rather, ought the monuments of gratitude and reverence of a city like Boston to be reared.

If any of you have been readers of Tolstoï, you will see that I passed into a vein of feeling similar to his, with its abhorrence of all that conventionally passes for distinguished, and its exclusive deification of the bravery, patience, kindliness, and dumbness of the unconscious natural man.

Where now is *our* Tolstoï, I said, to bring the truth of all this home to our American bosoms, fill us with a better insight, and wean us away from that spurious literary romanticism on which our wretched culture— as it calls itself—is fed? Divinity lies all about us, and culture is too hide-bound to even suspect the fact. Could a Howells or a Kipling be enlisted in this mission? or are they still too deep in the ancestral blindness, and not humane enough for the inner joy and meaning of the laborer's existence to be really revealed? Must we wait for someone born and bred and living as a laborer himself, but who, by grace of Heaven, shall also find a literary voice?

And there I rested on that day, with a sense of widening of vision, and with what it is surely fair to call an increase of religious insight into life. In God's eyes the differences of social position, of intellect, of culture, of cleanliness, of dress, which different men exhibit, and all the other rarities and exceptions on which they so fantastically pin their pride, must be so small as practically quite to vanish; and all that should remain is the common fact that here we are, a countless multitude of vessels of life, each of us pent in to peculiar difficulties, with which we must severally struggle by using whatever of fortitude and goodness we can summon up. The exercise of the courage, patience, and kind-ness, must be the significant portion of the whole business; and the distinctions of position can only be a manner of diversifying the phenomenal surface upon which these underground virtues may manifest their effects. At this rate, the deepest human life is everywhere, is eternal. And, if any human attributes exist only in particular individuals, they must belong to the mere trapping and decoration of the surface-show.

Thus are men's lives leveled up as well as leveled down—leveled up in their common inner meaning, leveled down in their outer gloriousness and show. Yet always, we must confess, this leveling insight tends to be obscured again; and always the ancestral blindness returns and wraps us up, so that we end once more by thinking that creation can be for no other purpose than to develop remarkable situations and conventional distinctions and merits. And then always some new leveler in the shape of a religious prophet has to arise—the Buddha, the Christ, or some Saint Francis, some Rousseau or Tolstoï—to redispel our blindness. Yet, little by little, there comes some stable gain; for the world does get more humane, and the religion of democracy tends toward permanent increase.

This, as I said, became for a time my conviction, and gave me great content. I have put the matter into the form of a personal reminiscence, so that I might lead you into it more directly and completely, and so save time. But now I am going to discuss the rest of it with you in a more impersonal way.

Tolstoï's leveling philosophy began long before he had the crisis of melancholy commemorated in that wonderful document of his entitled "My Confession," which led the way to his more specifically religious works. In his masterpiece "War and Peace"—assuredly the greatest of human novels—the rôle of the spiritual hero is given to a poor little soldier named Karataïeff, so helpful, so cheerful, and so devout that, in spite of his ignorance and filthiness, the sight of him opens the heavens, which have been closed, to the mind of the principal character of the book; and his example evidently is meant by Tolstoï to let God into the world again for the reader. Poor little Karataïeff is taken prisoner by the French; and, when too exhausted by hardship and fever to march, is shot as other prisoners were in the famous retreat from Moscow. The last view one gets of him is his little figure leaning against a white birch-tree, and uncomplainingly awaiting the end.

"The more," writes Tolstoï in the work "My Confession," "the more I examined the life of these laboring folks, the more persuaded I became that they veritably have faith, and get from it alone the sense and the possibility of life. . . . Contrariwise to those of our own class, who protest against destiny and grow indignant at its rigor, these people receive maladies and misfortunes without revolt, without opposition, and with a firm and tranquil confidence that all had to be like that, could not be otherwise, and that it is all right so. . . . The more we live by our intellect, the less we understand the meaning of life. We see only a cruel jest in suffering and death, whereas these people live, suffer, and draw near to death with tranquillity, and oftener than not with joy. . . . There are enormous multitudes of them happy with the most perfect happiness, although deprived of what for us is the sole good of life. Those who understand life's meaning, and know how to live and die thus, are to be counted not by twos, threes, tens, but by hundreds, thousands, millions. They labor quietly, endure privations and pains, live and die, and throughout everything see the good without seeing the vanity. I had to love these people. The more I entered into their life, the more I loved them; and the more it became possible for me to live, too. It came about not only that the life of our society, of the learned and of the rich, disgusted me—more than that, it lost all semblance of meaning in my eyes. All our actions, our deliberations, our sciences, our arts, all appeared to me with a new significance. I understood that these things might be charming pastimes, but that one need seek in them no depth, whereas the life of the hard-working populace, of that multitude of human beings who really contribute to existence, appeared to me in its true light. I understood that there veritably is life, that the meaning which life there receives is the truth; and I accepted it."

In a similar way does Stevenson appeal to our piety toward the elemental virtue of mankind.

"What a wonderful thing," he writes,[1] "is this Man! How surprising are his attributes! Poor soul, here for so little, cast among so many hardships, savagely surrounded, savagely descended, irremediably condemned to prey upon his fellow-lives—who should have blamed him, had he been of a piece with his destiny and a being merely barbarous? . . . [Yet] it matters not where we look, under what climate we observe him, in what stage of society, in what depth of ignorance, burdened with what erroneous morality; in ships at sea, a man inured to hardship and vile pleasures, his brightest hope a fiddle in a tavern, and a bedizened trull who sells herself to rob him, and he, for all that, simple, innocent, cheerful, kindly like a child, constant to toil, brave to drown, for others; . . . in the slums of cities, moving among indifferent millions to mechanical employments, without hope of change in the future, with scarce a pleasure in the present, and yet true to his virtues, honest up to his lights, kind to his neighbors, tempted perhaps in vain by the bright gin-palace, . . . often repaying the world's scorn with service, often standing firm upon a scruple; . . . everywhere some virtue cherished or affected, everywhere some decency of thought and courage, everywhere the

---

[1] *Across the Plains:* "Pulvis et Umbra" (abridged).

ensign of man's ineffectual goodness—ah! if I could show you this! If I could show you these men and women all the world over, in every stage of history, under every abuse of error, under every circumstance of failure, without hope, without help, without thanks, still obscurely fighting the lost fight of virtue, still clinging to some rag of honor, the poor jewel of their souls."

All this is as true as it is splendid, and terribly do we need our Tolstoïs and Stevensons to keep our sense for it alive. Yet you remember the Irishman who, when asked, "Is not one man as good as another?" replied, "Yes; and a great deal better, too!" Similarly (it seems to me) does Tolstoï over-correct our social prejudices, when he makes his love of the peasant so exclusive, and hardens his heart toward the educated man as absolutely as he does. Grant that at Chautauqua there was little moral effort, little sweat or muscular strain in view. Still, deep down in the souls of the participants we may be sure that something of the sort was hid, some inner stress, some vital virtue not found wanting when required. And, after all, the question recurs, and forces itself upon us, Is it so certain that the surroundings and circumstances of the virtue do make so little difference in the importance of the result? Is the functional utility, the worth to the universe of a certain definite amount of courage, kindliness, and patience, no greater if the possessor of these virtues is in an educated situation, working out far-reaching tasks, than if he be an illiterate nobody, hewing wood and drawing water, just to keep himself alive? Tolstoï's philosophy, deeply enlightening though it certainly is, remains a false abstraction. It savors too much of that Oriental pessimism and nihilism of his, which declares the whole phenomenal world and its facts and their distinctions to be a cunning fraud.

A mere bare fraud is just what our Western common sense will never believe the phenomenal world to be. It admits fully that the inner joys and virtues are the *essential* part of life's business, but it is sure that *some* positive part is also played by the adjuncts of the show. If it is idiotic in romanticism to recognize the heroic only when it sees it labeled and dressed-up in books, it is really just as idiotic to see it only in the dirty boots and sweaty shirt of some one in the fields. It is with us really under every disguise: at Chautauqua; here in your college; in the stock-yards and on the freight-trains; and in the czar of Russia's court. But, instinctively, we make a combination of two things in judging the total significance of a human being. We feel it to be some sort of a product (if such a product only could be calculated) of his inner virtue *and* his outer place—neither singly taken, but both conjoined. If the outer differences had no meaning for life, why indeed should all this immense variety of them exist? They *must* be significant elements of the world as well.

Just test Tolstoï's deification of the mere manual

laborer by the facts. This is what Mr. Walter Wyckoff, after working as an unskilled laborer in the demolition of some buildings at West Point, writes of the spiritual condition of the class of men to which he temporarily chose to belong:

"The salient features of our condition are plain enough. We are grown men, and are without a trade. In the labor-market we stand ready to sell to the highest bidder our mere muscular strength for so many hours each day. We are thus in the lowest grade of labor. And, selling our muscular strength in the open market for what it will bring, we sell it under peculiar conditions. It is all the capital that we have. We have no reserve means of subsistence, and cannot, therefore, stand off for a 'reserve price.' We sell under the necessity of satisfying imminent hunger. Broadly speaking, we must sell our labor or starve; and, as hunger is a matter of a few hours, and we have no other way of meeting this need, we must sell at once for what the market offers for our labor.

"Our employer is buying labor in a dear market, and he will certainly get from us as much work as he can at the price. The gang-boss is secured for this purpose, and thoroughly does he know his business. He has sole command of us. He never saw us before, and he will discharge us all when the débris is cleared away. In the meantime he must get from us, if he can, the utmost of physical labor which we, individually and collectively, are capable of. If he should drive some of us to exhaustion, and we should not be able to continue at work, he would not be the loser; for the market would soon supply him with others to take our places.

"We are ignorant men, but so much we clearly see —that we have sold our labor where we could sell it dearest, and our employer has bought it where he could buy it cheapest. He has paid high, and he must get all the labor that he can; and, by a strong instinct which possesses us, we shall part with as little as we can. From work like ours there seems to us to have been eliminated every element which constitutes the nobility of labor. We feel no personal pride in its progress, and no community of interest with our employer. There is none of the joy of responsibility, none of the sense of achievement, only the dull monotony of grinding toil, with the longing for the signal to quit work, and for our wages at the end.

"And being what we are, the dregs of the labor-market, and having no certainty of permanent employment, and no organization among ourselves, we must expect to work under the watchful eye of a gang-boss, and be driven, like the wage-slaves that we are, through our tasks.

"All this is to tell us, in effect, that our lives are hard, barren, hopeless lives."

And such hard, barren, hopeless lives, surely, are not lives in which one ought to be willing permanently to remain. And why is this so? Is it because they are so dirty? Well, Nansen grew a great deal dirtier on his polar expedition; and we think none the worse of his life for that. Is it the insensibility? Our soldiers have to grow vastly more insensible, and we extol them to the skies. Is it the poverty? Poverty has been reckoned the crowning beauty of many a heroic career. Is it the slavery to a task, the loss of finer pleasures? Such slavery and loss are of the very essence of the higher fortitude, and are always counted to its credit— read the records of missionary devotion all over the world. It is not any one of these things, then, taken by itself—no, nor all of them together—that make such a life undesirable. A man might in truth live like an un-skilled laborer, and do the work of one, and yet count as one of the noblest of God's creatures. Quite possibly there were some such persons in the gang that our author describes; but the current of their souls ran underground; and he was too steeped in the ancestral blindness to discern it.

If there *were* any such morally exceptional individuals, however, what made them different from the rest? It can only have been this—that their souls worked and endured in obedience to some inner *ideal*, while their comrades were not actuated by anything worthy of that name. These ideals of other lives are among those secrets that we can almost never penetrate, although something about the man may often tell us when they are there. In Mr. Wyckoff's own case we know exactly what the self-imposed ideal was. Partly he had stumped himself, as the boys say, to carry through a strenuous achievement; but mainly he wished to enlarge his sympathetic insight into fellow-lives. For this his sweat and toil acquire a certain heroic significance, and make us accord to him exceptional esteem. But it is easy to imagine his fellows with various other ideals. To say nothing of wives and babies, one may have been a convert of the Salvation Army, and had a nightingale singing of expiation and forgiveness in his heart all the while he labored. Or there might have been an apostle like Tolstoï himself, or his compatriot Bondareff, in the gang, voluntarily embracing labor as their religious mission. Class-loyalty was undoubtedly an ideal with many. And who knows how much of that higher manliness of poverty, of which Phillips Brooks has spoken so penetratingly, was or was not present in that gang?

"A rugged, barren land," says Phillips Brooks, "is poverty to live in,—a land where I am thankful very often if I can get a berry or a root to eat. But living in it really, letting it bear witness to me of itself, not dishonoring it all the time by judging it after the standard of the other lands, gradually there come out its qualities. Behold! no land like this barren and naked land of poverty could show the moral geology of the world. See how the hard ribs . . . stand out strong and solid. No life like poverty could so get one to the heart of things and make men know their meaning, could so let us feel life and the world with all the soft cushions stripped off and thrown away. . . . Poverty makes men come very near each other, and recognize each other's human hearts; and poverty, highest and best of all, demands and cries out for faith in God. . . . I know how superficial and unfeeling, how like mere mockery, words in praise of poverty may seem. . . . But I am sure that the poor man's dignity and freedom, his self-respect and energy, depend upon his cordial knowledge that his poverty is a true region and kind of life, with its own chances of character, its own springs of happiness and revelations of God. Let him resist the characterlessness which often goes with being poor. Let him insist on respecting the condition where he lives. Let him learn to love it, so that by and by, [if] he grows rich, he shall go out of the low door of the old familiar poverty with a true pang of regret, and with a true honor for the narrow home in which he has lived so long." [1]

The barrenness and ignobleness of the more usual laborer's life consist in the fact that it is moved by no such ideal inner springs. The backache, the long hours, the danger, are patiently endured—for what? To gain a quid of tobacco, a glass of beer, a cup of coffee, a meal, and a bed, and to begin again the next day and shirk as much as one can. This really is why we raise no monument to the laborers in the Subway, even though they be our conscripts, and even though after a fashion our city is indeed based upon their patient hearts and enduring backs and shoulders. And

[1] *Sermons*, 5th Series, New York, 1893, pp. 166-167.

this is why we do raise monuments to our soldiers, whose outward conditions were even brutaler still. The soldiers are supposed to have followed an ideal, and the laborers are supposed to have followed none.

You see, my friends, how the plot now thickens; and how strangely the complexities of this wonderful human nature of ours begin to develop under our hands. We have seen the blindness and deadness to each other which are our natural inheritance; and, in spite of them, we have been led to acknowledge an inner meaning which passeth show, and which may be present in the lives of others where we least descry it. And now we are led to say that such inner meaning can be *complete* and *valid for us also,* only when the inner joy, courage, and endurance are joined with an ideal.

But what, exactly, do we mean by an ideal? Can we give no definite account of such a word?

To a certain extent we can. An ideal, for instance, must be something intellectually conceived, something of which we are not unconscious, if we have it; and it must carry with it that sort of outlook, uplift, and brightness that go with all intellectual facts. Secondly, there must be *novelty* in an ideal,—novelty at least for him whom the ideal grasps. Sodden routine is incompatible with ideality, although what is sodden routine for one person may be ideal novelty for another. This shows that there is nothing absolutely ideal: ideals are relative to the lives that entertain them. To keep out of the gutter is for us here no part of consciousness at all, yet for many of our brethren it is the most legitimately engrossing of ideals.

Now, taken nakedly, abstractly, and immediately, you see that mere ideals are the cheapest things in life. Everybody has them in some shape or other, personal or general, sound or mistaken, low or high; and the most worthless sentimentalists and dreamers, drunkards, shirks and verse-makers, who never show a grain of effort, courage, or endurance, possibly have them on the most copious scale. Education, enlarging as it does our horizon and perspective, is a means of multiplying our ideals, of bringing new ones into view. And your college professor, with a starched shirt and spectacles, would, if a stock of ideals were all alone by itself enough to render a life significant, be the most absolutely and deeply significant of men. Tolstoï would be completely blind in despising him for a prig, a pedant and a parody; and all our new insight into the divinity of muscular labor would be altogether off the track of truth.

But such consequences as this, you instinctively feel, are erroneous. The more ideals a man has, the more contemptible, on the whole, do you continue to deem him, if the matter ends there for him, and if none of the laboring man's virtues are called into action on his part,—no courage shown, no privations undergone, no dirt or scars contracted in the attempt to get them realized. It is quite obvious that something more than the mere possession of ideals is required to make a life significant in any sense that claims the spectator's admiration. Inner joy, to be sure, it may *have,* with its ideals; but that is its own private sentimental matter. To extort from us, outsiders as we are, with our own ideals to look after, the tribute of our grudging recognition, it must back its ideal visions with what the laborers have, the sterner stuff of manly virtue; it must multiply their sentimental surface by the dimension of the active will, if we are to have *depth,* if we are to have anything cubical and solid in the way of character.

The significance of a human life for communicable and publicly recognizable purposes is thus the offspring of a marriage of two different parents, either of whom alone is barren. The ideals taken by themselves give no reality, the virtues by themselves no novelty. And let the Orientalists and pessimists say what they will, the thing of deepest—or, at any rate, of comparatively deepest—significance in life does seem to be its character of *progress,* or that strange union of reality with ideal novelty which it continues from one moment to another to present. To recognize ideal novelty is the task of what we call intelligence. Not every one's intelligence can tell which novelties are ideal. For many the ideal thing will always seem to cling still to the older more familiar good. In this case character, though not significant totally, may be still significant pathetically. So, if we are to choose which is the more essential factor of human character, the fighting virtue or the intellectual breadth, we must side with Tolstoï and choose that simple faithfulness to his light or darkness which any common unintellectual man can show.

But, with all this beating and tacking on my part, I fear you take me to be reaching a confused result. I seem to be just taking things up and dropping them again. First I took up Chautauqua, and dropped that; then Tolstoï and the heroism of common toil, and dropped them; finally, I took up ideals, and seem now almost dropping those. But please observe in what sense it is that I drop them. It is when they pretend *singly* to redeem life from insignificance. Culture and refinement all alone are not enough to do so. Ideal aspirations are not enough, when uncombined with pluck and will. But neither are pluck and will, dogged endurance and insensibility to danger enough, when taken all alone. There must be some sort of fusion, some chemical combination among these principles, for a life objectively and thoroughly significant to result.

Of course, this is a somewhat vague conclusion. But in a question of significance, of worth, like this, conclusions can never be precise. The answer of appreciation, of sentiment, is always a more or a less, a balance struck by sympathy, insight, and good will. But it is an answer, all the same, a real conclusion. And, in the course of getting it, it seems to me that our eyes have been opened to many important things. Some of you are, perhaps, more livingly aware than you were an hour ago of the depths of worth that lie around you, hid in alien lives. And, when you ask how much sympathy you ought to bestow, although the amount is, truly enough, a matter of ideal on your own part, yet in this notion of the combination of ideals with active virtues you have a rough standard for shaping your decision. In any case, your imagination is extended. You divine in the world about you matter for a little more humility on your own part, and tolerance, reverence, and love for others; and you gain a certain inner joyfulness at the increased importance of our common life. Such joyfulness is a religious inspiration and an element of spiritual health, and worth more than large amounts of that sort of technical and accurate information which we professors are supposed to be able to impart.

To show the sort of thing I mean by these words, I will just make one brief practical illustration, and then close.

We are suffering today in America from what is called the labor-question; and, when you go out into the world, you will each and all of you be caught up in its perplexities. I use the brief term labor-question to cover all sorts of anarchistic discontents and socialistic projects, and the conservative resistances which they provoke. So far as this conflict is unhealthy and regrettable,—and I think it is so only to a limited extent,— the unhealthiness consists solely in the fact that one-half of our fellow-countrymen remain entirely blind to the internal significance of the lives of the other half. They miss the joys and sorrows, they fail to feel the moral virtue, and they do not guess the presence of the intellectual ideals. They are at cross-purposes all along the line, regarding each other as they might regard a set of dangerously gesticulating automata, or, if they seek to get at the inner motivation, making the most horrible mistakes. Often all that the poor man can think of in the rich man is a cowardly greediness for safety, luxury, and effeminacy, and a boundless affectation. What he is, is not a human being, but a pocketbook, a bank account. And a similar greediness, turned by disappointment into envy, is all that many rich men can see in the state of mind of the dissatisfied poor. And, if the rich man begins to do the sentimental act over the poor man, what senseless blunders does he make, pitying him for just those very duties and those very immunities which, rightly taken, are the condition of his most abiding and characteristic joys! Each, in short, ignores the fact that happiness and unhappiness and significance are a vital mystery; each pins them absolutely on some ridiculous feature of the external situation; and everybody remains outside of everybody else's sight.

Society has, with all this, undoubtedly got to pass toward some newer and better equilibrium, and the distribution of wealth has doubtless slowly got to change: such changes have always happened, and will happen to the end of time. But if, after all that I have said, any of you expect that they will make any *genuine vital difference* on a large scale, to the lives of our descendants, you will have missed the significance of my entire lecture. The solid meaning of life is always the same eternal thing,—the marriage, namely, of some unhabitual ideal, however special, with some fidelity, courage, and endurance; with some man's or woman's pains.— And, whatever or wherever life may be, there will always be the chance for that marriage to take place.

Fitz-James Stephen wrote many years ago words to this effect more eloquent than any I can speak: "The 'Great Eastern,' or some of her successors," he said, "will perhaps defy the roll of the Atlantic, and cross the seas without allowing their passengers to feel that they have left the firm land. The voyage from the cradle to the grave may come to be performed with similar facility. Progress and science may perhaps enable untold millions to live and die without a care, without a pang, without an anxiety. They will have a pleasant passage and plenty of brilliant conversation. They will wonder that men ever believed at all in clanging fights and blazing towns and sinking ships and praying hands; and, when they come to the end of their course, they will go their way, and the place thereof will know them no more. But it seems unlikely that they will have such a knowledge of the great ocean on which they sail, with its storms and wrecks, its currents and icebergs, its huge waves and mighty winds, as those who battled with it for years together in the little craft, which, if they had few other merits, brought those who navigated them full into the presence of time and eternity, their maker and themselves, and forced them to have some definite view of their relations to them and to each other." [1]

In this solid and tridimensional sense, so to call it, those philosophers are right who contend that the world is a standing thing, with no progress, no real history. The changing conditions of history touch only the surface of the show. The altered equilibriums and redistributions only diversify our opportunities and open chances to us for new ideals. But, with each new ideal that comes into life, the chance for a life based on some old ideal will vanish; and he would needs be a presumptuous calculator who should with confidence say that the total sum of significances is positively and absolutely greater at any one epoch than at any other of the world.

I am speaking broadly, I know, and omitting to consider certain qualifications in which I myself believe. But one can only make one point in one lecture, and I shall be well content if I have brought my point home to you this evening in even a slight degree. *There are compensations:* and no outward changes of condition in life can keep the nightingale of its eternal meaning from singing in all sorts of different men's hearts. That is the main fact to remember. If we could not only admit

[1] *Essays by a Barrister,* London, 1862, p. 318.

it with our lips, but really and truly believe it, how our
convulsive insistencies, how our antipathies and dreads
of each other, would soften down!   If the poor and
the rich could look at each other in this way, *sub specie
æternatis*, how gentle would grow their disputes! what
tolerance and good humor, what willingness to live and
let live, would come into the world!

APPENDIX I

DATES AND FAMILY NAMES[1]

1842.	January 11. Born in New York.
1857–58.	At School in Boulogne.
1859–60.	In Geneva.
1860–61.	Studied painting under William M. Hunt in Newport.
1861.	Entered the Lawrence Scientific School.
1863.	Entered the Harvard Medical School.
1865–66.	Assistant under Louis Agassiz on the Amazon.
1867–68.	Studied medicine in Germany.
1869.	M.D. Harvard.
1873–76.	Instructor in Anatomy and Physiology in Harvard College.
1875.	Began to give instruction in Psychology.
1876.	Assistant Professor of Physiology.
1878.	Married. Undertook to write a treatise on Psychology.
1880.	Assistant Professor of Philosophy.
1882–83.	Spent several months visiting European universities and colleagues.
1885.	Professor of Philosophy. (Between 1889 and 1897 his title was Professor of Psychology.)
1890.	"Principles of Psychology" appeared.
1892–93.	European travel.

[1] From *The Letters of William James*, vol. i.

1897.	Published "The Will to Believe and other Essays on Popular Philosophy."
1899.	Published "Talks to Teachers," etc.
1899–1902.	Broke down in health. Two years in Europe.
1901–1902.	Gifford Lectures. "The Varieties of Religious Experience."
1906.	Acting Professor for half-term at Stanford University. (Interrupted by San Francisco earthquake.)
1906.	Lowell Institute lectures, subsequently published as "Pragmatism."
1907.	Resigned all active duties at Harvard.
1908.	Hibbert Lectures at Manchester College, Oxford; subsequently published as "A Pluralistic Universe."
1910.	August 26. Died at Chocorua, N. H.

William James was the eldest of five children. His brothers and sisters, with their dates, were: Henry (referred to as "Harry"), 1843–1916; Garth Wilkinson (referred to as "Wilky"), 1845–1883; Robertson (referred to as "Bob" and "Bobby"), 1846–1910; Alice, 1848–1892.

He had five children. Their dates and the names by which they are referred to in the letters are: Henry ("Harry"), 1879; William ("Billy"), 1882; Herman, 1884–1885; Margaret Mary ("Peggy," "Peg"), 1887; Alexander Robertson ("Tweedie," "François"), 1890.

APPENDIX II

THE WORKS OF WILLIAM JAMES

The works of William James, from which have been taken the selections included in this volume, are:

1885. *Literary Remains of Henry James, Senr.*, with an Introduction by William James.

Houghton, Mifflin & Co., Boston.

1891. *Principles of Psychology.*

Vol. I: Scope of Psychology. Functions of the Brain. Conditions of Brain Activity. Habit. The Automaton Theory. The Mind-Stuff. Theory Methods and Snares of Psychology. Relations of Minds to Other Things. The Stream of Thought. The Consciousness of Self. Attention. Conception. Discrimination and Comparison. Association. Perception of Time. Memory.

Vol. II: Sensation. Imagination. Perception of "Things." Perception of Space. Perception of Reality. Reasoning. Production of Movement. Instinct. The Emotions. Will. Hypnotism. Necessary Truth and the Effects of Experience.

Henry Holt & Co., New York. Macmillan & Co., London.

1892. *Text-Book of Psychology.* Briefer Course.

Sensation. Sight. Hearing. Touch. Sensations of Motion. Structure of the Brain. Functions of

the Brain. Neural Activity. Habit. Stream of
Consciousness. The Self. Attention. Concep-
tion. Discrimination. Association. Sense of Time.
Memory. Imagination. Perception. Reasoning.
Consciousness and Movement. Emotion. Instinct.
Will. Psychology and Philosophy.

Henry Holt & Co., New York. Macmillan & Co.,
London.

1897. *The Will to Believe,* and Other Essays in Popular Philosophy.

The Will to Believe. Is Life Worth Living? The
Sentiment of Rationality. Reflex Action and Theism. The Dilemma of Determinism. The Moral
Philosopher and the Moral Life. Great Men and
their Environment. The Importance of Individuals.
Some Hegelisms. What Psychical Research Has Accomplished.

Longmans, Green & Co., London.

1898. *Human Immortality.* New Edition with Preface
in reply to his Critics, 1917.

Houghton, Mifflin & Co., Boston. Dent & Sons,
London.

1899. *Talks to Teachers on Psychology, and to Students on Some of Life's Ideals.*

Psychology and the Teaching Art. The Stream
of Consciousness. The Child as a Behaving Organism. Education and Behaviour. The Necessity of
Reaction. Native and Acquired Reactions. The
Laws of Habit. Association of Ideas. Interest. Attention. Memory. Acquisition of Ideas. Apper-
ception. The Will.

Talks to Students: The Gospel of Relaxation. On

a Certain Blindness in Human Beings. What Makes a Life Significant?

Henry Holt & Co., New York. Longmans, Green & Co., London.

1902. *The Varieties of Religious Experience. A Study in Human Nature.* The Gifford Lectures on Natural Religion, Edinburgh, 1901–2.

I. Religion and Neurology. II. Circumscription of the Topic. III. The Reality of the Unseen. IV. and V. The Religion of Healthy-Mindedness. VI. and VII. The Sick Soul. VIII. The Divided Self and the Process of its Unification. IX. and X. Conversion. XI., XII., and XIII. Saintliness. XIV. and XV. The Value of Saintliness. XVI. and XVII. Mysticism. XVIII. Philosophy. XIX. Other Characteristics. XX. Conclusion. Postscript.

Longmans, Green & Co., London.

1907. *Pragmatism. A New Name for Some Old Ways of Thinking.*

The Present Dilemma in Philosophy. What Pragmatism Means. Some Metaphysical Problems Pragmatically Considered. The One and the Many. Pragmatism and Common Sense. Pragmatism and the Conception of Truth. Pragmatism and Humanism. Pragmatism and Religion.

Longmans, Green & Co., London.

1909. *The Meaning of Truth. A Sequel to Pragmatism.*

Function of Cognition. The Tigers in India. Humanism and Truth. The Relation between Knower and Known. The Essence of Humanism. A Word More about Truth. Professor Pratt on Truth. Pragmatist Account of Truth. Meaning of

the Word Truth.   The Existence of Julius Cæsar.
The Absolute and the Strenuous Life.   Hébert on
Pragmatism.   Abstractionism and "Relativismus."
The English Critics.   A Dialogue.
Longmans, Green & Co., London.

1909. *A Pluralistic Universe.*   Hibbert Lectures at
    Manchester College.

I. The Types of Philosophic Thinking.   II. Monis-
tic Idealism.   III. Hegel and his Method.   IV. Con-
cerning Fechner.   V. Compounding of Consciousness.
VI. Bergson and his Critique of Intellectualism.   VII.
The Continuity of Experience.   VIII. Conclusion.
Appendix: A. The Thing and its Relations.   B.
The Experience of Activity.   C. On the Notion of
Reality as Changing.
Longmans, Green & Co., London.

1911. *Memories and Studies.*

Louis Agassiz.   Emerson.   Robert Gould Shaw.
Francis Boott.   Thomas Davidson.   Herbert Spencer's Autobiography.   Frederick Myers.   A Psychical Researcher.   Mental Effects of Earthquake.
Energies of Men.   The Moral Equivalent of War.
Remarks at a Peace Banquet (1904).   Social Value
of the College-bred.   The University and the Individual.   A Pluralistic Mystic.
Longmans, Green & Co., London.

1911. *Some Problems of Philosophy.*   A Beginning of
    an Introduction to Philosophy.

Philosophy and its Critics.   The Problems of
Metaphysics.   The Problem of Being.   Percept and
Concept.   The One and the Many.   The Problem of
Novelty.   Novelty and the Infinite.   Novelty and
Causation.

Appendix: Faith and the Right to Believe.
Longmans, Green & Co., London.

1912. *Essays in Radical Empiricism.* Edited by Ralph Barton Perry.

I. Does Consciousness Exist? II. A World of Pure Experience. III. The Thing and its Relations. IV. How Two Minds Can Know One Thing. V. The Place of Affectional Facts in a World of Pure Experience. VI. The Experience of Activity. VII. The Essence of Humanism. VIII. *La Notion de Conscience.* IX. Is Radical Empiricism Solipsistic? X. Mr. Pitkin's Refutation of Radical Empiricism. XI. Humanism and Truth Once More. XII. Absolutism and Empiricism.
Longmans, Green & Co., London.

1920. *The Letters of William James.* Edited by his son Henry James.

Vol. 1. I. Introduction. II. 1861-1864. III. 1864-1866. IV. 1866-1867. V. 1867-1868. VI. 1869-1872. VII. 1872-1878. VIII. 1878-1883. IX. 1883-1890. X. 1890-1893.

Vol. 2. XI. 1893-1899. XII. 1893-1899 (continued). XIII. 1899-1902. XIV. 1902-1905. XV. 1905-1907. XVI. 1907 1909. XVII. 1910.

Appendices: Three Criticisms for Students. Books *The Letters of William James* in one volume.
The Atlantic Monthly Press, Boston.

THE END

The Best of the World's Best Books

COMPLETE LIST OF TITLES IN

THE MODERN LIBRARY

For convenience in ordering use number at right of title

MODERN LIBRARY GIANTS

A series of full-sized library editions of books that formerly
were available only in cumbersome and expensive sets.
THE MODERN LIBRARY GIANTS REPRESENT A
SELECTION OF THE WORLD'S GREATEST BOOKS

These volumes contain from 600 to 1,400 pages each